CAMBRIDGE STUDIES IN
MEDIEVAL LIFE AND THOUGHT

Edited by M. D. Knowles, Litt.D., F.B.A.
*Emeritus Regius Professor of Modern History in the
University of Cambridge*

NEW SERIES VOL. XIII

THE SECULAR CLERGY
IN THE
DIOCESE OF LINCOLN
1495-1520

THE SECULAR CLERGY
IN THE
DIOCESE OF LINCOLN
1495-1520

BY

MARGARET BOWKER

*Lecturer in History in the University of
Cambridge and Fellow of Girton College*

CAMBRIDGE
AT THE UNIVERSITY PRESS
1968

CAMBRIDGE UNIVERSITY PRESS
Cambridge, New York, Melbourne, Madrid, Cape Town, Singapore, São Paulo

Cambridge University Press
The Edinburgh Building, Cambridge CB2 8RU, UK

Published in the United States of America by Cambridge University Press, New York

www.cambridge.org
Information on this title: www.cambridge.org/9780521042918

© Cambridge University Press 1968

First published 1968
This digitally printed version 2008

A catalogue record for this publication is available from the British Library

Library of Congress Catalogue Card Number: 68–10147

ISBN 978-0-521-04291-8 hardback
ISBN 978-0-521-07014-0 paperback

TO JOHN

CONTENTS

PREFACE

My greatest debt is to Professor Kathleen Major, whose extensive knowledge of the Lincoln diocesan and chapter archives has saved me from many errors and stimulated me into further investigations. The mistakes that remain are my own. I am also grateful to Girton college for the financial assistance of a research fellowship and grant, and to undergraduates of the college who have helped me in the enormous task of indexing the sixteenth-century clergy of the diocese; in particular I owe special thanks to Miss Sally Stallworthy and Miss Frances Huggett. Dr H. S. Bennett, Miss B. F. Harvey, Dr G. R. Elton, Professor D. Joslin, Dr M. Kelley, Dr R. Schofield, Mrs J. Howarth, Dr J. N. L. Myres, and Professor M. D. Knowles have been especially generous of their time in helping me to unravel many points of particular difficulty. The staff of the Lincoln Record Office have extended to me both friendship and great assistance, and I am indebted to them for the extensive use I have been allowed to make of their books and manuscripts.

Most of the material in this book has not appeared before in print, but parts of the chapter on non-residence formed an article in the *Journal of Ecclesiastical History* and my thanks are due to the editor for permission to use it again. Some of the material in the first chapter figures in my introduction to Bishop Atwater's Court of Audience book, which has been printed by the Lincoln Record Society.

Finally, my mother has given me much practical help for which I am very grateful. Miss Gurley has exercised much patience in typing the manuscript and has rendered invaluable assistance in helping me to compile the index. Without the constant encouragement and support of my husband this book would not have been possible at all.

M.B.

LIST OF ABBREVIATIONS

Note: Full details of the manuscript sources cited in the footnotes will be found in the Bibliography, see below pp. 214–27. References to manuscripts are to documents in the custody of the Lincoln Record Office unless otherwise stated.

A.A.S.R.P.	*Associated Architectural Societies Reports and Papers.*
A.A.S.R.P. xxvIII	A. Percival Moore, 'Proceedings of the Ecclesiastical Courts in the Archdeaconry of Leicester, 1516–1534', *Associated Architectural Societies Reports and Papers*, vol. xxvIII, part I, 1905, 117 ff., part II, 1906, 593 ff.
D.N.B.	*Dictionary of National Biography.*
Emden, *Oxford*	A. B. Emden, *A Biographical Register of the University of Oxford to* A.D. *1500*, 3 vols. Oxford, 1957–1959.
Emden, *Cambridge*	A. B. Emden, *A Biographical Register of the University of Cambridge to* A.D. *1500*. Cambridge, 1963.
Le Neve	*Jo. Le Neve. Fasti Ecclesiae Anglicanae, Lincoln Diocese, I*, new edition compiled by H. P. F. King. London, 1962.
L. and P.	*Letters and Papers, Foreign and Domestic, of the Reign of Henry VIII preserved in the Public Record Office, the British Museum and elsewhere*, vol. I, catalogued by J. S. Brewer, 2nd edition by R. H. Brodie, 1920; vols II–IV, catalogued by J. S. Brewer, 1864–72.
Lincolnshire Pedigrees	*Lincolnshire Pedigrees*, ed. A. R. Maddison, 4 vols., Harleian Society, 1902–6.

L.R.S.	*Lincoln Record Society.*
L.R.S. 5, 10	*Lincoln Wills 1271–1530*, ed. C. W. Foster, Lincoln Record Society, vol. 5, 1914, vol. 10, 1918.
L.R.S. 12	*Chapter Acts of the Cathedral Church of St Mary of Lincoln*, ed. R. E. G. Cole, Lincoln Record Society, vol. 12, 1915.
L.R.S. 33, 35, 37	*Visitations in the Diocese of Lincoln 1517–1531*, ed. A. Hamilton Thompson, 3 vols., Lincoln Record Society, vol. 33, 1940; vol. 35, 1944; vol. 37, 1947.
L.R.S. 61	*The Book of the Court of Audience of Bishop William Atwater, 1514–20*, ed. M. Bowker, Lincoln Record Society, vol. 61, 1967.
Longden 1–xvi	H. I. Longden, *Northamptonshire and Rutland Clergy*. 16 vols. Northampton 1938–52.
P.R.O.	Public Record Office.
O.H.S.	Oxford Historical Society.
Salter	*A Subsidy Collected in the Diocese of Lincoln in 1526*, ed. H. Salter, Oxford Historical Society, vol. LXIII, 1913.
Valor Ecclesiasticus	*Valor Ecclesiasticus*, 6 vols. Record Commission, 1825–34.

NOTES

MAGISTER and DOMINUS. The titles *Magister* and *Dominus* were used in diocesan documents to distinguish the master of arts from all others who did not hold that degree. These titles have been retained.

DATING. The year began on 25 March; the discrepancy with modern dating has been shown as 1514/15.

PLACE-NAMES. An attempt has been made to give the place-names their modern form, but the variations in the spelling of names and the frequent omission from the diocesan documents of any indication of their county has made identification hazardous. No attempt has been made to modernize surnames.

TEXT-TABLES. In order to keep the tables in their exact position in the text, the table notes have had to be placed in some instances on the following page and in one instance on the preceding page.

INTRODUCTION

Very little detailed work has been done on the state of the secular clergy just before the Reformation. The general studies of the Reformation have drawn heavily on the evidence of contemporary literature; where diocesan material has been used, it has often been treated too cursorily, and it has not been possible to estimate whether the examples derived from it are typical or exceptional.[1] In consequence we know a great deal about what contemporaries thought about the church, but rather less about how their attitude was formed, and how accurate they were in their assessment.[2] We know that some early Tudor writers considered the clergy ignorant, immoral, non-resident and negligent in their duties. We do not know how many clerks actually conformed to this pattern. We know that the citizens of London were scandalized by Hunne's case, but not whether other scandals of a similar nature were occurring outside the metropolis. The unpopularity of the ecclesiastical courts is well attested by the events which led up to the indictment of the clergy for their participation in ecclesiastical jurisdiction in 1532, but we are still largely ignorant of the structure of the courts and their proceedings.[3] Wolsey is seen to dominate the early sixteenth-century church and to exemplify its worst abuses, and we are apt to forget that there were other bishops and other churchmen who were less flamboyant but much more typical.

It will be a long time before sufficient work is done on the diocesan archives for a more balanced picture of the church in the

---

[1] The same view has been expressed by A. G. Dickens, *Lollards and Protestants in the Diocese of York 1509–1558* (Oxford, 1959), p. 1. The same author in *The English Reformation* (London, 1964) also remarks on how little is known about the secular clergy (p. 51).

[2] One of the best discussions about the state of the church, mainly derived from literary sources but drawing, where possible, on diocesan material, is H. Maynard Smith, *Pre-Reformation England* (London, 1938); there are also useful chapters in P. Hughes, *The Reformation in England* (London, 1950), vol. 1.

[3] A. Ogle, *The Tragedy of the Lollards' Tower* (Oxford, 1949); for some account of the workings of the ecclesiastical courts, see B. L. Woodcock, *Medieval Ecclesiastical Courts in the Diocese of Canterbury* (Oxford, 1952).

early sixteenth century to emerge. This study is an attempt to sketch such a picture from one diocese only for the episcopates of Bishops Smith, Wolsey and Atwater 1495–1520/1. Until other studies are undertaken, we shall not know whether Lincoln was typical, or whether the differences between dioceses were so great that no diocese can be taken as typical. Lincoln was not likely to be unrepresentative of the English church in the conduct of its ecclesiastical courts,[1] but its ordination figures, the quality of its incumbents and the number of non-residents may vary a good deal from other sees, if only because of its proximity to London and the inclusion of the University of Oxford within its boundaries. It is also impossible to know whether the clergy were improving their standards in the early sixteenth century or whether these were deteriorating. Comparative data for the early fifteenth century are frequently not available, and, in consequence, it is hard to know how the situation in the church was changing. Some evidence survives to suggest that the educational standards of the clergy had improved; had their moral standards improved as well?

The documentary evidence available also places its own limitations on our knowledge. Some attempt has been made to show how a diocese was run, but too little material survives of the administration of the archdeaconry and the deanery for a complete study of diocesan administration to be possible. An attempt has been made to reconstruct the background to ordination and the way in which newly ordained deacons and priests acquired benefices. But, here again, the documentary evidence is lacking at a critical point. Statistics are available to indicate the number of men ordained and instituted, but they are not available for their education, particularly if they did not proceed to university. As a result we are left with a picture of clerical education which relies partly on figures and partly on inference. Finally the question of the care of the churches has been considered and an attempt has been made to estimate the amount of non-residence, concubinage and neglect in both the parish and the collegiate churches. The documentary evidence on these matters is much fuller: an

---

[1] L.R.S. 61, pp. 1 ff.

estimate can be made of clerical income from the subsidy of 1526, though this is likely to be an underestimate. There are also court and visitation books which enable the historian to reconstruct some kind of picture of parish life. But the limitation to visitation material, in particular, is that it relies on complaints. The visitor is told what the parish thought to be wrong. It shows, therefore, the tolerance or exasperation of the parishioners rather than the actual state of affairs. A visitation return does not indicate where the priest had deviated from the canonical norm; it indicates only where the parishioners were dissatisfied with him. The returns are useful in showing the limits of anticlericalism. They cannot be taken as giving a definitive guide to the state of the parochial clergy.

In spite of these limitations, it is hoped that this study and particularly the statistical material contained in it will provide a starting point from which it may be possible to arrive at a more accurate description of the state of the church in the early six-teenth century. Occasionally it has not proved possible to indicate exactly how some of the statistics have been compiled: a figure of the number of men ordained, for instance, is given, but not the names of all the ordinands counted in it; but four appendices which contain evidence of more general interest have been in-cluded. It is hoped that, as similar material from other dioceses is published, comparative studies will at last be able to be made.

No attempt has been made to study the clergy after 1520/21 when Bishop Atwater died, to be succeeded by Bishop Longland. Longland's episcopate spanned the break with Rome, and it was felt that the impact of the Reformation could not properly be estimated until the condition of the church before the break was more fully understood. It would be all too easy to attribute to the Reformation changes which had been taking place before it.

CHAPTER I

THE DIOCESE AND ITS
ADMINISTRATION

Colet in his famous convocation sermon was not afraid to criticize the ecclesiastical dignitaries before whom he preached:

Moreover these that are in the same dignities, the most part of them doth go with so stately a countenance and with so high looks that they seem not to be put in the humble bishopric of Christ but rather in the high lordship and power of the world.[1]

On other occasions he was reputed to have described them as 'wolves in sheep's clothing',[2] and, though his outspokenness may have made him exceptional, it is clear that his dissatisfaction with the ecclesiastical hierarchy was shared by others. The papacy and the whole system of papal taxation were criticized by Erasmus, Fish and Starkey,[3] and the 'spiritual pre-eminence' of the Holy See was called in question, in a somewhat inarticulate fashion, by many of the Lollards.[4] Within the episcopacy itself there were stirrings of conscience, and a certain uneasiness at the way in which sees were left without a resident bishop. Fox, while Bishop of Winchester, bemoaned the thirty years in which he had neglected his duties towards his cathedral offices and his bishoprics. He particularly regretted that he had devoted time to the furtherance of a war for which, he said, he had 'no little remorse in my conscience'.[5] Bishop Smith of Lincoln in a letter to Sir Reginald Bray lamented his enforced absence from his diocese for ten years because of his presidency of the Council of the Marches.[6] Nor was this mere rhetoric. When the opportunity came, either through old age, redundancy or disgrace, many 'courtier' bishops returned

---

[1] *The Thought and Culture of the English Renaissance*, ed. E. M. Nugent (Cambridge, 1956), p. 360.
[2] H. Maynard Smith, *Pre-Reformation England* (London, 1938), p. 29.
[3] *Ibid.* pp. 13–21.
[4] A. G. Dickens, *Lollards and Protestants in the Diocese of York 1509–1558* (Oxford, 1959), p. 9.   [5] Maynard Smith, *op. cit.* p. 27.
[6] Westminster Abbey Muniments, no. 16038.

to their dioceses in order to devote to them such belated care as
health and old age would allow.[1]

Criticism of papal exactions and of the secular employment of
the bishops was not new. It had been a feature of the reforming
movement of the thirteenth century, and an ingredient of anticlerical criticism thereafter.[2] But, by the sixteenth century, indig-
nation at the conduct of ecclesiastical affairs, especially at the church
courts, was marked. Hunne's case and the Commons Supplication Against the Ordinaries[3] indicated that this criticism was no
longer simply the concern of poets like Chaucer; it had apparently
become a national issue. The unpopularity of the courts, their
fees and of the whole system of penance was such that it could be
used as a stick with which to beat the clergy and prepare them for
submission.[4] Henry's victory over the pope and the clergy in
1534 seemed sudden and dramatic, but it was, in a sense, inevitable. By the sixteenth century the church was exceedingly legalistic
in outlook with the inevitable corollary that the ecclesiastical courts
occupied a prominent place within it. Two factors interacted to
produce this legalism: the developments in the late thirteenth and
fourteenth centuries within the diocesan administrative machine,[5]
and the tendency for this machine to be run by lawyers rather
than by theologians. Until further diocesan studies are undertaken,
it will not be certain whether the church was more legalistic by
the early sixteenth century than ever before, or whether the increase in criticism reflects not an increase in provocation, but a
lower level of tolerance, which may have been brought about, at
least in part, by royal encouragement.[6] But a study of the Lincoln

[1] Maynard Smith, op.cit. p. 27; this evidence is born out at Lincoln, see
below, p. 17.

[2] J. R. H. Moorman, Church Life in England in the Thirteenth Century (Cambridge, 1946), pp. 210 ff.

[3] For a consideration of the importance of these, see A. Ogle, The Tragedy
of the Lollards Tower (Oxford, 1949).

[4] J. J. Scarisbrick, 'The Pardon of the Clergy of Canterbury 1531', Cambridge Historical Journal, XII (1956), 22 ff.; for a modification of this interpretation see A. G. Dickens, The English Reformation (London, 1964), p. 104.

[5] C. Morris, 'The Commissary of the Bishop in the Diocese of Lincoln',
Journal of Ecclesiastical History, X, no. 1 (1959), 50 ff.

[6] Dickens, The English Reformation, p. 88.

diocese reveals the complexity of the structure of the English church and the consequent stresses inherent within it.

I. THE DIOCESE AND THE CHURCH

A diocese as large and difficult to handle as Lincoln was likely to require a number of people to administer it, and to present a special challenge. The diocese included part of Hertfordshire and the whole of Huntingdonshire, Bedfordshire, Buckinghamshire, Oxfordshire, Rutland, Northamptonshire, Leicestershire and Lincolnshire. This vast area was divided into eight archdeaconries which usually coincided with the county boundaries, but Lincolnshire was divided into the archdeaconries of Lincoln and Stow, and Hertfordshire and Rutland were included in the archdeaconries of Huntingdon and Northampton respectively. To the difficulty of size was added that of communication. Lincolnshire, in particular, was notorious for its bad roads, and, even in the summer, it might be hazardous for the bishop to make contact with parts of his diocese;[1] Longland wrote to Wolsey, in September 1528, that he had written to the prior of Spalding and sent his chancellor to see him 'for the waters in the Fens are now great and dangerous'.[2] Within any one county, there were wide differences of economic activity and fortune.[3] These brought in their wake ecclesiastical problems which were peculiar to certain archdeaconries. The weavers of Buckinghamshire were probably responsible for the persistence of Lollardy in that county;[4] some counties suffered more heavily from depopulation than others, and, in consequence, the bishop had to decide whether to allow the incumbent to continue in the parish, and, if he did so, he had to make sure he received an adequate stipend.[5]

The presence, within the diocese, of powerful religious houses

[1] J. W. F. Hill, *Tudor and Stuart Lincoln* (Cambridge, 1956), pp. 1-3.
[2] C. Wise, *Rockingham Castle and the Watsons* (London, 1891), p. 24.
[3] J. Thirsk, *English Peasant Farming* (London, 1957), *passim*.
[4] *Acts and Monuments of John Foxe*, ed. S. R. Cattley with an introduction by G. Towneshend, IV (London, 1837), 208 ff.
[5] M. Beresford, *The Lost Villages of England* (London, 1954), pp. 337 ff.; for a consideration of some of these problems see below, p. 144.

and collegiate churches could also embarrass the bishop. Trouble arose in 1501 when the prior of St John of Jerusalem was accused of usurping episcopal jurisdiction in certain parishes; he claimed that he had a papal privilege giving him the right to correction and probate over all his tenants in England; the bishop complained that the prior had extended this privilege and had absolved excommunicates and given letters testimonial (both episcopal functions). He also asserted that the prior had granted probate to those who were not his tenants since they were not distinguished by having displayed the sign of the cross on the doors of their houses.[1] Special negotiations had to be conducted with the abbots of Ramsey and Peterborough to settle with them the procedure to be adopted for criminous clerks, convicted within their liberties; it was agreed that the abbots should transfer the offending clerks to the bishop's prison, but the abbot of Peterborough was quick to point out that he was doing the bishop a favour, and demanded that the bishop: 'entyr in yor said commission that I shalbe alowed for my costes and charges for the conveance of them and a place assigned where thei shall rest'.[2] It was, perhaps, because the diocese was a difficult one to administer that it had the reputation of requiring the personal residence of its bishop. Silvester Gigli, the Italian bishop of Worcester, writing to Wolsey to congratulate him on his advancement to York from Lincoln, said that he had hoped that 'he himself would have had the diocese of Lincoln but he hears from Ammonius that it demands personal residence'.[3] Certainly Wolsey himself had not taken this view very seriously; he never seems to have entered the diocese as bishop of Lincoln, but it is interesting that he did not attempt to hold the see in plurality and that it was subsequently given to someone, William Atwater, who could and did reside.

Whoever held the see of Lincoln held a position of importance within the church. He had a dual role: not only was he ultimately responsible for the administration of the largest diocese in the country; he was also the link in ecclesiastical matters between that diocese and the pope, the archbishop of Canterbury and, increasingly, the king.

[1] Register 24, fo. 216.   [2] *Ibid.* fo. 179 v.   [3] *L. and P.* I, pt. II, no. 3197.

Contacts between the see of Lincoln and Rome were few in this period. Papal power had ceased to be exercised through provision except in the case of bishops who were provided to their sees. More real was the exercise of papal power through grants of privileges or dispensations. Certain dispensations, particularly from residence, were obtained from the Holy See,[1] and a few appeals were made to Rome.[2] Contrary to the popular view in the sixteenth century, only slight sums of money left the country for Rome. Little was paid even in the annual tribute of Peter's Pence.[3] The bishop himself had to pay heavy service taxes to Rome on his appointment, and it is estimated that the bishop of Lincoln paid £1,536 on his translation for common and petty services and other expenses.[4] The clergy, although protected by the king from income taxes payable to Rome, in fact contributed to the subsidy of a tenth levied by the king in 1502 and given by him for a crusade against the Turk. The Lincoln clergy contributed £2,759 of a total of £12,131 raised.[5] Indulgences administered in England for warfare against the Turks between 1487 and 1495, and for the Jubilee and rebuilding of St Peter's, left few traces in the diocese. The indulgence for St Peter's in 1517 raised about £1,144 from the country as a whole, and the Lincoln diocese probably contributed about one fifth of this sum.[6]

If the pope seemed far away, the papal legate did not. Wolsey's plans for reform received little support in the diocese, and his threatened interference with its administration resulted in an indenture between himself and Bishop Longland: Wolsey promised not to interfere in the granting of probate to the wills of those with goods valued at under £10, and he also promised not to meddle in vacancies, matters of correction, visitations, exemptions and sequestrations. As a result he had little authority in the diocese: his impotence was underlined by the fact that he was

[1] See, for example, Register 24, fos. 100, 102v, 157v, 159v, 176v, 177, 200, 202v, 203v, 204v, 205, 207v, 218v, 219v, 222, 223v–9; Register 25, fos. 12, 65v, 67v, 75v, 79v, 82v.
[2] Protocols of Appeal, Box 74, 1514; Register 25, fo. 65.
[3] W. E. Lunt, *Financial Relations of the Papacy with England 1327–1534* (Cambridge, Mass., 1962), pp. 1–53, 717.
[4] *Ibid.* p. 304.   [5] *Ibid.* pp. 159–60.   [6] *Ibid.* pp. 596–611.

not allowed to have an apparitor within it to keep a watchful eye on his rights.[1] It is not clear what prompted the indenture since there are few signs of Wolsey's activity in the diocese before 1523. But the indenture appears to have been successful in limiting the legate's interference since there are no traces of his intervention in the affairs of the diocese and only one known appeal to his court.[2]

More apparent in the diocese was the authority exercised by the archbishop of Canterbury. If Wolsey overshadowed Archbishop Warham in the state, he did not wholly succeed in doing so in the church. Warham's administration of the see of Lincoln during a vacancy was governed by the agreement made between the dean and chapter of Lincoln and the archbishop of Canterbury in 1261.[3] By this agreement the dean and chapter nominated three or four of its canons from whom the archbishop chose one as his official. The official took an oath both to the archbishop and to the dean and chapter. Rights of jurisdiction and visitation were reserved to the dean in certain areas, and the archdeacons were entitled to a third of the bishop's part of sequestrations and a quarter of his synodals.[4]

There is no *sede vacante* material following Wolsey's resignation in the chapter act book and none in Warham's register.[5] But the procedure is fully apparent in the vacancies caused, first by the death of William Smith in January 1513/14, and later by the death of William Atwater in February 1520/21. The dean and chapter immediately notified the archbishop of the death of the bishop, and submitted four names from which one was chosen as the official; the official submitted accounts of the procurations, fruits of vacant benefices and fees from the probate of wills due to the archbishop by reason of the vacancy.[6] But his administration was not easy. After the death of Bishop Smith, John Constable was

---

[1] Bishops' Possessions, Manorial: unnumbered box.

[2] *A.A.S.R.P.* xxviii, pt. ii, 638.

[3] I. J. Churchill, *Canterbury Administration* (C.H.S, 1933), i, 169 ff.

[4] *Ibid.* ii, 42 ff.

[5] In fact Wolsey was translated to York on the same day on which William Atwater was provided to the see of Lincoln, though Atwater was not consecrated and did not receive temporalities until a little later.

[6] Lambeth Palace, Register Warham, ii, fos. 284v ff.

appointed official. He wrote a letter to the archbishop, which indicates clearly the delicacy of his position. After stating that he enclosed accounts of procurations, he went on to point out:

mi Lord certeyne poor places be so greatly dekeyd that neyther in tyme of the last vacacon nor syth at eny tyme they have payd eny procuraties and now being in moch more dekeye I have remitted them unto your mercy. Dyverse odre places ther be also wher I upon ryght urgent causes have nott taken the hole procuracye but such somme as I withoutt clamoure myght conveniently gett, humbly besechyng your grace to considre the povertie and dekeye of the seyd places and of your goodnes to pardon them clerely[1] . . . I must also besehe your grace take noo displeasour that I have not visited such places as wer this yere visited by the late busshop of the diocese for it is directly ageynst the composicon betwixt you and the Deane and Chapitor of Lincoln.[2]

Though the chapter was not militantly hostile to the archbishop's claims to administration, as it had once been, it is clear that it watched the official with care. Since he was one of the resident canons, the chapter could make the close uncomfortable for him if they thought his administration was at fault.

The archbishop of Canterbury also enjoyed, in theory, the probate of wills where the deceased had *bona notabilia* in more than one diocese. The precise nature of the archbishop's prerogative in this respect was the subject of a dispute when William Atwater was appointed to the see in 1514. The origin of the dispute, according to an embittered account of it in the register of Hugh Oldham, bishop of Exeter, lay in an attempt by Cardinal Morton to treat goods as 'notable', *notabilia*, if they were valued at £5 or even less.[3] The suffragans objected to this claim, and the case was submitted to Rome.[4] While judgement at Rome was awaited, the king made an attempt to resolve the deadlock by ordering that, for the next three years, the archbishop should only have probate if the deceased left goods or debts, or both, in more than one diocese to

[1] A list of the places most likely to have been affected may be found in Lincoln MSS. Subsid. 1, 3, 4, 5, 6; accounts of the procurations are contained in Lambeth Palace, Register Warham, II, fos. 284 ff.

[2] Cj. 2, fo. 7 a.

[3] D. Wilkins, *Concilia Magnae Britanniae* (London, 1737), III, 653.

[4] Lambeth Palace, CM./VI/75.

the value of £10 or more. Similarly, he should only have the administration of the goods of intestates if they were valued at £10 or more.[1] The ten pound assessment of *bona notabilia* was accepted, and this valuation formed the basis for an agreement between Warham and Wolsey, then bishop of Lincoln.[2] To safeguard his prerogative, the archbishop was to have an apparitor in each archdeaconry who would enforce his rights. But on occasions the apparitor might not succeed in laying claim to the probate of a will due to the archbishop. Bishop Atwater granted probate to the will of Ralph Bowman of Uppingham on 4 September 1516 even though the registrar noted that the deceased had *bona notabilia in diversis diocesis provincie Cant' ultra xx^{li}*.[3]

The clergy of the diocese had to be represented by proctors at the convocation of Canterbury, but little was achieved beyond assent to taxation.[4] Hopes that convocation would take serious note of the clamour for reform were thwarted by disagreements between the archbishop and the legate as to their respective roles in achieving it.[5] But convocation provided an opportunity for the clergy from one diocese to meet those of another. Usually such contacts were of a formal nature but on occasions one diocesan bishop might come into conflict with another. The bishop of Ely became involved in a tithe dispute in the Lincoln diocese, during Atwater's episcopate,[6] and special arrangements had to be made regulating the bishop's jurisdiction over the new college of Corpus Christi at Oxford, founded by the bishop of Winchester. It was agreed that all episcopal rights appropriately belonged to the bishop of Winchester.[7]

The king was not aloof and detached from diocesan affairs; his interference in the probate dispute with Canterbury indicates that he was claiming the role of mediator and judge even in a case

---

[1] Lambeth Palace, CM./XI/83.

[2] Lambeth Palace, CM./XI/85; this agreement was upheld in the indenture between Longland and Wolsey, see above, p. 8.

[3] Register 25, fo. 87. For details of the archbishop's apparitors see Somerset House, Probate Act Books I, *passim.*

[4] Convocations, Box I, 1501, 1505, 1509, 1516, 1519, 1522.

[5] Wilkins, *Concilia*, pp. 660–1.

[6] Register 25, fo. 77.   [7] *Ibid.* fo. 94 v.

which he had allowed to go to Rome. His permission had to be obtained before the prior of Newburgh could procure bulls and apostolic letters in connexion with the appropriation of the church of Epworth.[1] Foreigners could not hold benefices in England without his licence, and they paid a double share of taxation for the privilege.[2] To the clergy, the king must have seemed an ever present and hard master, as the burden of taxation which he put upon them increased. Between 1512 and 1518, they were asked to pay six subsidies of a tenth and the weight of this taxation was oppressive:[3] the resident canons of Lincoln cathedral, who were accustomed to receiving £20 or more per annum from the common fund, only received £6 in 1514, and the accounts noted:

Causa exilitatis...hoc anno quam diversis annis precedentibus est causa decimarum et subsidii domino Regi et Archepiscopo Ebor' concessorum.[4]

The king could not afford to tax the clergy so harshly that he risked losing the cooperation of the diocese. He had subtle means of maintaining control but he still relied on a large measure of spontaneous consent and support. At the level of the parish, he had enough benefices to make his patronage worth courting, but not enough to give him control of the parochial clergy.[5] The sympathetic assistance of the diocesan was to be expected because he was nominated by the king. Though the procedure of provision created the illusion that it was the pope who provided the bishop to his see, it deceived no one.[6] A steady succession of civil servants were appointed to the bishopric of Lincoln. Their administration creates the impression of self-sufficiency, but the method of their appointment leaves little doubt that their loyalty to the crown was strong, and that they were unused, and, in many cases, unable, to act against the wishes of the king. As yet an occasion when they might have to choose between two masters had not arisen.[7]

---

[1] Register 25, fo. 65.   [2] Ibid. fo. 86.
[3] Lunt, *Financial Relations of the Papacy with England*, pp. 161–2.
[4] Bj. 3. 3, 1514 (no foliation); for other effects of royal taxation, see below pp. 142 ff.   [5] See below, p. 67.
[6] A. H. Thompson, *The English Clergy and their Organisation in the Later Middle Ages* (Oxford, 1947), pp. 31–9.
[7] Dickens, *The English Reformation*, p. 43.

2. THE BISHOPS OF LINCOLN AND THEIR ADMINISTRATIVE ASSISTANTS

The bishops of Lincoln in the fifteenth century had much in common. Fleming, Gray, Alnwick, Rotherham and Russell had been in the royal service and the others had powerful patrons: Marmaduke Lumley was a close supporter of Cardinal Beaufort, and Chedworth was a follower of William Waynflete.[1] Four were lawyers and three were theologians.[2] Three were Oxford graduates and four were from Cambridge, and some of them were connected with one another; William Gray (bishop of Lincoln 1431–6) went to the council of Sienna with his predecessor Richard Fleming, and one of Gray's successors, John Chedworth, had also been his chaplain.[3] The first three sixteenth-century bishops of Lincoln, William Smith, Thomas Wolsey and William Atwater, were, like their predecessors, graduates and royal servants, and they appear to have known each other and to have worked together.

Smith was the only one of the three whose family had any pretensions to rank. He was the fourth son of Robert Smyth of Peckhouse in Prescot, Lancashire,[4] and he was one of the few early sixteenth-century bishops to be drawn from a county family which may be loosely described as gentry.[5] Wolsey and Atwater had lowlier but more typical origins. Wolsey was the son of an Ipswich butcher,[6] and Atwater was described as being from Cannington in Somerset,[7] though the clearest indication of his paren-

[1] See Emden, *Oxford*, II, 697, 809; III, 1610; *Cambridge*, pp. 11, 133, 377, 491.
[2] The lawyers were Gray, Alnwick, Lumley, Russell; the theologians were Fleming, Rotherham and Chedworth.
[3] Fleming, Gray and Russell were at Oxford; Alnwick, Lumley, Chedworth and Rotherham were at Cambridge, see Emden, *loc. cit.*
[4] Emden, *Oxford*, III, 1721.
[5] J. J. Scarisbrick, 'The Conservative Episcopate in England 1529–1535' (Cambridge, Ph.D. thesis, 1956), p. 2. Dr Scarisbrick shows that Charles Booth, Geoffrey Blythe, Henry Standish, Cuthbert Tunstal, Robert Sherborn and perhaps John Harman *alias* Vesey were the only other bishops with gentle backgrounds, cf. L. B. Smith, *Tudor Prelates and Politics 1506–1558* (Princeton, 1953), pp. 12 ff. Mr Smith is primarily concerned with those holding sees after the break with Rome, which accounts for the difference in his findings.
[6] Emden, *Oxford*, III, 2077.   [7] *L. and P.* I, pt. I, no. 438 (3 m. 25).

tage seems to connect him with Wells; a John Atwater of Wells left the bishop 'my next best gilte pece', and it is possible that William was his son.[1] His family was not armigerous—a defect which he remedied himself in 1509 by acquiring his own coat of arms.[2]

All three early sixteenth-century bishops went to Oxford; Smith was a canon and civil lawyer[3] and Wolsey and Atwater were theologians.[4] All three contributed in a particular way to the advancement of education. Smith founded Brasenose College, Oxford and made gifts to Lincoln College, Oxford, as well as founding two grammar schools.[5] Wolsey founded Cardinal College and attempted to found a college at Ipswich on the model of Winchester.[6] Atwater is not known to have founded any schools or colleges, but he was responsible for persuading William Horman to write his *Vulgaria* printed by Pynson in 1519.[7] He also seems to have been the scholar of the group. Smith bequeathed many books to Brasenose, but they are scarcely marked at all, and show little sign of having been read. Atwater's books, on the other hand, are heavily annotated in his own hand, either to enable him to lecture from them, or as a result of his attending lectures.[8] There is no evidence that he knew any Greek, and, though his handwriting shows humanist influences, he seems, like Smith, to have favoured the old learning rather than the new. But he was not out of touch. His notes include a consideration of whether it was better to study law or theology,[9] and he tried at one point to outline the relationship between faith and doubt and concluded: *fides non excludit omnem dubitationem sed vincentem dubitationem.*[10]

---

[1] *Somerset Medieval Wills 1383–1500*, ed. F. W. Weaver (Somerset Record Society, 1901), p. 389.

[2] Bodleian Library, MS. Ashmole 858, fos. 9, 17.

[3] Emden, *Oxford*, III, 1721.   [4] Emden, *Oxford*, I, 73; III, 2077.

[5] Emden, *Oxford*, III, 1721; R. Churton, *Lives of William Smyth Bishop of Lincoln and Sir Richard Sutton Knight, Founders of Brasen Nose College* (Oxford, 1800), *passim*.   [6] Emden, *Oxford*, III, 2077.

[7] *Horman's Vulgaria Puerorum*, ed. M. R. James (Roxburghe Club, 1926), p. 3.

[8] For a list of these books, see Emden, *Oxford*, I, 73.

[9] Brasenose College Library, UB. S. I. 27.

[10] *Ibid.*

Smith and Wolsey owed their advancement to a powerful patron. It is unlikely that Smith was educated in the household of Margaret, Countess of Richmond, but he enjoyed her later favour; he was presented to benefices by her,[1] and it is significant that, although he was a royal servant of some standing, he took little part in public affairs after her death.[2] Wolsey was fortunate in having the support first of the Marquis of Dorset, and then of Sir Richard Nanfan.[3] Atwater had a variety of patrons; it is possible that at Magdalen he became acquainted with Waynflete and that this friendship accounts for his election to an Eton fellowship in July 1482.[4] Thereafter he probably owed his advancement to Smith and to Wolsey: he acted as commissary for Smith, when Smith was appointed Chancellor of the University of Oxford,[5] and he had been at Magdalen with Wolsey. An early association between the two may account for the fact that Atwater's main promotions followed Wolsey's rise to power. Whatever the relationship between them, it was thought by the university of Oxford to be close enough for letters to be sent to Atwater urging him to use his influence with Wolsey to help the university to overcome its perennial problems of money, sanitation, plague and privileges.[6]

Faithful service to the crown distinguished all three bishops. None of them had served in a parish and all had served the crown. Smith was keeper of the hanaper of the chancery, and a member of Prince Arthur's council in the Marches of Wales, of which he was subsequently president until his retirement in 1512. Recognition of the value of his service came in the form of innumerable canonries and deaneries including that of St. Stephen's chapel, Westminster. In 1493 Smith was promoted to the bishopric of Lichfield and Coventry before his subsequent translation to Lin-

---

[1] Cf. D.N.B. *ad loc.*

[2] See below, p. 18.

[3] A. F. Pollard, *Wolsey* (London, 1929), p. 13.

[4] He was also bursar and precentor of the college for a period, see Eton College Audit Rolls, 19, 20, 21, 22, 23, *passim.*

[5] *Epistolae Academicae*, ed. H. Anstey, II (O.H.S. xxxvi, 1898), 655–6.

[6] Bodleian Library MS. 282, fos. 13, 32v, 37v, 40v.

coln in 1495.[1] Wolsey had been chaplain to Henry Deane, who was for a short time archbishop of Canterbury, and then to Sir Richard Nanfan, deputy of Calais. But his distinction lay in diplomacy: in 1508 he took part in a number of minor missions to Scotland and the Netherlands, and, after being appointed almoner to the king in 1509, he took an ever increasing share in organizing the war against France. Like Smith he held a large number of benefices including the deanery of St Stephen's, but Lincoln was his first bishopric.[2] Atwater's services to the crown were less spectacular; a large number of preferments came to him while he was still chancellor's commissary at Oxford,[3] but he does not seem to have entered royal service until his appointment as dean of the chapel royal in 1508.[4] Thereafter he is found engaged in minor business, until his preferment to the see of Lincoln, in September 1514, following Wolsey's translation to York.

Atwater was at least in his middle sixties when he was appointed to the see of Lincoln, and he may have been older;[5] he could reasonably regard the see as a form of retirement, and, though he was very active in administering it, he was not torn between a series of conflicting duties, as Smith, in particular, appears to have been. Atwater made occasional appearances at Convocation, the house of Lords and the Council, but the greater part of his time was spent in his diocese.[6] Smith after his appointment to Lincoln

---

[1] Emden, *Oxford*, III, 1721; C. A. J. Skeel, *The Council in the Marches of Wales* (London, 1904), pp. 30 ff.

[2] Emden, *Oxford*, III, 2077; Pollard, *Wolsey*, pp. 13 ff.

[3] For a list of these, see Emden, *Oxford*, I, 73.

[4] Cf. Emden, *loc. cit.*; Dr Emden suggests that Atwater was appointed to the chapel royal in 1502 and held it until his death; in fact Geoffrey Symeon was dean until his death in August 1508 (P.R.O. REQ. 1./3/fo. 161; for Symeon's death, see A. 3. 2, fo. 21.)

[5] The inscription on Atwater's tomb was said to have recorded that he died on 4 February 1520/1 in his eighty-first year: *obiit anno aetatis suae octogesimo primo* (British Museum, Lansdowne MSS. 978, fo. 183); the inscription has now disappeared, and it is impossible to know whether Atwater died in his eighty-first year, or, more probably, his seventy-first; his itinerary if that of a septuagenarian is remarkable.

[6] An itinerary for Bishop Atwater is appended to my edition of his court of audience book, *L.R.S.* 61, pp. xxiv ff.

still continued as president of the council of the Marches of Wales; he was often in a dilemma to know where his responsibilites lay. On one occasion Smith was on his way to visit the dean and chapter of Lincoln when he received an order from the prince of Wales to return to Bewdley.[1] It may have been this incident which prompted him to write to Sir Reginald Bray; he drew Bray's attention to the ruinous state of his cathedral church and the non-residence of parsons and vicars as well as the 'unkind dealing of many in his diocese'.[2] Clearly he thought that there was much he could and should be doing in his diocese, and his absence from it caused him some anxiety. Wolsey was not apparently worried in the same way.[3]

In fact, the evidence suggests that Smith, either in spite of his anxieties or because of them, visited the diocese and administered it himself on a number of occasions. He was not a complete absentee, like Wolsey, nor as diligent a diocesan as Atwater. He personally held ordinations eleven times during an episcopate of nineteen years,[4] while Atwater held five in the six and a half years during which he was bishop.[5] Smith also visited his cathedral church in 1501, 1503, 1507 and 1510;[6] five Leicestershire deaneries were visited by him in person in September 1510,[7] and it is possible that he visited the monastic houses of Ashridge, Irthlingburgh, Chacombe, Wroxton and St Frideswide's.[8] Little visitation material of any kind survives from his episcopate but it is very unlikely that the extant fragments represent the sum of Smith's involvement. Casual references to him also suggest further activity: he was partly responsible for the rebuilding of the episcopal manor at Liddington;[9] his motto and shield can still be seen in places in the hall and windows. An account book survives of the expenses he incurred while staying

---

[1] Churton, *Lives of William Smyth of Lincoln and Sir Richard Sutton*, p. 112.
[2] Westminster Abbey Muniments, no. 16038.
[3] Wolsey was personally installed in 1509 as dean of Lincoln, A. 3. 4, fo. 30 v.
[4] Register 24, fos. 16, 19, 23 v, 27, 28, 44 v, 45, 52, 63 v, 65, 75 v.
[5] Register 25, fos. 111 ff.
[6] Register 24, fo. 230; A. 3. 2, fo. 71; Vj. 6, fo. 1; A. 3. 4, fo. 26.
[7] Viv. 5, fos. 70 v–92.
[8] Religious Houses 2.   [9] *L.R.S.* 14, p. xxiv.

at Banbury in October 1508; he had had his leggings repaired before he left London at a cost of 2s., and on arrival at Banbury he employed a barber, at a cost of 4d., before entertaining at least twenty people to dinner and supper over the week-end. He appears to have lived well, and to have enjoyed a varied diet which included beef, whale, mutton, pork, salt and stockfish and salmon, besides the usual chickens, eggs and butter.[1] From Banbury he could supervise the arrangements for his new foundation of Brasenose, and it is possible that he spent the last years of his life there.

Atwater had never been so heavily involved in affairs of state as Smith and he was older when provided to Lincoln: these two circumstances made it easier for him to devote his considerable energies to the diocese. Between 1515 and 1520, he spent fifteen and a half months at Old Temple, Holborn, and most of the rest of his time at one of his manors in the diocese. He devoted more time to the southern part of the diocese than to the northern, but this was probably because he preferred to be near to London.[2] It seems likely that during his episcopate he visited every archdeaconry in the diocese, although nothing survives, except a visitation monition, to indicate that he went to Northampton.[3] Nine visitations of deaneries or religious houses were made for him by special commissaries, and eighteen by his vicar general, but at least one hundred and three were conducted by him in person.[4] To the lower clergy this activity must have been as amazing as it was unexpected; the curates of St Paul's Bedford were caught unawares by the bishop, and, in 1518, they had to appear before the chancellor becaue they failed to meet the bishop with a procession when he visited the church. They were ordered to say a mass for his well-being, and to give 2d. to the shrine of St Hugh at Lincoln.[5]

Little evidence survives of the pastoral side of the bishop's

[1] Bishop's Accounts, Misc. 18, passim.
[2] For his itinerary, see above, p. 16n.
[3] Visitation Monitions 1500–1739, June 1519.
[4] Vj. 6, fos. 32 v ff.; L.R.S. 33, 35, 37, passim; this figure includes places visited twice and is approximate as there are occasions when a visitation may be inferred though no actual records of it survive (see L.R.S. 33, pp. 141 ff.)
[5] Cj. 2, fo. 56v.

duties. Probably most of the routine work of confirmations, dedications of churchyards and the receiving of vows of the religious was left to suffragans.[1] Yet though he was a theologian and not a lawyer Atwater took some interest in the legal side of a bishop's work. Bishops of Lincoln by 1500 had two courts: a consistory court, the presidency of which was invariably delegated and to which came cases brought at the request of two parties, and a court of audience. Atwater held his own court of audience eighty-four times out of a total of 133 occasions on which it is known to have sat.[2] Obviously the very name of the court would imply that it was proper for the bishop to preside, but it was nevertheless unusual for a diocesan to do so. Records of over 220 audience cases have survived for the episcopate of Atwater's successor, John Longland, but he only appears to have presided in two of them.[3] To the court of audience came a variety of cases, either on appeal from the court of the bishop's commissary or archdeacon, or as a result of a direct intervention by the bishop, sometimes as a consequence of his visitation. No appeal could be made to the court of audience from the consistory court.

On occasions Atwater delegated the hearing of part, or all, of a case to a deputy, usually his chancellor. The delegation followed no recognizable rule, and it looks as though he simply gave to his deputy any work for which he had neither the time nor the inclination.[4] But the activity of Atwater, and the anxiety Smith appears to have felt at his prolonged absences, raise the question of how important the presence of the bishop in the diocese actually was. Did he bring to the conduct of affairs an authority and experience which were really noticed? Or were the bishop's deputies so efficient that the absence of the diocesan was hardly significant?

Smith and Fox certainly thought that their presence in their

[1] See below, p. 25.

[2] Cj. 2, *passim*.

[3] Cj. 3, *passim*; Cj. 4, *passim*; for the two occasions on which Longland presided see Cj. 3, fos. 21, 22.

[4] For a fuller discussion of the procedure of the court of audience and its relationship to other courts in the diocese, see my edition of Bishop Atwater's court of audience book, *L.R.S.* 61, pp. ix ff.

dioceses was in some way desirable and necessary;[1] Smith, in particular, saw a relationship between the decay of churches and the non-residence of incumbents on the one hand and the absenteeism of the bishop on the other. Fox when he resided in his diocese also devoted his attention to keeping a check on his non-resident clergy. The connexion may be important.[2] Frequently the fabric repairs necessary in parish churches were the responsibility of the religious houses which had appropriated them.[3] Similarly the incumbents most likely to be non-resident were those who had power enough, through family influence or royal service, to force the pope or a bishop to grant them a dispensation to hold cures in plurality.[4] In both cases, therefore, specifically mentioned by Smith, powerful interests might be involved. The bishop might have to force a well-known religious house, from outside the diocese, to appear before him to answer for the ruin of its appropriated churches, and it might be necessary to sequester the fruits of those churches if his citation was ignored; alternatively he might need to force a non-resident either to show his dispensation or to reside in his church. In either case, the bishop or his deputy required all his authority; that of the bishop was increased by his reputation at court and the royal favour he would be thought to have enjoyed. A chancellor or vicar general acting for him in his absence would be unknown and possibly unheeded. Even when the bishop resided the problem was real enough. Bishop Atwater had great difficulty in compelling religious houses and non-resident clergy to appear before him. Nearly half of those cited to appear before his court did not do so, and a note of *non comparuit* was entered by their names;[5] of those who did appear, some took a long time: the vicar of Ashwell could not be found when he was due to appear before the bishop in September 1518. He was cited again but nothing more was heard from him until the farmer of the living appeared before the bishop on 9 April 1519 and admitted that the vicar had received letters of

---

[1] See above, pp. 4, 17.
[2] *Register of Richard Fox Bishop of Durham 1494–1501*, ed. M. P. Howden (Surtees Society, 1932), p. xlv.
[3] See below, p. 132.   [4] See below, p. 99.   [5] Cj. 2, fos. 77v ff.

citation and promised that he would appear before Whitsuntide.[1] Atwater was presiding in person over the court and was known to have the confidence of Wolsey; if his orders could be ignored, those of a deputy were likely to have been treated with contempt.

When Richard Mayhew of Hereford returned to his diocese to reside in it, he devoted much of his time to dealing with cases of heresy and to trying to discipline the vicars choral of his cathedral church.[2] In complicated cases of this kind the presence of the bishop was desirable and sometimes essential. There might be no precedents which would guide the judge, and important personages or powerful interests could be involved; the case of Richard Thornton presented just this problem. He had wandered around the diocese of Lincoln preaching without a licence; he claimed to hold an exhibition from the queen to preach, and he appears to have gone from diocese to diocese doing so; his orders were in question and any investigation into them would require the cooperation of the registrar at York, where he said he had been ordained. If Thornton was speaking the truth and he really did have the queen's support, any move against him would provoke royal displeasure. If he was insane, the case was still a serious one and required the support of other diocesans in whose dioceses he had also offended.[3] The bishop was probably the only person who could risk trying to unravel a case of this kind.

The bishop could also bring flexibility to diocesan affairs. There is a marked contrast between his conduct of cases in his court of audience and that of his subordinates in the archdeaconries. Bishop Atwater never imposed full public penance on an offender. If full penance was imposed, the offender, according to a fifteenth-century formulary book, had to go before the cross in procession, carrying a burning candle, and receive chastisement from the curate at the four corners of the churchyard.[4] The

[1] *Ibid.* fo. 76v.

[2] *Register of Richard Mayhew, Bishop of Hereford*, ed. A. T. Bannister (Canterbury and York Society, 1921), p. v.

[3] Cj. 2, fos. 100a ff. See also below, pp. 41, 112, for further mention of Thornton.

[4] Formulary 2, fo. 27. For a fuller consideration of this question see my introduction to the court of audience book, *L.R.S.* 61, pp. xv ff.

bishop still demanded that the penitent go in the procession bare-headed, and sometimes clothed only in his shirt, but he was to offer his candle at the High Altar and he was not told to undergo the discipline in the churchyard;[1] on occasions he might, in addition, have to give money either for the rebuilding of the Fosse Dyke, a canal linking Lincoln and the Trent, or to the shrine of St Hugh, and sometimes special prayers or fasting would be ordered.[2] In contrast the commissary in the archdeaconry of Leicester, William Mason, who also acted as president of the bishop's consistory court,[3] was still ordering the discipline.[4] Perhaps the contacts which the bishop had with events in London made him more sensitive to public opinion, and more ready to meet it; at any rate he seems to have used his discretion and departed from the accepted penitential formulae.[5] A deputy either did not have such discretion or he did not care to use it. He had to remember that he might, at any time, have to account for his actions to the bishop on whom he depended for his appointment.[6] In consequence the danger for the diocese in the absence of the bishop lay in the tendency of subordinates to play for safety, to perform their duties in a routine, even mechanical, fashion, with the corollary that they might be ignored by the powerful, and appear harsh and unreasonable to the parishioner. Atwater brought to his diocese a warmth and spirituality which make his visitation injunctions, in particular, notable;[7] he also brought the weight of his authority and discretion. His deputies, and those of other non-resident bishops, lacked some of these qualities: it was perhaps for that reason that the highest offices

[1] Cj. 2, *passim*.

[2] Cj. 2, fos. 34v, 36v, 56v, 74, 88, 90v, 98v, 107, 107v.

[3] See below, p. 26.   [4] Viv. 5, fo. 25.

[5] Bishop Alnwick rarely seems to have ordered the discipline, see A. H. Thompson, *The English Clergy and their Organisation in the Later Middle Ages*, pp. 206 ff. When a penitent is simply asked to undergo *publicam penitenciam* it is hard to know exactly what was involved and whether it included the discipline or not; in Atwater's court book most penances are more fully and less ambiguously given.

[6] Bishop Fitzjames was ultimately responsible for his chancellor's conduct of the Hunne affair, see A. Ogle, *The Tragedy of the Lollards Tower*, pp. 68 ff.

[7] D. Knowles, *The Religious Orders in England*, III (Cambridge, 1959), 68–9.

eluded them. Smith and Atwater perceived that their actual presence was of consequence in the diocese; Wolsey did not. As a result some sees, particularly those collected by the cardinal in the early sixteenth century, were probably suffering from being run by deputies, and never enjoying the authority as well as the wisdom of a more experienced and senior man.[1]

For routine affairs, the deputies employed by the bishop were adequate enough; there is no question of their competence in handling day-to-day administration. Duties which could only be performed by persons in episcopal orders were carried out by suffragans: their most important duty was that of ordination, in which they worked in close association with the bishop's chancellor. The suffragan actually ordained the candidates but the chancellor was responsible for examining the ordinands.[2] The bishop paid the suffragan his expenses, which could be as little as 3s. 4d. or as much as £1. 15s.,[3] but the suffragan gave to the bishop all the money he had taken in fees for his performance of other strictly episcopal functions.[4] He blessed newly elected abbots, for which he charged 33s. 4d., and he rededicated churchyards which had been defiled by the shedding of blood; this was a more expensive procedure, and in the case of Little Bitham cost as much as £3. 6s. 8d.[5] No evidence survives of the activities of the suffragan in confirming the children of the parishes which he passed on his way to ordination, but since this was normal procedure and did not involve fees, it probably was not neglected but simply went unrecorded.[6]

The duties of a suffragan were not particularly onerous, and did not require a special knowledge of theology or canon law. It was usual in the Lincoln diocese for the bishop to employ two suffragans at a time and they were often from religious orders.

[1] It would be particularly interesting to have a diocesan study of the diocese of Worcester, which was held by foreigners between 1497 and 1535, besides a study of the effect of Wolsey's absence on his dioceses.

[2] Bishop's Accounts, Rentals, 1, fo. 12v: 'pro expensis magistri Cancellarii Suffragenei Willelmi Spenser et Willelmi Miller ac servientium suorum tempore celebracionis ordinum die sabbati iiii^{or} temporum in prima ebdomada xl^{mo} apud Bukden'. For the significance of the chancellor's presence see below, p. 25.

[3] *Ibid.* fo. 12v.   [4] *Ibid.* fo. 9v.   [5] *Ibid.* fo. 9v.

[6] W. Lyndwood, *Provinciale* (Oxford, 1679), Lib. I, tit. 6, cap 5.

They were rarely graduates, and sometimes they worked in more than one diocese. Thomas Ford, an Austin canon and bishop of Achonry in Ireland, acted for Smith in the early years of his episcopate; he also seems to have acted in the Lichfield diocese.[1] He was without help in Lincoln until the appointment of Augustine Church, abbot of Thame and bishop of Lydda in Palestine, in 1501.[2] According to his commission, Thomas Ford was supposed to act in the archdeaconries of Lincoln, Stow, Leicester, Huntingdon and Rutland after 1501, thereby leaving Augustine the archdeaconries of Oxford, Buckingham, Bedford and Northampton.[3] But this division did not work out in practice. Augustine took an ordination at Lincoln in March 1503, and Thomas ordained at Oxford in March 1505.[4] In fact Thomas ceased to act as a suffragan in the diocese after 1505. Augustine was alone until the appointment of John Bell, bishop of Mayo in Ireland, in 1507; he too was an Austin canon who served several dioceses and continued to serve in Lincoln until about 1529.[5] John was left on his own between 1512 and 1514; in December 1514 Roger Smyth, abbot of Dorchester, was appointed to help. He held the titular see of Lydda in Palestine and also seems to have acted as a suffragan for the diocese of Salisbury;[6] he, too, served Longland, and, though he had ordained in many archdeaconries under Atwater, Longland commissioned him to work particularly in the archdeaconries of Oxford, Bedford and Buckingham.[7] Atwater appears to have thought that two suffragans were insufficient and in 1516 he asked the pope that John Bransfort, from the monastery of Bury St Edmunds, be consecrated as a suffragan for the diocese.[8] It is

---

[1] Register 24, *passim*: D. Knowles, *The Religious Orders in England*, III, 493.

[2] Knowles, *op. cit.* p. 494; Register 24, fo. 29.

[3] Register 23, fo. 217v.   [4] Register 24, fos. 34v, 48v.

[5] Knowles, *op. cit.* p. 493; for a very helpful note on Longland's suffragans, see *Chapter Acts of the Cathedral Church of St Mary of Lincoln 1520–1536*, ed. R. E. G. Cole (Lincoln Record Society, 12, 1915), p. xiv.

[6] W. Dugdale, *Monasticon Anglicanum* (London, 1817), VI, pt. I, 323: Dugdale was under the impression Roger died in 1518 or 1535; the earlier date is impossible as Longland commissioned him to act as suffragan in 1521 (Register 26, fo. 69) and 1535 seems the most probable date of his death (Cole, *loc. cit.*).

[7] Register 26, fo. 69.   [8] *L. and P.* II, pt. I, no. 2535.

not clear whether the pope granted the request, but by 1519 John, bishop of Ario, is found acting in the diocese; he was probably the monk for whose consecration the bishop had asked.[1] Longland retained the practice of having three suffragans where possible. This development may have become necessary because of the other commitments of suffragans; at any rate it is hard to see how the work had increased so much as to demand the services of three men when, under Bishop Smith, one had frequently sufficed.[2]

Suffragans, although they were in episcopal orders, were less important in the diocese than the bishop's other deputies: his vicar general, official principal, commissary general and his chancellor. The suffragans could only ordain on the authority of the bishop himself or his vicar general or chancellor.[3] Only once was a suffragan present in the bishop's household, and they appear to have enjoyed little status.[4] The bishop's other deputies were of greater consequence, though the distribution of power between them is hard to unravel; there was apt to be a distinction between theory and practice, and the loss, in many cases, of the original commissions to these deputies further complicates questions of their precise power.

In theory the vicar general acted as the bishop's *alter ego* in his absence. His powers included those of episcopal visitation (with the powers of correction subsequent upon it), the right to hold synods of the clergy, to empower religious orders to proceed to elections and the authority to receive the vows of religious and to transfer them, where appropriate; vicars general could absolve from ecclesiastical penalties and had charge of those clerks convicted of secular offences who were imprisoned in the bishop's prisons and might wish to proceed to purgation. They were often given powers of probate and the right to hear appeals, as well as having the right to conduct the bishop's correspondence and to receive the resignations of incumbents. They were also empowered to inquire into the rights of patrons and admit to benefices those clerks whom they had found suitable. They were responsible for

[1] Register 25, *passim.*
[2] Cole, *op. cit.* p. xiv.
[3] Register 24, fos. 1–93 v.
[4] Cj. 2, fo. 62.

sending letters asking the archdeacon to induct to a benefice and they issued letters testimonial and dimissory. The one limit to their power was its duration: it lapsed the moment the bishop set foot in the diocese.[1] The official principal was a more permanent deputy. His office did not lapse on the return of the bishop but he presided for him over the consistory court, which heard cases brought at the instance of two parties. No appeal lay from the consistory to the bishop, since the official sat merely as a substitute for the bishop, and the court was regarded as the bishop's own. The bishop's other court, his court of audience, was either held by him in person or by his chancellor or commissary general, both of whom had powers of correction and probate. They also had the right to hear appeals or to intervene in a case with which the bishop was particularly concerned.[2]

It was always possible for an overlap to occur between the respective duties of these officers: an instance case might come before the chancellor in the audience court only for it to be found to have already gone before the official principal in the consistory court. In a marriage case, for example, which came before the vicar general in 1529, the man involved asserted that the woman had been cited to appear before the consistory court at Stamford; the case was left to the consistory.[3] Another matrimonial case in the same year was thought to belong more appropriately to the consistory court and was adjourned to it.[4] In practice the danger of duplication was averted in a variety of ways. Under both Smith and Longland, the offices of vicar general, commissary general, chancellor and official principal were often combined and held by the same man.[5] The only occasions, in either episcopate, when any separation was made, were when the vicar

---

[1] The commissions to Lincoln vicars general are not as full as this (see Register 24, fos. 97v, 210; Formulary 3) but, since the intention is clearly to grant to the vicar general all episcopal power except that of collating to benefices, the commissions should not be taken as exhaustive; for a very full commission, see that of Wolsey to Brian Higden, 1514 (A. H. Thompson, *The English Clergy*, pp. 197 ff.).

[2] C. Morris, 'A Consistory Court in the Middle Ages', *Journal of Ecclesiastical History*, XIV, no. 2 (1963), 151–5.

[3] Cj. 4, fo. 34.   [4] *Ibid.* fo. 44v.

[5] Register 24, fos. 104, 132v, 163, 169v, 210, 229; Register 26, fo. 274.

generalship had lapsed and the bishop was in his diocese; on at least one occasion when this happened, the office of commissary general was given to someone who had not been vicar general;[1] this was a short and simple expedient which was probably designed to enable the vicar general to have a rest, freed from the jurisdictional duties of the commissary by the separate grant. There would have been no need to free him of the duties of official principal, since he, in practice, delegated them to a permanent deputy who was known as the president of the consistory court.[2] In this way two purposes were served: during the absence of the bishop from his diocese, one man performed all his jurisdictional functions, with the result that there could be no confusion about his ultimate authority; the only possible confusion lay in ascertaining in which capacity the deputy was acting. When the bishop was in his diocese, the office of vicar general lapsed, that of official principal continued to be delegated, and help was given to the bishop in the conduct of his court by a specially appointed commissary general.

Bishop Atwater took this process of amalgamation a stage further; not only did he appoint Richard Roston as chancellor, commissary general and official principal; Roston also combined these offices with a *permanent* vicar generalship.[3] He was described as vicar general when the bishop was in the diocese, and it is probable that he continued to admit candidates to benefices notwithstanding the bishop's presence; this may account for admissions being made in two different places in the diocese on the same days.[4]

[1] Register 26, fo. 190; there are examples of a short-lived but separate commissary generalship under Smith: in 1501 Henry Wilcocks acted as commissary general though Charles Booth was combining the other offices, *Liber Albus Civitatis Oxoniensis*, ed. W. P. Ellis and H. E. Salter (Oxford, 1909), p. 97, and William Mason may well have done the same (Emden, *Cambridge*, p. 395).

[2] C. Morris, 'A Consistory Court in the Middle Ages', *Journal of Ecclesiastical History*, xiv, no. 2 (1963), 154; William Mason held this office, see Proxies, 1490–1598, Box. 71.

[3] No commissions survive of the exact terms of Atwater's appointments but it is absolutely clear from the court of audience book that Roston held all these appointments whether or not the bishop was *in remotis*. For his designation as vicar general and chancellor see Cj. 2, *passim*; for the combination of commissary general and chancellor see Cj. 2, fos. 78, 84v.

[4] For a note on the dating of institutions see my appendix to the court of

Richard Roston, though not in episcopal orders, was almost a second bishop: he held the court of audience even when the bishop was in the diocese, and he conducted visitations in the diocese. Perhaps his peculiar appointment, which did not survive the death of his master, marks an early recognition of the fact that the diocese was too large for any one man to administer. It needed to be permanently divided or its administration had to be delegated.[1]

The men holding these combined offices held a decisive position in the diocese. All of them were lawyers. James Whitstones, who acted as vicar general to Smith between 1495 and 1500, was a canon lawyer and held degrees from Cambridge and Bologna. He, like Smith, owed his promotion to Margaret, Countess of Richmond, of whose council he eventually became president; he appears to have given up his vicar generalship when he went into her service, and he probably spent most of his time in Leicester, where he was dean of the Newarke college.[2] Charles Booth, vicar general from 1500 to 1508,[3] was also a graduate of Cambridge and Bologna, but he was a civil and not a canon lawyer. Like Smith he was a member of Prince Arthur's council, and he became chancellor of the council in the Marches of Wales in 1502.[4] He was succeeded in the diocese of Lincoln by Henry Wilcocks,[5] who was a doctor of civil law with some diocesan experience;[6] he had been official to the archdeacon of Oxford in 1501 and had acted as commissary general, probably during the residence of the bishop in the diocese, in 1501 and 1507.[7] He was still vicar general in 1515,[8]

audience book, *L.R.S.* 61, p. xxiv; the bishop is unlikely, for instance, to have been responsible for both the institutions made on 21 May 1520, one at Brickhill and one at Old Temple (Register 25, fos. 35, 49, 58).

    [1] For another example of a permanent vicar generalship, see I. J. Churchill, *Canterbury Administration*, I, 594; for Roston's visitations see *L.R.S.* 33, 35, 37, *passim*.   [2] Emden, *Oxford*, III, 2039.

    [3] The earliest mention of Booth as vicar general, chancellor, official principal and commissary general is found in Register 24, fo. 153 (10 August 1500); the last mention of him in this capacity was in 1508 (A. 3. 3, fo. 6 v).

    [4] Emden, *Cambridge*, p. 77; he later became bishop of Hereford.

    [5] Register 23, fo. 377 v.   [6] Emden, *Oxford*, III, 2047.

    [7] Bishop's Accounts, 7, *passim*; *Liber Albus Civitatis Oxoniensis*, ed. W. P. Ellis and H. E. Salter, p. 97.   [8] Cj. 2, fo. 23 v.

but he then retired to the archdeaconry of Leicester, where he was a conscientious archdeacon and personally visited his clergy on a number of occasions.[1] In 1515, Richard Roston succeeded him. He may well have been a relative of Bishop Smith, since he sometimes is described as 'Richard Roston *alias* Smith'.[2] He was a graduate of the university of Cambridge and was a doctor of canon law; his experience was mainly of diocesan affairs.[3] He acted as commissary for the archdeaconries of Huntingdon and Bedford in the years 1499–1500 and he resided at the cathedral between 1504 and 1511, taking his full share of responsibilities.[4]

Legal training fitted a vicar general for the conduct of routine episcopal duties; Booth and Roston both conducted visitations for the bishop, and the evidence suggests that they did so thoroughly and conscientiously.[5] Roston also presided over the bishop's court of audience, but it was here that the limitations of a deputy are seen. Because of the peculiar nature of his appointment, Roston could refer a case to the bishop whenever he liked, without having to prorogue it or refer it out of the diocese. The bishop was usually at hand and could be asked for his opinion in a difficult case. Roston sometimes took advantage of this opportunity:[6] one occasion on which he did so is particularly interesting. It came before Roston on 3 December 1517. Alice Riding of Eton appeared before the court and confessed that she had had a child by a priest, which she had suffocated and buried under a pile of straw in her father's orchard. The case was a difficult one, not only because a priest was implicated, but also because an ecclesiastical offence and a secular crime were both involved: the ecclesiastical court had to deal with the incontinence and the failure to baptize the child before its death; the secular courts would be concerned with the homicide; the seriousness of the case was aggravated in the bishop's eyes by the fact that the child was born

[1] *A.A.S.R.P.* xxviii (1905), 127–43.
[2] *L. and P.* i, pt. i, no. 438, 218.   [3] Emden, *Cambridge*, p. 493.
[4] Bishop's Accounts, 7, *passim*; A. 3. 2, fo. 100; A. 3. 3, *passim*; A. 3. 4, *passim*.
[5] *L.R.S.* 33, 35, 37, *passim*; Vj. 5, *passim*.
[6] For another complicated case in which the bishop was called in to give judgement see Cj. 2, fo. 39v.

on the feast of the Purification. No doubt it was these factors, taken with the simplicity of the girl, which caused Roston to refer the case to the bishop: the scribe carefully noted:

hec omnia Dominus iniunxit pro offensis ad suam correctionem spectantibus homicidio penitus omittendo cum quo noluit ullo modo intromittere.[1]

We do not know how Roston would have dealt with the case had the bishop not been there, but the bishop had an authority which might be useful if there was any dispute about the respective jurisdiction of the royal and ecclesiastical courts. A deputy left to handle a diocese, without the knowledge that his diocesan was near at hand, might well choose to leave a case of this kind alone, at least until the royal courts had finished with it. Few can have wished to have had something like Hunne's case on their hands, and the corollary must have been that they proceeded with the utmost care when persons of consequence were involved. Yet the vicars general and chancellors inevitably became the symbols of ecclesiastical jurisdiction and attracted a certain unpopularity in consequence. Under Bishop Longland, the chancellor was murdered by Lincolnshire rebels in the Pilgrimage of Grace; his predecessors had been treated more lightly; one man tore up his citation to appear before the audience court, and another called the chancellor a false judge, but opposition had not yet turned from contempt and contumacy to open violence.[2]

The machinery of the diocesan administration seemed cumbersome and provoked greater resentment and discontent at the level of the archdeaconry. Responsibility for diocesan affairs in the archdeaconry was shared between the archdeacon and the bishop's commissary. The commissary had cognisance of all cases belonging to the bishop; Bishop Smith ordered his commissaries to inquire into the dispensations of non-residents, and to certify their names to the bishop, or his chancellor, before Easter each year; the commissary was also to sequester the fruits of a rectory, if the rector refused to repair it, and he accounted to the bishop for the money due from vacant benefices, the mortu-

[1] Cj. 2, fo. 51v.   [2] Cj. 2, fo. 57v; Cj. 4, fo. 21.

aries of priests and farmed churches. He also had probate of wills, jurisdiction over moral offences and, on occasions, on a special mandate from the bishop or his deputy, he might have the right of visitation.[1] The evidence suggests that commissaries were, in fact, doing all these things. The commissary for the Leicester archdeaconry was active in searching out moral offenders, and cases of fornication, usury, divination, heresy, defamation and neglect to receive the sacraments came before him.[2] The commissary in the archdeaconry of Buckingham was granting probate of a large number of wills every year, and administering the goods of those who died intestate.[3] Accounts survive from the commissaries of all archdeaconries testifying to their zeal in collecting and accounting for the bishop's dues from vacancies, farmed churches and probate fees.[4] William Mason, on a special commission from the bishop, visited the archdeaconry of Leicester as a commissary.[5] In performing this duty, he was coming close to the preserve of the archdeacons and their deputies, the archdeacon's officials. The archdeacon's duties were less jurisdictional and more pastoral than those of the commissary. He was the *oculus episcopi* with a general duty of supervising the clergy, particularly through visitation; he also administered the sacraments to sick clergy and was responsible for seeing that their duties were being properly performed.[6] But the archdeacon also had his own court, and to it came the instance cases of the diocese; in particular he was likely to hear a large number of cases of breach of contract, defamation and tithe—cases, in fact, in which the dispute was between two parties and brought at the instance

[1] For a commission to commissaries see Register 24, fo. 216; for a particularly helpful discussion of their duties, see C. Morris, 'The Commissary of the Bishop in the Diocese of Lincoln', *Journal of Ecclesiastical History*, x, 50 ff.

[2] *A.A.S.R.P.* xxviii (1905), 603 ff.

[3] Aylesbury Record Office, D/A/We, 1–224.

[4] Bishop's Accounts Misc. 6, *passim*; ibid. 7, *passim*; Bishop Fuller's Transcripts, fos. 132–44; Bishop's Accounts, Rentals, 1, fo. 11; Bodleian Library, MSS. Barlow, 54, fo. 47v.

[5] Viv. 5, *passim*.

[6] A. H. Thompson, 'Diocesan Administration in the Middle Ages: Archdeacons and Rural Deans', *Proceedings of the British Academy* (1943), pp. 191 ff.; Lyndwood, *Provinciale*, Lib. I, tit. 10, cap. I and II.

of one of them. In addition the archdeacon, like the commissary, had probate jurisdiction and the right to correct moral failings.[1] In consequence, there could be considerable rivalry between the archdeacon and commissary for probate and moral cases. Disputes between them in the fourteenth century had been bitter.[2] By the sixteenth century, the hostility between them had been largely overcome by a process of amalgamation: the same man deputized for the archdeacon as his official and acted as bishop's commissary. William Mason combined the offices for the archdeaconry of Leicester in 1509,[3] and John Silvester succeeded him in both.[4] Robert Halam was both official and commissary for the Lincoln archdeaconry in 1515,[5] and, in 1519, John Cocks and Robert Gostwick acted in both capacities in the archdeaconries of Buckingham and Northampton respectively.[6] But, though disputes about the respective responsibilities of archdeacon and commissary were largely a matter of the past, the issues confronting both were considerable.

The archdeacon and the commissary had courts of first instance. They provided a preliminary hearing for the majority of ecclesiastical cases which never proceeded to the consistory or audience court. In cases of correction, or office cases, as they were called, the jurisdiction of which was shared by the archdeacon and commissary, the initiative in detecting a case lay with the church authorities. The archdeacon or commissary had to find out enough about the case to be able to bring charges; the material for them might be elicited at a visitation, or it might come from information laid by the incumbent of the parish, or by an officer whose duty it was to ferret out cases and to cite defendants, the apparitor. Occasionally local rumour reached the court, and action was taken on it.[7] But, in all office cases, the responsibility for not issuing citations frivolously, and for not charging on inadequate evidence,

---

[1] Morris, 'The Commissary of the Bishop in the Diocese of Lincoln', *Journal of Ecclesiastical History*, x, 59 ff.

[2] Morris, *loc. cit.*   [3] Viv. 5, *passim.*

[4] Convocation, Box I, 1519.   [5] *L.R.S.* 5, p. xiii.

[6] Bodleian Library, MS. Browne-Willis, 14, fos. 12, 14; Visitation Monitions 1500–1739, 16 June, 1519; see appendix I for list of known commissaries.

[7] As in the case of Alice Riding q.v. (Cj. 2, fo. 51v).

lay squarely with the ecclesiastical court itself. Few though the court books are, they suggest that, in order to be sure of fulfilling their duty of correction, the ecclesiastical courts were acting too officiously. In a court of first instance, a number of cases were likely to be denied and a proportion of defendants would not have shrunk from perjury. But the number of cases dismissed because the charge had not been sustained in court was too high for either explanation to be wholly convincing. In the prebendal court of Buckingham between 1493 and 1504, of a total of twenty-eight cases, fourteen were denied, nine had no sequel, and only five were admitted and the accused put to penance.[1] In the cases included among the visitation returns of the archdeaconry of Leicester, about one third of the defendants denied the charges against them and succeeded in purgation.[2] In contrast, in the bishop's audience court, 1525–7, of fifty-seven charges brought, only eight were denied and the remaining forty-nine admitted.[3] It looks as though the archdeaconry courts were being too active.

The probable explanation for their activity lay in the financial gains to be made from citing a man to appear before the court, irrespective of his guilt. Fees for citation were considerable, and they could quickly increase if a second citation was necessary because the defendant had not appeared in answer to the first; sparse though the evidence about fees is, it would suggest that a citation cost at least 8*d*. and the charge was born by the defendant in all cases. James Pegge was cited to appear before the archdeacon of Leicester in 1510, but he could not be found; he was then cited a second time (*viis et modis*), but still with no result; when he eventually appeared, after being suspended from church, he had run up a large bill. The scribe noted *soluit pro feodo curie viz pro ii citacionibus et una suspencione iis iiid*.[4] His failure to appear before the court and his subsequent suspension may have been due to a temporary absence, and have been quite unintentional, yet he was bound to pay for the consequences, even before the court had pronounced on his guilt or innocence

---

[1] Cj. 1, *passim*.
[2] Viv. 5, *passim*.
[3] Cj. 3, *passim*.
[4] Viv. 5, fo. 45v.

in the original charge against him. In this case the two citations cost 8*d.* each and suspension 11*d.*; in another case 11*d.* is the sum given for suspension and the absolution from it.[1] Henry Hynd, a butcher, was in the same situation as James Pegge; he denied the charges against him, but then did not appear on the appropriate day to proceed to purgation; he was charged with a bill which included 11*d.* for absolution from the suspension he had incurred.[2] Johanna Pudsey of Buckminster was even more hardly dealt with: she admitted a charge of fornication, showed that she had already been corrected for it, but was charged a fee for a citation which should not have been made at all.[3] John Davy of the parish of St Martin and St Nicholas was accused of fornication; he eventually purged himself of the charge, but, as he had failed to appear when cited on one occasion, he had to pay a fee for a double citation.[4] The apparitor and the registrar shared the fees, and it was very properly at the door of the apparitor that contemporary literature placed the blame for 'fictitious' citations.[5] But the effect of the apparitor's greed was felt not only by the aggrieved defendant but also in the ecclesiastical courts themselves. Contempt of court became commonplace. Archdeacons and commissaries had the utmost difficulty in forcing those who were guilty of a moral offence to appear before them, with the result that faults went uncorrected for a considerable time. On 30 October 1509 Agnes Hogkyn was before the commissary, accused of the serious offence of committing adultery with a curate who was also her confessor; the case was adjourned until 7 December, when Agnes did not appear; she subsequently failed to appear on 13 January, 25 January, 16 February and only appeared again on 9 March.[6] Richard Dalle of Illston on the Hill was reported at the visitation of the archdeacon for having given Margaret Cowper a child; he appeared before the archdeacon and admitted the charge on 24 November 1510. He refused to do the imposed penance and continued to see the girl in question. In June 1511 he admitted to these offences, but did not appear when called before the court

---

[1] Viv. 5, fo. 35.   [2] *Ibid.* fo. 3.   [3] *Ibid.* fo. 94.   [4] *Ibid.* fo. 39.
[5] Maynard Smith, *Pre-Reformation England*, pp. 82–3.
[6] Viv. 5, fo. 25.

on two occasions in August; he eventually appeared in November and agreed to marry the girl. It had taken the archdeacon a year to correct him.[1] In half of the cases which came before the archdeacon and of which the sequel is reported, there is a record of a failure to appear in answer to a citation; sometimes the accused took two or three months to appear, and occasionally, as with Richard Dalle, it took much longer to bring him to court.[2] The effect, therefore, of the zeal of the apparitor and his officiousness in issuing citations was that it brought curial procedure into disrepute, thereby hampering the archdeacon in his work of correction.

But it was not only those responsible for citations who were defeating the best interests of the courts. The archdeacon and the commissary were doing the same. By insisting on the full penitential formulae, including the discipline, they were continuing an unpopular practice which many tried to avoid by commutation.[3] It is hard to be certain of the extent of commutation since it is not always recorded, and it figured in the commissary's accounts under the innocent heading of *corrections*. In the accounts of the commissary for Oxford in 1500, under the heading of correction, a subheading is given of 'Fines for the redemption of penance'. A woman of Burford was charged 3s. 4d. and a Thomas Tanner of Bicester paid 6s. 8d.[4] They were fortunate; Bartholomew Hoose of Melton Mowbray paid the commissary of Leicester 13s. 4d. for the commutation of his penance.[5] On a number of occasions, the bishop was forced to acquiesce in a demand for commutation, particularly when it was made by someone with rank or connexions;[6] the archdeacon and commissary were subject to greater pressure, if only because they lacked episcopal status and power. Their deputies were even more vulnerable. A report made to the vicar general when he visited Boston makes this abundantly clear: the parishioners said,

quod nichil habent detegere eo quod dominus Thomas Porter decanus decanatus Holand sedebat et tenebat curiam nomine domini officialis

[1] *Ibid.* fo. 62v.   [2] Viv. 5, *passim.*   [3] See above, p. 21.
[4] Bishop's Accounts, Misc. 6, fo. 4 ff.   [5] Cj. 3, fo. 23v.
[6] See my introduction to Bishop Atwater's court of audience book, *L.R.S.* 61, p. xvi.

Archidiaconi Linc' et coram eo omnia erant detecta et multa defunc-
torum testamenta erant probata. Dicunt eciam quod multa crimina
sunt detecta de tempore in tempus coram officiali sed nulla propterea
sit correctio nisi pecuniaria. Quia non erat visum hic quod aliquis hic
publice penituit nisi pauperimus fuerit.[1]

Fear and officiousness, two of the attributes of petty officialdom,
were combining to bring the ecclesiastical courts, in particular,
into disrepute.

Yet a fault in the judge of the court might be a virtue at visitation; a scrupulous attention to detail, and an anxiety that nothing
be hidden from the archdeacon, only to be revealed to the bishop,
might make an archdeacon a poor judge and a good visitor. At
any rate certain archdeacons, or their officials, were visiting all
parts of their jurisdiction with the utmost care and regularity.
The official of the archdeacon of Buckingham held a chapter of
clergy every month in varying places in his archdeaconry, and
heard complaints and frequently dealt with the cases arising from
them.[2] The archdeacon of Leicester visited deaneries with care,
and, though records have not survived for other archdeaconries,
it is unlikely that visitations were neglected, if only because they
brought to the visitor or his deputy a valuable source of income,
procurations.[3]

Very little evidence survives to indicate how useful the rural
deans were at this period; the names of a few of them have survived, by chance, in the records, but there is no indication of
what they were doing.[4] Similarly there were a host of minor

---

[1] Vj. 5, fo. 48 v.   [2] Aylesbury Record Office, D/A/V. 1, passim.
[3] A.A.S.R.P. xxviii (1905), 127–43. It is perhaps significant that only one of
the commissaries of whom anything is known in this period (for a list, see
appendix, p. 185.) was a theologian. All the rest held a degree in canon or civil
law, or both. The archdeacons had a more varied background (see John Le Neve,
Fasti Ecclesiae Anglicanae 1300–1541, compiled by H. P. F. King (London, 1962),
pp. 6 ff.) but their tendency to appoint the bishop's commissaries as their own
officials had the effect of bringing lawyers to prominence.
[4] What is known of rural deans in this period has been summarized by
A. H. Thompson, 'Diocesan Administration in the Middle Ages: Archdeacons
and Rural Deans', Proceedings of the British Academy (1943), pp. 191 ff., and
W. Dansey, Horae Decanicae Rurales (Rivington, 1844); for mention of the
election of rural deans see Aylesbury Record Office, D/A/We/1, fo. 242 v.

diocesan officials of whom little is known. William Giles, for example, was constantly with the bishop and may have been his chaplain, but nothing is known of him beyond that he was given a benefice by Bishop Smith and appears to have continued to serve Bishop Atwater. Giles was clearly one of the bishop's household from whom clerks were selected for special missions.[1] Some of these received rapid promotion, like John Burges, who was at Magdalen with the bishop, and was appointed by him to conduct a number of special visitations and was collated by him to the treasurership of the cathedral.[2] Less fortunate was Thomas Swain, who died in the service of the bishop without having attained much recognition.[3]

Perhaps the most important of these household officials was the bishop's registrar. Frequently little is known about this important official but we know something about Edward Watson, who kept the bishop's records for the greater part of this period. He was not a priest and he was married to Bishop Smith's niece; he held considerable lands and he was a lawyer and had a reputation for kindness.[4] He is commemorated by a brass at Liddington and he appears to have been the father of many children. The episcopal visitation returns, the court of audience books and most of the registers of Smith and Atwater are in his hand. Much of what we know of the clergy in this period is contained in the records he so carefully kept.

[1] Cj. 2, *passim*; Register 23, fo. 305.
[2] Emden, *Oxford*, I, 308; for the dispute about the tenure of the treasurership in which he was involved, see below, p. 170. For his visitations, see *L.R.S.* 35, pp. 98, 101, 105, 111; *L.R.S.* 37, pp. 32, 95.
[3] Cj. 2, fos. 54, 58; *L.R.S.* 35, pp. 158, 174, 178; *L.R.S.* 37, pp. 44, 116.
[4] C. Wise, *Rockingham Castle and the Watsons* (London, 1891), pp. 19 ff.

CHAPTER II

THE WAY TO A BENEFICE

I. ORDINATION

Why is a man ordained? At any time this is a difficult question
to answer, but for the early sixteenth century little evidence survives of individual aspiration, of the sudden stirrings of vocation
or the ruthless calculations of the ambitious. Ordination might be
the first step in a career of selfless devotion or the first rung on the
ladder of political and social advancement. The church provided
almost unique opportunites which, in themselves, gave ample
reasons for ordination; dispensations from residence enabled priests
to study at a university on the fruits of a benefice which they had
never seen, and a degree provided an entrée to positions of power
in both church and state. Ordination was, therefore, both the outward expression of a calling to the cure of souls, and, at the
same time, the means of acquiring an assured income and a position in society which might otherwise be unattainable. When the
church in the late sixteenth century was seen to provide a 'mean
employment',[1] when its prizes were less glittering and it had
ceased to be a means of political advancement, a much higher
premium was put on a more obviously pastoral vocation.

Whatever their motives, men were offering themselves for ordination to the priesthood in considerable numbers between February 1495/6 and December 1520. A total of 2609 deacons were
ordained priest in the diocese during this period.[2] All of them
were seculars, since the Lincoln ordination lists noted religious
separately. Large though the numbers seem, even in so extensive
a diocese, they are proportionately slightly lower than those for
some other dioceses. Direct comparisons are complicated by the
fact that registrars did not always follow the same rules in com-
posing their lists; some included the religious with the seculars,

[1] C. Hill, *Economic Problems of the Church from Archbishop Whitgift to the Long
Parliament* (Oxford, 1956), pp. 208 ff.
[2] Register 24, fos. 1–94: Register 25, fos. 7–12, 111–37.

[38]

and others kept them apart; there is also some difficulty in comparing Lincoln with a diocese less than one sixth of its size. But, if religious are included in the figures to facilitate comparison, and relative size may be determined by contrasting the number of parishes in a diocese, then it would seem that fewer were ordained priest at Lincoln than elsewhere:

Diocese	Average number ordained priest inclusive of religious at one ordination	Number of parishes as a fraction of the number of parishes in the Lincoln diocese[1]	Estimated average of the total number ordained at one ordination if size of diocese same as Lincoln
Lincoln	30[2]	—	30
Exeter	13[3]	$\frac{1}{3}$	39
Hereford	7[4]	$\frac{1}{7}$	49
Bath & Wells	10[5]	$\frac{1}{4}$	40
Ely	8[6]	$\frac{1}{16}$	128

Both Ely and Lincoln might be supposed to have ordained a large number of men on letters dimissory, as a result of the inclusion of a university within their boundaries: this was the case at Ely, where 75% of all ordinands were strangers to the diocese, often studying at Cambridge; but in Lincoln the university of Oxford did not have so profound an effect; on an average only two or three deacons out of thirty were ordained on letters

[1] This estimate is made on the basis of the number of parishes per diocese given in Hughes, *The Reformation in England*, pp. 32–3.

[2] Register 24, fos. 1–94; Register 25, fos. 7–12, 111–37.

[3] A. E. Mumford, *Hugh Oldham 1492?–1519* (London, 1936), p. 104.

[4] *Register of Thomas Myllyng 1474–1492*, ed. A. T. Bannister (Canterbury and York Society, 26, 1920) 154–84; the average for the episcopate of Richard Mayhew was eight, see *The Register of Richard Mayhew 1504–1516*, ed. A. T. Bannister (Canterbury and York Society, 27, 1921), 237–72.

[5] *Registers of Oliver King and Hadrian Castello, Bishops of Bath and Wells*, ed. H. C. Maxwell-Lyte (Somerset Record Society, 54, 1939), pp. 8, 84; the figures are based on the ordination lists which have been printed.

[6] Cambridge University Library, Ely Diocesan Documents, G. 1. 6, Register of John Alcock, fos. 223 ff; incomplete lists survive for the episcopate of Nicholas West, G. 1. 7, fos. 80 ff.

dimissory, though on one occasion, in March 1503/4, sixteen Cambridge graduates were ordained at once.[1]

The appearance of a man's name on an ordination list marked the first occasion, in many instances, on which the ecclesiastical authorities took cognizance of him. But behind the formal entry of his name there lay, for each candidate, the preliminaries of acquiring the learning and title which were the necessary prerequisites to being ordained at all. He had also to cope with the purely practical difficulties of providing himself with the money for the fees, clothes and travel which were the inevitable concomitants of ordination. Ordination appears to have been an expensive business. Humphrey Garrad of Wold left Edmund Walles 26s. 8d. in order to buy himself a gown if he ever became a priest, and he promised to meet the expenses incurred in obtaining any dispensations he might need.[2] William Maydwell left 5s. to Thomas Temple to become a priest:[3] the bequest cannot have gone very far towards providing the necessary robes and fees. A robe cost as much as 12s., and fees were usually 6s. 8d.[4] Travel might also have presented something of a problem. Ordinations were usually held at one of the bishop's manors, at Liddington, Buckden, or Lincoln, and occasionally at a religious house. To avoid unnecessary inconvenience, the bishop or his suffragan sometimes held an ordination twice in the same month but at two different places; in March 1508/9, the suffragan went first to All Saints, Northampton, and then to Banbury.[5] Conditions at both Buckden and Liddington were very cramped, and the problems of accommodation were considerable. Though three-quarters of the candidates for any ordination were drawn from a fifty mile radius, they would still have had to spend one or two nights *en route*, particularly if a form of pre-ordination examination was held.

The social background of those who sought ordination varied

---

[1] Register 24, fo. 43.
[2] Longden, v, 179.   [3] *Ibid.* IX, 187.
[4] Bishop's Accounts, Rentals, I, fo. 13. For the requirements of clerical dress see Lyndwood, *Constitutiones Legatinae D. Othonis et D. Otheboni* (Oxford, 1679), p. 37.
[5] Register 24, fos. 73 v–5 v.

considerably: there were a few, like John Talbot, who came from noble families even though they might be illegitimate members of them;[1] many more, like Bishop Smith himself, had connexions among the landed gentry: Robert Bedyngfeld, for instance, was son of Sir Edmund Bedyngfeld of Oxburgh, and several gentry families eventually presented one of their number to benefices.[2] But the social background of the majority of ordinands is obscure and it is probable that many were from humble families like Bishop Atwater himself. Little is known of the educational qualification of many ordinands. It had been enacted at the council of Oxford that no one was to be admitted to orders without first being examined.[3] The purpose of the examination was to test whether the candidate was old enough to be a priest (he had to be twenty-five), and whether he was morally suitable, and had reached a certain educational standard. It was also necessary that he should be able to show that he had a means of livelihood, either in the form of a title to a benefice or in a private income of not less than 5 marks *per annum*. A similar examination was held before any priest was admitted to a benefice. There is no direct evidence at Lincoln to indicate that the ordination examination was being held, though it is certain that candidates for admission to benefices were examined. The case of Richard Thornton indicates that ordination examinations were being held at York. Thornton was said to have confessed that: 'M. doctor Tate examined hym and admytted hym to the order of prestehode in a lytle house beside thaff[4] chapitre house of the mynster.'[5] It seems very unlikely that York was the only diocese to examine, and the care with which titles were noted and some dispensations recorded in the register indicates that a form of scrutiny was practised at Lincoln. As we shall see, some of the morally unsuitable slipped through the net,[6] and it is probable that some deacons were ordained priest under age. It was a recognized practice to allow

---

[1] See below, p. 45.

[2] Longden, II, 53; see also below, appendix II, p. 187.

[3] Lyndwood, *Provinciale*, Lib. I, tit. 5; see also H. S. Bennet, 'Medieval Ordination Lists in the English Episcopal Registers', *Essays presented to Sir Hilary Jenkinson*, p. 20.

[4] *Sic* for *that of*.   [5] Cj. 2, fos. 100 ff.   [6] See below, p. 116.

scholars to proceed to orders before they were twenty-five,[1] and
the eight dispensations recorded in Smith's register are unlikely
to represent the total granted. The youngest recipient was Edward
Staples, a student aged fifteen, and most of the others whose
dispensations were noted were also scholars:[2] one dispensation
allowed Richard Baker to proceed to orders even though he was
blind in his left eye. His misfortune was thought to have been
caused by a mixture of illness and study.[3] But it was difficult to
be sure of a date of birth, and, however well intentioned the
examiner, he was likely to have been misled about the age of an
ordinand on a number of occasions.

It was easier to test a candidate's educational qualifications. But
there is some doubt about the adequacy of the standard required,
and whether the examination achieved the desired result of keeping
the illiterate and the ignorant out of orders. The education of the
priesthood was strongly criticized throughout the sixteenth century. Thomas Starkey wrote that:

there ys...a grete faute wych ys the ground of al other almost, and
that ys concernyng the educatyon of them wych appoynt themselfe to
be men of the Church. They are not brought up in virtu and lernyng
as they schold be, nor wel approvyd therin before they be admytted to
such hye dygnyte...for commonly you schal fynd that they can no
thyng dow but pattyr up theyr matyns and mas, mumblyng up a
certayn number of wordys no thynge understoode.[4]

Starkey's criticisms had a long history. The later Middle Ages
had been greatly concerned with the problem of educating the
priesthood. In the fourteenth century, the aim was primarily to
improve technique. Manuscripts were produced which instruc-
ted the priest exactly how he should conduct himself in the con-

---

[1] The desirability of granting dispensations to young scholars was recog-
nized in the Constitution *Cum ex eo* of Boniface VIII, see L. Boyle, 'The
Constitution "Cum ex eo" of Boniface VII: Education of Parochial Clergy',
Medieval Studies, 24 (Toronto, 1962), 268 ff.

[2] Register 24, fos. 202v, 218v, 222v, 223, 227, 229, 240, 269.

[3] *Ibid.* fo. 156v.

[4] *A Dialogue between Cardinal Pole and Thomas Lupset, Lecturer in Rhetoric at
Oxford, by Thomas Starkey*, ed. J. M. Cowper (E.E.T.S. extra series, XII, 1878),
132.

fessional, and how he was to perform the other functions of his office.[1] In the fifteenth century a number of colleges were founded at both Oxford and Cambridge with the purpose of improving the general level of clerical education by increasing the number of graduates.[2] By the end of the fifteenth century, the aim was not merely to instruct in technique and to give a selected few a university education. It had become more ambitious. By 1494 William de Meltham in a treatise for ordinands was concerned that they should have a knowledge of grammar, an appreciation of scripture, and, above all, an intellectual curiosity which would ensure a growth in understanding and provide a means of amusement in the long winter evenings in a remote parish.[3] He wanted all priests not merely to know how to perform the duties expected of them, but to be able to explain why they were performing them at all. This note is sounded again and again in Erasmus, More and Starkey, and there was an increasing emphasis in the sixteenth century on the need to read the scriptures fluently.[4] Starkey required a priest not only to say mattins but to understand fully what it was he was saying. The difficulty of the period is, then, that it is one of transition, in which standards were changing; the idea of what was desirable and normal was being re-examined. It is all too easy to assume that this process of re-examination, and the increase in the volume of criticism of clerical education which accompanied it, indicate a decline in standard rather than a change in standard. As a result there is a tendency to assert, paradoxically, that, though there were more educational opportunities in the fifteenth century, yet the clergy remained as ignorant as ever.[5] The reverse may be true. Sir Thomas More may have been right in asserting that large numbers could read and that the English

[1] W. A. Pantin, *The English Church in the Fourteenth Century* (Cambridge, 1955), pp. 190 ff.

[2] Viz. Lincoln college, All Souls and Magdalen at Oxford, and King's, Queens', St Catherine's and Jesus at Cambridge.

[3] Hughes, *The Reformation in England*, p. 85.

[4] T. W. Baldwin, *William Shakespere's Small Latine and Lesse Greek* (Illinois, 1944), I, 75 ff.

[5] See especially J. Simon, *Education and Society in Tudor England* (Cambridge, 1966), p. 32: 'while the standard of lay education rose during the later middle ages there was no like improvement in the education of the clergy.'

clergy were better educated than their European counterparts.[1] His observation does not necessarily conflict with Starkey's criticism.[2] More is not demanding exactly the same standard as Starkey; he is indicating that the goals of the fourteenth and fifteenth centuries have been achieved. He is not asserting that understanding has yet followed. Indeed it would be at least a century before the parochial clergy could live up to the high standards expected of them by the early humanists and their successors.[3]

The level of education required of a priest is, therefore, undergoing change, and it is often difficult to know by what standard critics of the clergy are judging them. Nor is the evidence adequate enough to test their subjective judgements by other criteria. The only figures which are available for clerical education are of the number of graduates who were presented to benefices. They have been taken as providing a useful comparative guide between one period and another and of indicating the highest standard achieved. Yet these figures are very difficult to interpret, and have frequently been cited too hastily. They tend to seem small and to lend weight to the criticism of a more serious deficiency throughout the priesthood as a whole.[4] But, in fact, their meaning can only be gauged if they are compared with earlier figures of graduates and an indication of progress or deterioration can be definitely established.

Between 1421 and 1431, in the Lincoln diocese, laymen presented 7 graduates to livings, but they made 191 other presentations.[5]

---

[1] *The Dialogue of Sir Thomas More Concerning Tyndale*, ed. W. E. Campbell (London, 1927), pp. 214–15.

[2] Cf. L. Stone, 'The Educational Revolution in England 1560–1640', *Past and Present* no. 28 (July 1964), 42. Professor Stone dismisses More's comment that half the population could read as 'alarmist nonsense'.

[3] See, for instance, J. S. Purvis, *Tudor Parish Documents of the Diocese of York* (Cambridge, 1948), pp. 96 ff. Cf. A. G. Dickens, 'Aspects of Intellectual Transition among the English Parish Clergy of the Reformation Period: A Regional Example', *Archiv. für Reformationsgeschichte*, 43 (1952), 51 ff.

[4] Hughes, *The Reformation in England*, I, 84; M. Deanesly, *The Lollard Bible* (Cambridge, 1920), pp. 158 ff.

[5] E. F. Jacob, 'On the Promotion of English University Clerks during the Later Middle Ages', *J. Eccl. History*, I (1950), 183.

Between 1495 and 1520, they presented 261 graduates to livings and 1168 non-graduates.[1] The percentage of graduate presentations, therefore, rose from $3\frac{1}{2}\%$ to approximately $11\frac{1}{2}\%$. If graduate numbers are to be used as the test of the educational attainments of the clergy, then the position had notably improved during the course of the fifteenth century.

But figures of the number of graduates presented represent only the educational *élite*: they include only those who had received at least the degree of M.A. They do not include those who had received the degree of B.A., or those who had not actually graduated, though they had spent some time at the university. In ecclesiastical documents the designation *magister* is reserved for those who were masters of arts; those who were bachelors of arts, those who had some university training, and those who had none are all referred to as *domini*. When Wolsey was presented to a living in July 1508, for example, he was not described as a *magister* because there was some doubt whether he had become a master of arts by then.[2] He would, therefore, be excluded from all figures of graduates because he was not designated as such. Amongst those presented to benefices who are thought not to have been graduates there were then many B.A.s and a considerable number of clerks who went up to the university for a year or two and never proceeded to a degree at all. It is estimated that only one third of the total number who matriculated ever proceeded even as far as the degree of B.A., and only one sixth to that of M.A.[3] So, in addition to the number of known graduates presented to livings, there was a much larger number presented who had been to university for

[1] Registers 23 and 25, *passim*. In all 791 graduates were presented but these figures are of *presentations*; several graduates received more than one living and therefore only 609 persons are involved of whom: 211 graduated in arts; 99 graduated in canon law; 79 graduated in civil law; 66 graduated in theology; 38 graduated in both laws; 4 graduated in medicine; 1 graduated in music. 110 are described as *magistri* but I have been unable to trace their degrees. In addition to the above there was John Talbot who held the degrees of B.A., M.D., D.C.L., D.Th., and defies classification!
[2] *Register Richard Mayhew*, ed. A. T. Bannister, p. 275; Emden, *Oxford*, III, 2077.
[3] H. Rashdall, *The Universities of Europe in the Middle Ages*, ed. F. M. Powicke and A. B. Emden (Oxford, 1936), III, 347, 349n.

a period. They did not necessarily leave the university because they were not up to the standard.[1] Shortage of money was one of the reasons most likely to compel a student to abandon his studies.[2] The pages of Oxford university registers abound with cases of debt,[3] and a clerk who did not manage to obtain a good benefice would have had difficulty in keeping himself at a university for long. Yet these men had received some form of higher education, even though they were not *magistri*. They were more likely to reside in the parish than the average graduate,[4] and an estimate of clerical education which overlooks them makes little sense.

Certainly they could read vernacular literature, and they would be severely handicapped in the university course if they had any difficulty in reading and writing in Latin. Any criticism of them was likely to be directed to the nature of the curricula which they had followed. The arts course was the most popular; it was also the necessary preliminary to any other degree. It was a general training which could be used later as the basis for a more specialized study. It varied in length, but it was normal to take at least four years before incepting as a bachelor in arts, and a further three to obtain the degree of master of arts. During the first four years, the study of the old and new logic formed the most important part of the syllabus, and grammar and rhetoric, though officially retained within it, were assumed to have been covered to a considerable extent at school. Arithmetic, geometry, music and metaphysical and natural philosophy were studied in courses for the degree of M.A.[5]

[1] Cf. Hughes, *The Reformation in England*, p. 84; Dr Hughes has based his calculations on the number of degrees given at Oxford, which would seem, in the light of Dr Emden's researches, a great deal too low.

[2] E. F. Jacob, 'University Clerks in the Later Middle Ages, the Problem of Maintenance,' *Bulletin of the John Rylands Library*, XXIX (1926), cf. Hughes, *The Reformation in England*, p. 84, who suggests that the clerks who did not complete a degree were unable 'to pass the leaving examination'.

[3] See, especially, O.U. Reg. D, 1485–1505, fos. 5, 5v, 9v, 11v, 24v, 26.

[4] See below, p. 97.

[5] Strickland Gibson, *Statuta Antiqua Universitatis Oxoniensis* (Oxford, 1931), pp. lxxxviii ff.; see also J. Fletcher, 'The Oxford Arts School in the Fifteenth Century' (Oxford, D.Phil. thesis, 1961).

Clearly the arts course was little more than a general training which More defended on the grounds that it was worthy 'to wait and as handmaids to give attendance upon divinity'.[1] But few stayed on at the university to read for a higher degree in either divinity or law and, for many, the arts course, or part of it, was the only training which they had.[2] How adequate a preparation was it for a parish priest? It would be a mistake to judge it solely in terms of the subjects and books actually studied. Then, as now, there were educational opportunities which did not depend on the quality of the set books. Friendships made, and discussions amongst students, all played their part in forming a mature mind capable of assessing problems even if not possessed of all the technical information necessary to solve them. But it would be wrong to assume that, because the arts course did not include any formal training in theology, the undergraduate was left in total ignorance of the rationalia of his faith. The statutes of some of the colleges provided for the reading of the Bible at meals, and the attendance of students at masses and other services of the church. At Balliol, for instance, it was ordered that:

singulis diebus Dominicis et festis, Magister, Socii et Scholastici, in propriis superpelliciis et capiciis secundum suum gradum, intersint matutinis cum suis laudibus, missae et vesperis et completorio, eam invicem plano saltem cantu pro numero devote et solemniter celebrantes.[3]

Similarly at Oriel and Merton, attendance at mass was obligatory. At Oriel there was provision *De lectione Bibliae* at meals. The liturgy of the church and part, at least, of the Bible would become extremely familiar to the students.[4] Their understanding of both would have been broadened at Oxford by the sermons preached at St Mary's by a theologian on Sundays and saints' days, which they were bound to attend. Some of these sermons have survived. They seem stilted and affected but they nevertheless convey an

---

[1] *The Dialogue of Sir Thomas More Concerning Tyndale*, ed. Campbell, Bk. I, ch. 22, p. 82.
[2] See above, p. 45 n.
[3] *Statutes of the Colleges of Oxford* (H.M.R.C., 1853), Balliol College, p. 9.
[4] *Ibid.* Oriel College, p. 7.

impression of great erudition[1] combined with some good advice.[2] If an undergraduate could keep awake through them, he might have learned a lot.

Changes were also taking place which would have improved the standards of those who never got to a university at all. Clearly this group were likely to include some who lacked the technique to perform their priestly functions adequately, as well as some who did not have the understanding, both of the functions themselves and of the Bible, which the humanists believed necessary. Yet changes were in progress, below the level of the university, which greatly affected this group: new schools were being founded, and the printing press was being used as a means of teaching the clergy the fundamentals of the faith. Kingsford drew attention to the large number of schools founded in London in the fifteenth century, and in this respect the city does not appear to have been an exception.[3] In some counties in the diocese, schools were founded and new opportunities provided. Northamptonshire had only one school on the death of Edward III but it had acquired a further five by the accession of Henry VIII.[4] Buckinghamshire gained three new schools in the fifteenth century; the most famous was Eton but there were others at Thornton and Buckingham.[5] William Waynfleet founded a school at Wainfleet in Lincolnshire in 1459; this brought up the number of schools in the county to at least ten besides those in the city.[6] Many sixteenth-century bishops were benefactors of learning and Bishop Smith founded two schools.[7] Professor Jordan's survey of charitable bequests for general educational purposes gives further corroborative

[1] See, for example, B. M. Harleian MS. 5398, fos. 46–58, for an erudite sermon by Reginald of Gloucester which contains a multitude of quotations.
[2] Good advice was given to students in a sermon by John Haynton in the mid-fifteenth century: 'confert discipulis ad doctrinam seipsos studiosos exhibere. Sed ad hoc 4^{or} precipue conferunt; primo ut discipuli perauditis magistrorum lectionibus matutinis, vigiliis attendant...confert eis 2° cum sociis conferre...confert eis 3° per seipsos subtiliter inquirere...sed 4° confert praecipue discipulis divina influentia' (ibid. fo. 20v).
[3] C. L. Kingsford, Prejudice and Promise in Fifteenth Century England (London reprint, 1962), p. 36.   [4] V.C.H. Northamptonshire, II, 201 ff.
[5] Ibid. Buckinghamshire, II, 147.   [6] Ibid. Lincolnshire, II, 422 ff.
[7] Maynard Smith, Pre-Reformation England, pp. 31–2.

evidence. He shows that bequests increased notably in the early sixteenth century, and they reached a level in 1530 which was not reached again until the seventeenth century.[1] Recent work has also substantiated this conclusion,[2] though it has been thought that the laity, particularly the gentry, benefited from the improved facilities rather than the clergy.[3] There is some evidence to suggest that parents destined their children for the priesthood at an early age, and the special protection which benefit of clergy, for instance, afforded may have had the effect of marking the clergy out as a caste.[4] But it is hard to imagine any school in the late fifteenth century actively discouraging intending clerks from joining its ranks. Society was not so rigidly classified. Gentlemen intending to follow a business career needed a basis of grammar and required a certain fluency in Latin and French; a training in both would help a clerk and each could adopt the occupation of the other.[5] Where a school was simply for the townsfolk, it is reasonable to suppose that some of its pupils eventually became priests, and that the intending clerk as well as the gentleman benefited from an increase in the number of schools.[6]

It is very difficult to connect any one individual with any of these schools, except Eton and Magdalen, because school lists have not survived. But evidence has survived of at least thirty schools in the diocese[7] and many more may have existed.[8] Some of these

[1] W. K. Jordan, *Philanthropy in England* (London, 1959), p. 373. It should, however, be noticed that all types of education are included in this figure and that colleges and universities benefited more than schools throughout the period 1501–30.   [2] J. Simon, *Education and Society in Tudor England*, pp. 19 ff.

[3] *Ibid.* p. 32.   [4] See below, p. 121.

[5] H. G. Richardson, 'Business Training in Medieval Oxford', *American Historical Review*, XLVI (1940), 259 ff.

[6] For an interesting example of a town school on the boundaries of the Lincoln diocese, which had enjoyed a precarious existence until satisfactorily endowed in 1479, see J. Lawson, *A Town Grammar School through Six Centuries* (Oxford, 1963), pp. 13 ff.

[7] For the schools in the remaining counties see V.C.H. *Hertfordshire*, II, 47; *Huntingdonshire*, II, 167; *Bedfordshire*, II, 149; *Leicestershire*, III, 243; *Oxfordshire*, I, 40 ff. See also R. S. Stanier, *Magdalen School* (Oxford Historical Society new series, III, 1940), 12 ff.; for a more optimistic reckoning of the Oxford facilities by a seventeenth-century antiquarian, see P. J. Wallis, 'The Wase School Collection', *Bodleian Library Record* (1952–3), pp. 78 ff.

[8] Simon, *Education and Society in Tudor England*, p. 4.

schools, like that at Boston, were primarily concerned with song, and some were petty, or ABC, schools rather than sophisticated grammar schools. Contemporaries tried to distinguish between these various types of school and in the foundation of Magdalen college, Oxford, the distinction between the song school and the grammar school was very clear.[1] The aim of each was different: the song school was mainly concerned with the choristers, while the ABC or petty school was for teaching children to read in the vernacular before they attempted the Latin grammar which distinguished the grammar school. But the distinction became blurred in practice.[2] Song schools had instructors in grammar, since most choristers were required to have a knowledge of both, and, since no syllabuses have survived for the period, we do not know which schools were exclusively concerned with Latin grammar.[3] Where there was no formal grammar school, the petty school may have attempted to go beyond teaching in the vernacular, and similarly, where a petty school was weak, the grammar school may have had to teach the elementary principles of reading. But even the grammar schools of the diocese could, without strain, have taught the hundred priests who were ordained each year had it not been for their unusual geographical distribution, and for their jealous and monopolistic attitude.

Within Lincolnshire, the chancellor had control of all schools except those of the prebends,[4] and this may well have had the effect of discouraging new foundations. Huntingdonshire had no grammar schools outside the town, because an early charter gave the city school a monopoly, and, throughout the diocese, the smaller villages were but poorly served.[5] The only chances for

[1] Stanier, *Magdalen School*, p. 42.
[2] Cf. L. Stone, 'The Educational Revolution in England 1560–1640', *Past and Present*, no 28 (July 1964), 42. For a discussion of the role of Song Schools, see A. H. Thompson, *Song Schools in the Middle Ages* (S.P.C.K., 1942), p. 6.
[3] See 'The Chantry Certificates for Lincoln and Lincolnshire returned in 1548 under Act of Parliament I Edward VI', ed. C. W. Foster and A. H. Thompson, *A.A.S.R.P.* XXXVI–XXXVII (1921–5), 33, 36.
[4] H. Bradshaw and C. Wordsworth, *Statutes of Lincoln Cathedral*, I, *The Black Book* (Cambridge, 1892), 284.
[5] V. C. H. *Huntingdonshire*, II, 167 ff.; for other monopolies see Simon, *Education and Society in Tudor England*, pp. 20 ff.

the bright villager were that a wealthy parent or relative would send him away from the village to a grammar school,[1] or that his promise would result in his winning a scholarship for grammar and singing, such as those available at the Burghersh and Buckingham chantries.[2] As it was, many ordinands must have received their education at petty schools or at the hands of the local parish priest. Thomas Hartwell of Brayfield, who was a master of grammar, had such a school, and left money to his scholars on his death;[3] money was left also in John Hinton's will to provide for the religious teaching of the children of the parish.[4] The quality of the teaching would have varied considerably from place to place, and it is difficult to gain a clear idea of the syllabus even in a grammar school. The earliest syllabuses available date from the 1520s and presuppose printed text-books. In this respect, too, the period 1495–1520 was a transitional one: the potentialities of printed text-books and the need for a consequent change in educational method was gradually becoming apparent. The syllabuses of the 1520s owe much to the ideas of Colet and Erasmus, and cannot be taken as constituting a norm at that date and certainly not for an earlier one.[5] It is probably safe to assume that the backward child never got to school at all, that the petty school leaver was literate, and that a few could read and understand some words of Latin. It is interesting, for example, that a seaman accused of heresy claimed that 'he understandith noo Latyn but he can rede Englyshe'.[6] A seaman would have had fewer chances of schooling than an intending priest though ports were becoming centres of education by the end of the fifteenth century.[7] But his literacy

[1] H. G. Richardson, 'Business Training in Medieval Oxford', *American Historical Review*, XLVI (1940), 267–8.
[2] V. C. H. *Lincolnshire*, II, 427–9; see also F. L. Harrison, *Music in Medieval Britain* (London, 1958), pp. 30 ff. for other opportunities available.
[3] Longden, VI, 189. Another master of grammar who may have kept a school was Robert Lee of Caldecote (Register 23, fo. 375 v).
[4] Longden, VII, 33.
[5] For a full account of the early Ipswich–St Paul's syllabuses see T. W. Baldwin, *William Shakspere's Small Latine and Lesse Greeke* (Illinois, 1944), I, 75 ff. See also R. S. Stanier, *Magdalen School*, pp. 41–2.
[6] Cj. 4, fo. 16.
[7] See Lawson, *A Town Grammar School through Six Centuries*, p. 13.

serves as a warning against assuming too low an educational standard for the priesthood. The product of the grammar school should, like the graduate, have understood Latin. It was the ordinand, therefore, who had no more than the petty school behind him, and whose educational attainment was no higher than that of the seaman, who would have been in particular difficulties, and for whom Starkey's criticism may have been justified. The Bible, the liturgy, the works of the fathers and the medieval schoolmen were all in Latin, and, unless their content was made available to a priest in English, his literacy would have been of little assistance to his understanding of his faith.

Help of a practical and technical kind was, by 1500, coming from the printing press. Caxton, de Worde, Pynson, and Berthelet all published a large number of devotional and educational works, many of which were in the vernacular. The printing press made possible a wider dissemination of knowledge than had hitherto been available. It put an understanding of the faith within the reach of any who could read English; it meant that the humanists' ambitions could one day be realized.[1]

The early printers were well aware of the special needs of their time. Caxton, in particular, carefully investigated the potential market for his projected publications.[2] It would be interesting to know what percentage of his devotional books found their way to parish priests. All too few books which have survived bear any marks of ownership, and many devotional publications went to laymen and to religious houses: one of the copies of the *Summa Angelica*, now in Lincoln Cathedral Library, was given by William Smith, rector of Belton, to the Carthusians of Axholme.[3] But some works were written specifically for the parish priest and it is hard to see what use could be made of them by anyone else. Books to guide the priest in the confessional and volumes of sermons had been circulating in England for well over a century.[4]

[1] H. S. Bennett, *English Books and Readers 1475–1557* (Cambridge, 1952), p. 65. For a short consideration of the impact of printing see D. M. Loades, 'The Press under the Early Tudors', *Cambridge Bibliographical Society*, IV, pt. 1 (1964), 29 ff.
[2] Bennett, *op. cit.* p. 17.   [3] Lincoln Cathedral Library, S.S. 2. 15.
[4] Pantin, *The English Church in the Fourteenth Century*, pp. 220 ff.

But a manuscript was a rarity and beyond the reach of those whose need might be the greatest.[1] Not so the unbound printed devotional works which were selling in John Dorne's bookshop in Oxford for a penny. Lives of the saints and the folio editions of the articles of the faith, to say nothing of volumes of sermons, were being sold for sums well within the range of the most ordinary priest.[2] But obviously it took time for both author and reader to appreciate the enormous potentialities of the printed book. Only gradually did the appreciation of the possibilities which it presented come to be realized: England could boast of few presses in comparison with the Continent.[3] By 1483, Magdalen school was producing grammarians who, in their turn, produced easier grammars for use within the school and outside it.[4] By the turn of the century, William de Meltham of York had produced his treatise for ordinands[5] and Bishop Atwater himself was responsible for goading William Horman, a headmaster of Eton, to write his *Vulgaria* to facilitate the learning of Latin.[6] The church, by the first decade of the sixteenth century, was making a serious attempt to use the press to educate both those who had, and those who had not, the opportunity of going to a grammar school or university. Are there any signs that Lincoln clergy who were not graduates actually owned any of these books or profited from them?

Printed books lacked binding and even the most common were all too easily destroyed, together with any marks of ownership which they might have borne. It is also unusual to find books mentioned in wills. Nicholas Bradbridge, for instance, was chancellor of Lincoln in 1512[7] and a doctor of theology who had studied at Oxford and Turin and had been headmaster of Eton.[8]

[1] H. E. Bell, 'The Price of Books in Medieval England', *Transactions of the Bibliographical Society*, XVII (1936–7), 312 ff.

[2] *The Day Book of John Dorne*, ed. C. R. L. Fletcher (Oxford Historical Society, v, 1885), 71 ff.

[3] H. Guppy, 'The Evolution of the Art of Printing', *Bulletin of the John Rylands Library*, 24 (1940), 232.

[4] Stanier, *Magdalen School*, pp. 25 ff.

[5] Hughes, *The Reformation in England*, p. 84.

[6] *Horman's Vulgaria Puerorum*, ed. M. R. James (Roxburghe Club, 1926), p. 3.

[7] A. 3. 4, fo. 47 v.   [8] Emden, *Oxford*, I, 241.

It is inconceivable that he owned no books, yet his will does not mention them.[1] There is therefore unlikely to be a great deal of evidence about the effect of the printing press on the diocesan clergy. The fact that any evidence has survived at all indicates that printed books were reaching some parish priests, even though it is impossible to say how many of the clergy were affected. William Maydwell, vicar of Welford, left to his patron, the abbot of Sulby, some works on canon law, grammar and devotion.[2] Robert Richardson, who served Easton Neston for nearly thirty years, left to the prior of Blackfriars, Northampton, his book of sermons,[3] and John Symmond, rector of Maidford, had a book on the life of Christ.[4] Andrew Yong, who collected three livings[5] but was not apparently a graduate, left an unspecified number of books,[6] as did another of his fellow clergy, William Hamsworth of Lowick.[7] Nicholas Grene of West Halton, who also appears to be undistinguished, owned a volume of Aquinas[8]—one wonders whether he had read it. Alexander Agneson, rector of Muston in Leicestershire, had a very interesting collection of books; he left to two chaplains some collected sermons, and one of them was bequeathed a copy of the *Distructorium Viciorum*, a work in which criticism of the clergy savours of Lollardy.[9] Perhaps Agneson was an owner of 'many books of heresy', as was William Kent, rector of Stony Stanton.[10] Gilbert Croke, rector of St Mary Magdalene, Lincoln, left books,[11] as did two Buckinghamshire clerks.[12] Some-

---

[1] *L.R.S.* 12, pp. 159–60.

[2] Register 23, fo. 203; Longden, IX, 187.

[3] Register 23, fo. 178; Longden, XI, 195–6.

[4] Register 23, fo. 224v; Longden, XIII, p. 135.

[5] He held Burwell, Wyberton and Bennington (Register 23, fos. 78v, 111v, 145).

[6] *L.R.S.* 10, p. 206.

[7] Register 23, fo. 214v; Longden, VI, 129.

[8] Register 25, fo. 26; Lincoln Cathedral Library, S.S. 2. 18.

[9] *L.R.S.* 10, p. 6. For a later example of a non-graduate with an interesting library, see A. G. Watson, 'A Sixteenth Century Collector: Thomas Dackomb 1496–1572', *Transaction of the Bibliographical Society*, V, XVIII, no. 3 (1963), 205.

[10] J. Fines, 'Heresy Trials in the Diocese of Lichfield 1511–1512', *J. Eccl. History*, XIX (October, 1963), 171–2.

[11] A. 3. 2, fo. 121v; Croke left a copy of the *Distructorium Viciorum* to the vicar of Gt Gaddesden.   [12] Aylesbury Record Office, D/A/We. 36, 47v.

times these books became the nucleus of a parish library and provided the incumbent with material for his sermons. William Skelton, treasurer of Lincoln cathedral, left: 'certaine books to be chenyd in the quere or in the librarie as it shall please them that be necessarye to them that use preching there'. His bequest included two books on preaching, a concordance and, unusually, a Bible.[1] There is scarcely any evidence at all of ownership of a vernacular Bible. A French vernacular Bible, in two volumes, was bequeathed by a layman, Edward Cheyne of Bedford, to his son.[2] While several copies of the New Testament in English have survived,[3] very few contain any mark of identification, presumably as a precaution against heresy proceedings.[4]

Slight though this evidence is, it is an indication that the press was having some effect on the parishes. It may also explain why there is so little criticism of the educational standards of the clergy in the visitation returns and presentation deeds of the diocese, and why there is no mention of them in the bishop's register.[5] One of the few exceptions was John Kale. He was presented by John Thornton to the vicarage of Shabbington in Buckinghamshire in 1504. He swore on being admitted that he would:

per unum annum integrum det suum studium arti grammaticali et circa maiorem cognicionem sacramentorum ac sacramentalium propter meliorem reformacionem parochianorum dicte vicarie sue.[6]

It would appear that John's learning was not sufficient to satisfy the bishop in 1504. But nearly twenty years later we find him

[1] A. 3. 2, fo. 12v.
[2] *The Bedfordshire Wills and Administration Proved at Lambeth Palace and in the Archdeaconry of Huntingdon*, ed. F. A. Page-Turner (Bedfordshire Historical Record Society, II), 21 ff.
[3] See especially H. O. Coxe, *Catalogi Codicum Manuscriptorum Bibliothecae Bodleianae*, part II (Laud Misc. MSS.), nos. 24, 25, 36, 182, 207, 361, 3883.
[4] One exception is a complete vernacular Bible owned by Geoffrey Blythe, bishop of Lichfield and Coventry (M. R. James, *Catalogue of the MSS of Corpus Christi College, Cambridge*, vol I, Cambridge, 1912, no. 147).
[5] Cf. J. Simon, 'A. F. Leach on the Reformation', *British Journal of Educational Studies*, 3, no. 2 (May 1955): 'the fact that ecclesiastical legislators intended a grammar school to be kept is one thing; the fact that visitation records reveal neglect of obligations and statutory duties is another.'
[6] Presentation Deeds, 1504, no. 144.

among the *magistri*, apparently as a graduate at Oxford who had also studied at Cambridge.[1] His case serves to indicate the difficulty of accepting an isolated example at its face value. Ignorance is not always permanent and may sometimes be amended.

A study of the visitation records reveals few other priests failing to meet the educational requirements of either the bishop or the parish. Informed comment on the church tended to make much of the gulf between intelligent layman and the average parish priest,[2] and, clearly, there was likely to be little in common between Sir Thomas More and Alexander Agneson. But this distinction, though real enough to the sixteenth-century humanist, was not yet apparent at the more humdrum level of the parish. The opportunities for education were as limited for the layman as they were for the priest, and a critical layman could make his criticism heard, if he had a mind to, at the visitation of the bishop. But the parishioners of most Lincoln parishes were as unpretentious as their pastors, and they appear to have been much more concerned with a priest's sociability and morality than with his lack of education. In only two parishes does any kind of dissatisfaction appear: at Wrawby in Leicestershire, the curate was *minus doctus*, and, at Spalding, the prior was said to provide priests for the church who were *minus idoneos et indoctos*.[3] Two priests at Leicester abbey were said to be ignorant and one was reported at Markby Priory,[4] but the ignorance of the religious would not affect the parishes unless the priests concerned had the cure of souls. One of them, John Leicester, a canon of Leicester abbey, may be the same as the Magister John Leycestre who was presented to the church of Oddington in 1520.[5] But, if he was, he too had become a *magister* since the visitation in 1518. It is unlikely that the same man is involved, but the case, like that of John Kale, serves to illustrate the fact that it was obstinate ignorance rather than an initial inadequacy which was criticized. The report from Markby stated that the ignorant brother, besides being scarcely

---

[1] Salter, p. 237; *Register of the University of Oxford 1505–1571*, ed. T. Boase (O.H.S. I, 1884), 87.
[2] Dickens, *The English Reformation*, p. 12; Maynard Smith, *Pre-Reformation England*, pp. 40 ff.   [3] *L.R.S.* 33, pp. 60 and 89.
[4] *L.R.S.* 35, p. 186; 37, p. 12.   [5] Register 25, fo. 49.

able to read, understand or write, would not 'dare operam litteris ac ideo manet indoctus'.[1] The printing press gave the authorities and the parish the right to expect that a priest, after ordination, would give some of his time to improving his understanding of scripture; in 1529, Convocation specifically ordered him to spend two or three hours, at least three days a week, in approved devotional reading.[2] The standards were changing as the opportunities for education improved. It would take time for a parish to adjust to the change; to learn to expect understanding as well as the technical knowledge necessary to the priestly office. The scarcity of examples in the visitation returns may well reflect the transition: they should not obscure the fact that, in spite of the progress, there was still a long way to go. The increase in the number of schools, and of the number of men going to the universities, clearly had an effect at the parochial level, and it is likely that the standard of education amongst the clergy was higher than it had ever been. But from the diocesan evidence it is equally clear that there were limitations to the scope of these improvements, and that these limitations were a potential danger to the church. Education was a haphazard affair; it was a matter of chance whether there was a good school available for the intending priest. It was also largely a matter of parental choice. Men are not born in cassocks, and unless they were destined for the ministry from birth they might miss even the limited opportunities which were available to them. Some of the Lincoln wills indicate that parents sent their sons to school for the specific purpose of sending them into the priesthood. Robert Blawe of Toft by Newton, whose will is dated 3 April 1530, wished that:

the sayd Richerd...shall have my eldest sonne and hys parte for to fynd hym att scolle and makyng hym a prest yff it please God to send hym hellyght (health).[3]

Sometimes it was more than one member of a family who was marked out for the priesthood. Several examples of two brothers becoming priests are provided by the diocese. Thomas Bexwell

[1] L.R.S. 37, p. 12. [2] Wilkins, Concilia, III, 722.
[3] L.R.S. 10, p. 176; see also ibid. p. 114.

of Harrowden had a brother who was rector of Cublington;[1] Matthew Wynyngton of Little Oakley had a brother as rector of Wadenhoe.[2] Seth Atturclif was well placed with a brother who was abbot of Croxton; the abbot provided him with several of his livings.[3] John Appleyard of Kelstern had a brother who was vicar of Barrow on Humber and rector of Ulceby.[4] Similarly there were livings which remained within one family. Somerby was in the hands of the Waldebys[5] and Astwood stayed with the Wyddyns.[6] Ordination was not just for the younger son; it was a useful way of providing for any son who had no claim to any other employment; in consequence the priesthood appeared as a career rather than a vocation.

If parents lacked the necessary foresight to send their sons to school in preparation for a priestly career, the defects of education had to be made good at a later stage. This could be a difficult and unpopular proceeding. The poor clerks of the cathedral were bound by statute to go to school, no matter what their age. They did not take kindly to it. On 28 June 1503, four clerks, Richard Lane, Robert Rede, Robert Gentill and John Felde, were all summoned before a small meeting of the chapter and rebuked for not observing their duties, nor attending divine service, nor going to school.[7] A year later all the poor clerks were accused of not going to school and were ordered to do so under pain of deprivation.[8] The vicars choral of the cathedral were not made to go to school unless they were obviously in need of it. Hamo Thwyng had been admitted as vicar choral in 1491 and had sworn 'to use his diligence to learn the organ and descant and grammar within the year following'.[9] In 1507 at the episcopal visitation, Richard Roston said the poor clerks were 'indocti ac inhabiles' and were being badly taught by an unsuitable instructor to whom they paid little or no attention.[10] The school attended by the poor clerks

[1] Register 23, fo. 164; Longden, II, 89.
[2] Register 23, fo. 165; Longden, XV, 147.
[3] Register 23, fos. 172v, 179v, 227v, 243.
[4] Register 23, fos. 43v, 105v, 108.
[5] Register 23, fos. 130v, 147.
[6] Register 23, fos. 320, 335v.
[7] A. 3. 2, fo. 66.
[8] Ibid. fo. 96v.
[9] V.C.H. Lincolnshire, II, 432.
[10] Vj. 6, fo. 2v.

was in the city; their reluctance to go to school may, in part, have been caused by the unwelcome exertions of a walk down the hill and back.

While the parents may take the credit for educating their sons, their action must nevertheless have lent considerable weight to the view that the priesthood was a means of self-aggrandizement, a career like any other for which there was nothing either strange or improper in parents making the selection. In such a situation the heart-searchings of More must have been rare if not unique. Very few testators made provision for any kind of alternative choice. One of the few exceptions was William Foster of Gosberton, who left money for his son to go to school, as a training for the priesthood, but made provision for him 'yf he be no prest'.[1] It was also a fault of the education which was received that it had to concentrate on literacy and Latin, and it was left to reformers like Meltham and More to point out that the priesthood demanded so high a standard of devotion and probity,[2] that it could not be undertaken automatically, and, if undertaken, only by 'better laymen and fewer'.[3] While the priesthood was regarded as an automatic career for some, even the improvements in education brought about by the printing press might go wide of the mark. The devout would have bought books and read them, but the indifferent would not.

Finally it is difficult to believe that many of the priests, trained in this way, could have made much progress in understanding the faith without vernacular Bibles. The Latin of the Vulgate is not particularly easy, and, while an understanding of the content of the offices was necessary, it was not so essential as an awareness of the foundation of the faith. Where a priest's Latin was not very good he had to rely on summaries of the faith as contained in the creed, and the limited comments upon it which were to be found in the devotional literature. These comments usually took the form of a consideration of the consequences of faith or the lack

[1] L.R.S. 5, p. 47.
[2] Dickens, *The English Reformation*, pp. 45–6; Hughes, *The Reformation in England*, pp. 85, 88n.
[3] *A Dialogue of Sir Thomas More Concerning Tyndale*, ed. Campbell, p. 215.

of it, since the bulk of devotional works concentrated on *exempla* and the lives of the saints[1] rather than on telling, in the vernacular, the stories of the gospel. This limitation was admitted at the time and it seems to be borne out by the absence of any evidence of vernacular scriptures in the diocese.[2] The transition from literacy to understanding would prove difficult, until the fear that heresy would result from the reading of the New Testament was replaced by a greater fear that superstition would result if the Bible was not read and known.

The church could afford this second-hand knowledge only for as long as there were no probing questions from parishioners, subjected to other influences as strange to the parish as they were hostile to the church. The printing press created a strong presumption that the parish would cease to be such a closed unit; the career of Martin Luther, and, eventually, the English break with Rome, increased the likelihood that the influences to which it would be subject would strain the clergy to the uttermost. The danger is clearly revealed in one of the cases which came before the bishop's court of audience. An apprentice was accused in 1527 of possessing one of Wycliffe's works; he confessed he had found it on the village rubbish dump and had hoped that someone might read it to him. In fact no one did read it, except his priest, but the care with which the accused was warned not to harbour heretical books indicates that the authorities recognized the danger.[3] The church could not rely on the continued ignorance of a parish as a safeguard against heresy for very long. But it was ultimately only when the survival of a Protestant, Anglican church depended on the priesthood and its ability to engage in apologetics that the bishops organized a programme of comprehensive education of their clergy. As long as the danger to the church of heresy and

---

[1] For a consideration of this, see Dickens, *op. cit.* pp. 1 ff.

[2] *A Dialogue of Sir Thomas More Concerning Tyndale*, ed. Campbell, p. 214; More, however, thought that many laymen possessed vernacular Bibles. See also Deanesly, *The Lollard Bible*, for a full, if pessimistic, consideration of this subject; it should, however, be noted that Miss Deanesly only investigated wills which are not a very reliable source for books (see above, p. 53); library catalogues reveal the existence of a considerable number of vernacular copies of the New Testament, see above, p. 55 n.   [3] Cj. 3, fo. 43 v.

doubt was comparatively slight, the education of the clergy could be left to chance.

It was never intended that a priest should depend on chance for a livelihood. Before ordination a priest was supposed to have a title or a guaranteed living of not less than 5 marks. If his own means totalled that amount, then his title was said to be that of his patrimony; if his own means were not sufficient, then he had to be guaranteed a living in the form of either a benefice or a curacy. As the greatest patrons of livings, the religious orders were in fact in a position to guarantee a considerable number of titles.

Very few ordinands were ordained on the strength of their own private means.[1] Thomas Durdent of Denham was ordained *ad titulum patrimonii sex marcarum* and Thomas Nevyll of Althorpe to the title of his patrimony of 8 marks.[2] But these were exceptions. Most ordinands took their titles from religious houses. Usually the nearest house was taken or the nearest house of any size. Robert Wright of Flixborough was ordained to the title of Thornholme, which was the nearest significant house to his home; Robert Walter probably took Markby for the same reason.[3] If an ordinand was studying he appears to have taken his title from a house in his university rather than one near his home; Geoffrey Hardy of Boston was at Cambridge and gave the title of Saint John the Evangelist in the city;[4] the same was true of William Boton of Kimcote and Richard English of Spalding.[5] In a few cases there is no obvious reason for the title given. Thomas Smythe of Bigby in Lincolnshire took his title from Sawley in Yorkshire;[6] James Tomlinson of Gainsborough took Ulverscroft when there were some nearer and more obvious houses, presumably available

---

[1] Cf. in the thirteenth century, when the proportion appears to have been higher; see especially J. R. H. Moorman, *Church Life in England in the Thirteenth Century* (Cambridge, 1946), pp. 24 ff.

[2] Register 25, fos. 8 v, 132. The Durdent family were lords of the manor of Denham in the fifteenth century, V.C.H. *Buckinghamshire*, III, 255–61.

[3] Register 23, fo. 10.

[4] Register 23, fo. 12 v; Emden, *Cambridge*, p. 286.

[5] Register 23, fo. 10; Emden, *Cambridge*, pp. 81, 665.

[6] Register 23, fo. 12 v.

to him.[1] In cases of unusual title, it is possible that the title may have been determined by the availability of livings. But many houses do not appear to have considered this factor at all.

House	Order	Number of titles given 1514–20/1	Number of presentations made of those to whom titles given 1514–20/1	Number of presentations made of those with other titles 1514–20/1
Bardney	Benedictine	9	1	2
Crowland	Benedictine	2	0	6
Godstow	Benedictine	1	0	7
Ramsey	Benedictine	1	0	6
Garendon*	Cistercian	44	0	0
Heynings	Cistercian	11	0	0
Louth Park	Cistercian	2	0	1
Chicksands	Gilbertine	1	0	4
Nocton	Augustinian	16	0	1
Osney	Augustinian	16	0	4
Ulverscroft	Augustinian	18	0	2
Northampton St James	Augustinian	17	0	0
Croxton	Premonstratensian	1	0	0
Axholme	Carthusian	1	0	0
		140	1	33

* Indicates extensive property outside the diocese.

There seems to be little relationship between the number of vacancies which a monastic house could be expected to have, whether in curacies or actual benefices, and the number of titles for ordination which it bestowed. Of 112 selected priests ordained under Bishop Smith, not one eventually received a benefice from the house which had given him a title at ordination.[2] This dis-

[1] Register 23, fo. 12v.
[2] A selection of priests was made from Smith's ordination lists; the choice was chiefly determined by the unusual quality of the name; with common names it is too difficult to be sure of correct identification; twenty-eight received benefices from other patrons.

crepancy is not explained by the number of men in religious orders who were being ordained. They were listed separately and it is unlikely that a large number of the ordinands went into religious orders after being ordained priest. Admittedly we do not know the names of all the curates in the diocese, and some houses may have been fulfilling their obligation by giving curacies to their ordinands. But an examination of the titles given by certain houses to those ordained under Bishop Atwater would seem to suggest that there was no relationship at all between vacancies and titles (see table opposite).[1]

There is no easy explanation for the figures in this table. Obviously in the case of Garendon, some of the ordinands may have received benefices outside the diocese from the house, but, until further figures are available, it is impossible even to guess at the mobility of the English clergy. Certainly at the level from which the bishops were drawn, it was nothing for a clerk to be ordained in one diocese and to receive all benefices from another. But at a lower level it is difficult to see how a Lincoln ordinand could hope to come to the notice of a patron unless he attracted the attention of a local magnate or religious house. Still more puzzling is the role of the religious orders in this practice. If the title was becoming largely a legal fiction, it was, for the priest, at worst, an inconvenient and largely unnecessary one. But what had the religious to gain from this blatant disregard for the spirit of the canon law, if not for the letter? It is possible that they received a proportion of the stipend which the ordinand eventually received[2] but, if this is so, there is no hint of it in monastic accounts. This may not be very significant, since monastic accounts were not always very explicit and concealment would have been easy. A further problem is the wider variation in practice, not only between orders, but also between houses of the same order. The Augustinians and Cistercians were giving many more titles than the Benedictines, Gilbertines, Premonstratensians or Carthusians though the Benedictines made more presentations. But among the Benedictines there were variations in practice: Bardney was

---

[1] Register 25, *passim*.
[2] Bennett, *Essays presented to Sir Hilary Jenkinson*, pp. 20–34.

the only house to present one of its own ordinands but it gave titles to more men than it presented; Crowland, Ramsey and Godstow did just the reverse and presented more men to benefices than it had given titles at ordination.

There are suggestions in contemporary literature that there was a certain amount of dissatisfaction over titles. Thomas More urged that fewer men be ordained and none 'but he that were, without collusion, sure of a living already'.[1] But he does not indicate what the collusion involved. Nor is there much evidence to indicate whether this practice resulted in a large number of priests being ordained without a means of livelihood. If this was so, it would leave little trace in the diocesan records, since most of the records are concerned with the parochial structure. There is only one case of a priest, apparently without a benefice, being brought before the bishop; he was clearly a clerical vagrant since he had been born in Lancashire, ordained at York, and preached in various places from Herefordshire to London without licence.[2] How exceptional he was it is impossible to say.

Whether it was the worst educated who had difficulty in getting a living depended ultimately on the patron. The haphazard nature of ordination, which left so much to chance, from the schooling of the ordinand to his understanding and perhaps his livelihood, would not have been so important had there been a careful screening of all ordinands before they were presented to benefices. If the unsuitable who had escaped the notice of the authorities at ordination could be kept from the parishes the evils of the system would be minimized. In fact such an examination was attempted, but it could be thwarted by a powerful patron.

2. PATRONAGE

It was the bishop's responsibility to see that unsuitable priests were not given the cure of souls. Before admitting a man to a benefice the bishop was required to satisfy himself that the candidate was

[1] *A Dialogue of Sir Thomas More Concerning Tyndale*, ed. Campbell, p. 220; see also Hughes, *The Reformation in England*, p. 88 n.

[2] Cj. 2, fos. 100 ff. See also above, p. 21, for further mention of the same priest.

suitable.[1] The definition of suitability was deceptively straight-forward: the candidate must be twenty-five years of age and ought to be known for the quality of his learning and the commendable nature of his way of life.[2] He had to be in orders and be capable of proceeding to priest's orders. If a candidate passed the bishop's scrutiny, then he was admitted to the benefice and letters ordering his induction were sent to the archdeacon or his official.

There seems to be little doubt that this procedure was followed. There is a note in the bishop's court of audience book that, in April 1527, Robert Strangwishe was admitted to the vicarage of St Nicholas Leicester. He promised at the time of his admission that he would appear before the chancellor

examinationem subiturum. Et quod si tunc non fuerit per eundem cancellarium repertus abilis ad curam animarum regendum quod tunc ad mandatum cancellarii ipsam vicariam resignabit.[3]

Usually the names of candidates for benefices were sent to the bishop and, if the candidate proved suitable, a note of his admission to a benefice was made in the register; a note was also made of his institution fee. The standard fee for an institution was 10s. unless some extraordinary difficulties were involved. If a living was exchanged for another, the charge was doubled, and, if any inquiries were necessary to ascertain what the rights of the patron or incumbent were, there might be other fees, usually 6s. 8d. to cover the registrar's expenses.[4] The fees resulting from inquiries into the patron's rights were probably met by the patron, but those of the institution by the aspiring incumbent.[5]

Apparently very few candidates for admission were rejected and none for unsuitability. One candidate was sent to learn grammar for a year[6] and one presentation deed bears the exceptional endorsement *Non expeditur ad hoc*.[7] The reason why this deed

[1] Lyndwood *Provinciale*, Lib. III, tit. 6, note k, see also Register 26, fo. 274.
[2] *Et quod sit commendandus scientia et moribus.*   [3] Cj. 3, fo. 43.
[4] Bishop's Rentals, I, fos. 6v ff.; Bishop Fuller's Transcripts, fo. 157.
[5] *Ibid.* It is interesting that inquiries of this kind still continued; references are made to them in the registers: see Register 23, fos. 56, 100, 175.
[6] Presentation Deeds, 1504, no. 144; see above, p. 55.
[7] *Ibid.* 1517, no 17.

was not expedited was not unsuitability. The candidate for admission was James Rowley and he was formally admitted to the benefice on 7 October, 1517.[1] Two months later James was dead and it is probable that he died before being inducted into his living by the archdeacon even though he had been admitted to it; a careful registrar was right to note such a detail, which might involve a dispute over fees during the vacancy. Technically James had never taken possession of the fruits of the benefice and they were owing to the bishop for the two months in which he had held the title to the living.[2]

If the bishop had the power to keep the blatantly unsuitable from the cure of souls, his power was nevertheless a very limited one. His was, at best, a negative voice; he might refuse a candidate for a benefice on the grounds of some canonical failing, but he had little power to improve the general standard of parish priests by collating his own nominees, even if he had wanted to do so. The bishop had only a limited number of livings in his own gift. If all possible livings are taken into consideration, the bishop appears to have had only fifty livings at his disposal.[3] This figure includes hospitals and chantries and the rights of nomination he possessed at Hemel Hempstead, Enstone, Goxhill, Little Coates, Stretton Magna and Laughton. Other livings might come to him by gift or through 'lapse of time'. If another patron had failed to present within six months of a vacancy, the presentation on that occasion 'lapsed' to the bishop. Bishop Atwater collated thirty people to livings and nineteen of these livings had come to him through lapse of time.[4] But there could be no certainty that patrons would neglect their rights in this way, and neglect was necessary on a very large scale if the bishop was to make a significant impact on his diocese by appointing to the parish men whom he believed to be suitable. For the most part he could do little more than assent to the candidates presented to him by the various patrons in the diocese.

[1] Register 25, fo. 17.
[2] Lyndwood, *Provinciale*, Lib. III, tit. 6, note g; induction was said to be to the *corporalem possessionem*.   [3] Toney's Repertorium, fos. 97v-8.
[4] Register 25, fos. 6, 13 v[2], 14, 15 v[3], 16, 16v, 17v, 18[2], 18v, 19v, 26v, 27, 32, 33, 34, 35, 35 v[2], 37, 38v, 40[2], 44, 48v, 51v, 53, 53 v, 54v, 56v, 61v, 62, 63v. A bishop was not said to 'present' a man to a living but to 'collate' him.

Nearly half of the patronage of the diocese was in the hands of the religious orders. This, in effect, meant that they had a decisive control of the parish churches. They could present devoted pastors to benefices or they could present the self-seeking and the unscrupulous. If the religious lacked friends at the dissolution, one reason must surely be that they had neglected to make them in the parishes from which the members of parliament were drawn. Neither pope nor bishop had the power to reform at the parochial level in the way the religious might have done by an enlightened exercise of their patronage.

This collective power was not equally distributed. At least one twelfth of the presentations made by the religious orders was made by the prior of St John of Jerusalem in England. St Albans and Ramsey also presented to a large number of livings, and, in particular areas, other houses were important. The Gilbertines of Chicksands in Bedfordshire exercised much of the patronage of that county, and, in Northamptonshire and Rutland, the houses of Peterborough and Thorney possessed considerable power. The large houses like Ramsey and Peterborough might present as many as seventy-five men to livings in twenty years while the smaller houses of local importance, like Crowland and Osney, would present about thirty.[1]

In contrast to the power of the religious, that of any group of laymen was puny. The crown over this period presented 123 men to livings, and the two bishops of Lincoln only eighty-five. Most of the patronage which was not in the hands of the religious was very widely spread among the laity and a variety of collegiate bodies such as the Oxford and Cambridge colleges. With the exception of the crown, no layman exercised decisively important power.[2] Most of them had but a handful of livings; typical was John Cheney of Chesham who presented to Cogenhoe and Drayton Beauchamp.[3]

The precise distribution of patronage varied a little from year

---

[1] All these figures are based on an analysis of Registers 23 and 25; the total number of presentations to parish churches for this period was 2,760; of these the religious presented about 1,331. [2] Register 23 and 25, *passim*.

[3] Register 23, fos. 182, 214v, 324v.

to year. This was because it was possible to grant away patronage rights for a certain number of years, usually for two incumbencies. In the Atwater period alone, forty such grants were made, twenty-six of which resulted in a transfer of patronage from a religious house to a secular priest or a layman.[1]

The incidence of patronage might vary a great deal. Bampton in the Bush, for example, became vacant four times between 1495 and 1520/1,[2] as did Bengeo.[3] Medmenham had four incumbents; two of its vacancies were caused by the death of the last vicar and two by resignation.[4] Friskney changed hands four times since three of its incumbents died.[5] Goldington had five incumbents, all but one of whom resigned—probably because the incumbent was bound to pay a former incumbent, John Stewart, a pension of 40s.[6] But usually a patron was lucky if he could present to a living more than once in ten years.

Nearly a quarter of those presented to livings under Bishop Smith were still in possession of them when the subsidy was assessed in 1526. Some of the incumbents had held their livings for twenty years; Thomas Stamp, who became rector of Aisthorpe in November 1498, was still the rector there in 1526, though the living was only said to be worth £4. 13s. 4d.[7] Thomas Kendall's rectory of Waddington St Peter was worth even less, yet he, too, was an incumbent of some twenty-seven years standing.[8] William Beley was the first vicar of Potterspury and was certainly there for nearly thirty years; he received £8 from this benefice and resided sufficiently to witness the wills of several of his parishioners.[9] John Roper, the first Lady Margaret praelector in divinity and a lecturer on philosophy, not surprisingly, held on to the vicarage of St Mary, Oxford, for nearly thirty years; the living was a convenient one for him, though it was not particularly

---

[1] Register 25, fos. 6, 13v[2], 14, 15v[3], 16, 16v[2], 17v, 18[2], 18v, 19v, 26v, 27, 32, 33, 34, 35, 35v, 37, 38v, 40[2], 41, 48v, 51v, 53, 53v[2], 54, 54v, 56v[2], 61v, 62v, 63v.   [2] Register 23, fos. 275v, 279, 279v, 282.
[3] Register 23, fos. 359, 365v; Register 25, fos. 56, 58v.
[4] Register 23, fos. 310, 317[2], 318.   [5] Register 23, fos. 32, 65v, 127, 133v.
[6] Register 23, fos. 390v, 399v, 406v, 407v, 408.
[7] Register 23, fo. 150; Salter, p. 40.   [8] Register 23, fo. 153v; Salter, p. 35.
[9] Register 23, fo. 173; Salter, p. 161; Longden, II, 57.

lucrative.[1] John Kale, whose ignorance of Latin grammar constituted a barrier to his acquiring Shabbington, stayed there for over twenty years.[2] Some of these 'obstinate' incumbents were not persistent in holding their livings because they lacked other opportunities; Robert Wadyluff, a member of the order of St John of Jerusalem, certainly had three livings, but this did not prevent him keeping a tight hold on the vicarage of Ravensthorpe for over twenty-five years.[3] A patron therefore could never be sure when the chance to bestow the favour of a living would come again. He had always to bestow it carefully.

Contemporaries often expressed the opinion that patrons did not use their patronage carefully enough. At the beginning of the fifteenth century, the University of Oxford was complaining that graduates were not being presented to livings. The archbishop of Canterbury was requested in 1438

Flexis igitur genibus, obnixius quo valemus exoramus ac petimus quatenus ad effectualem graduatorum promocionem oculos misericordie vestre convertere dignemini.[4]

This attempt, and others before it, had very little effect; between 1421 and 1431 very few graduates were presented to livings in the diocese. But by 1500 things had changed. Many graduates were presented[5] and the criticism directed against patrons struck another note. It was objected that livings were used simply as a means of social advancement. The fifteenth-century author of the *Destructorium Viciorum* complained

In these days, pastors and prelates of the Church tire and sweat to obtain dignities, one in the king's kitchen, another in a bishop's court and a third in the service of a temporal lord; but in the court of instruction in the Divine Law they labour least of all. And when, after long toil, they obtain a church through such occupations, they cease not to labour; but then they must be prebendaries, then archdeacons and

[1] Register 23, fo. 275v; Salter, p. 277; Emden, *Oxford*, III, 1590.
[2] Register 23, fo. 332v; Salter, p. 237; see also above, p. 55.
[3] Viz. Souldrop, Lower Stondon, Ravensthorpe (Register 23, fos. 175, 400v, 403v; Salter, p. 154; Cj. 2, fo. 30v).
[4] *Epistolae Academicae*, ed. H. Anstey, I (O.H.S. xxxv, 1898), 154.
[5] See above, p. 45.

then bishops. And when they have been raised to the highest rank within their reach, then so exhausted are they with their first fatigue that, by reason of the abundance of their service and toil, they can no longer keep watch over the flocks committed to them.[1]

This complaint was taken up in the sixteenth century, most notably by Colet in his famous Convocation Sermon of 1512. He spoke of the men of the church running 'almost out of breath, from one benefice to another', and he asked 'What other thing seek we nowadays in the Church than fat benefices and high promotions?'[2]

These criticisms reflect on the patron just as much as the priesthood. The breathlessly ambitious had to find a patron who would forward their ambition. Patrons cooperated because the ambitious man who achieved his goal, whether in church or state, was a useful ally and someone it was as well not to have offended. Patronage could easily become a form of talent spotting. Did this in fact happen and, if it did, what were its results?

Difficult though it is to find out about the men whom patrons presented to their livings, it is even more hazardous to try and construct the potential field from which a choice could have been made. We know who was appointed but not who was refused. But we do know for certain that, though there were more benefices vacant than there were ordained men to fill them, there were, nevertheless, great difficulties in acquiring a benefice.

Between 1496 and 1520/1, 2,760 parishes became vacant and a further 239 deaneries, hospitals and chantries. There were, therefore, no less than 2,999 vacancies in the diocese. To fill these vacancies only 1,655 men were ordained priest without actually possessing a benefice already.[3] If there had been no pluralism, there would have been too many vacancies, even allowing for the fact that some might be filled by priests ordained outside the diocese. The patron would have had difficulties in filling the livings at his

---

[1] G. R. Owst, *The Destructorium Viciorum of Alexander Carpenter* (S.P.C.K., 1952), p. 15.
[2] Quoted in H. J. Hillerbrand, *The Reformation in Its Own Words* (London, 1964), p. 305.
[3] These figures are based on an analysis of Registers 23, 24 and 25.

disposal. But this was far from being the case. All the available evidence indicates that there was pressure for benefices. Any ruse was worth trying in order to get one. Most of the intrigue remains hidden but occasionally we catch a glimpse of it. An indication of the pressure is provided by the case of Magister John Cordesmore. He appeared before the bishop himself on 18 October 1516 and requested the bishop to collate him to the rectory of Garsington in Oxfordshire; possibly his reason for the request was that he had relations in the neighbourhood.[1] He swore that the last rector was dead and that he held the necessary qualifications to hold the living. He admitted, however, that he held three benefices, one *in commendam* and two others of which he had resigned one. The bishop requested that he give proof of the previous rector's death and that he show adequate dispensation for this combination of livings; he was bound to do this not later than the Feast of the Purification 1516/17.[2] It must be assumed that these demands were beyond him or that he did not think the rectory worth the effort. He failed to appear before the bishop, and Magister John More was collated to the living.[3]

John Cordesmore had sufficient livings to give him a livelihood and, if he resided in them, plenty of interesting work. But there were many who were not so fortunate. Magister Geoffrey Hardy of Boston was ordained priest in April 1498.[4] He had graduated at Cambridge and held a degree in civil law.[5] He did not get a benefice of his own until March 1507/8 when he was presented to the vicarage of St Ives.[6] The intervening years he apparently passed as a curate at Kirton in Holland. The worst report that could be made of him was that when he visited the sick he took the Host to them but did not take the usual light.[7] Perhaps there were personal reasons which kept Geoffrey at Kirton, but it can hardly be said that he was canonically 'unsuitable' for a living.

[1] A Mathilda Cotismore lived at Britwell Salome (*L.R.S.* 33, p. 121).
[2] Cj. 2, fos. 15 ff.   [3] Register 25, fo. 46.
[4] Register 24, fo. 13.   [5] Emden, *Cambridge*, p. 286.
[6] Register 23, fo. 376v; he died shortly after receiving the living (*ibid.* fo. 378).
[7] Vj. 5, fo. 53; the report is unusual and it is possible that it was made because Geoffrey was unpopular.

Many others shared the same fate of serving a curacy for a very long time, sometimes even for life. It is very hard to trace curates and other lower clergy, and it would be dangerous to assume anything about those who disappear from view. But it is interesting that, of the twenty-six curates reported as serving Boston in 1500,[1] four were still there in 1526,[2] and, though eight eventually received a living, it took them some time. The first to move was William Kirke, who was given the living of Oadby in April 1504;[3] of the others, two had been presented by 1506,[4] one in 1509,[5] two in 1516/17,[6] one by 1526, and the remaining one simply became a curate at Grantham.[7] Nor does Boston appear to have been unusually bad in the prospects of promotion which it provided.

The curates of Grantham do not seem to have done much better. Of those whom it is possible to trace,[8] two stayed at Grantham from 1500 to 1526;[9] one was presented to a living by 1512[10] and another moved to a curacy at Wellingborough.[11] None of the curates at Fulstow in 1500 received a benefice though two moved their curacies.[12] The same picture emerges in Leicestershire. The names of some forty-two curates were recorded at the archidiaconal visitations of 1517. Many of these either stayed in the same curacy or simply moved to another curacy; at least nine curates stayed and about eleven moved. Only three appear to have received benefices.[13] The records of those ordained priest in the diocese tell the same story. Of 112 selected for investigation

---

[1] Vj. 5, fo. 48.   [2] Salter, pp. 66–7.
[3] Register 23, fo. 250.
[4] William Pynnell and Thomas Heryng (Register 23, fos. 106, 114v).
[5] Richard Stevynson (Register 23, fo. 214v).
[6] Richard Hardye and William Prat (Register 25, fos. 17v, 30).
[7] Salter, pp. 69, 153; John Gybon and John Adams.
[8] Vj. 5, fo. 68.   [9] William Lyall and James Shawe (Salter, p. 69).
[10] John Parker (Register 23, fo. 145v).
[11] John Parnell (Salter, p. 127).
[12] Vj. 5, fo. 32; John Graunt and Alan Smyth moved (Salter, pp. 20, 205).
[13] A.A.S.R.P. xxviii, 127 ff.; cf. Salter, pp. 99–106, 115–19.
The curate stayed in the parishes of Shangton, Whetstone, Church Langton, Stoke Chapel, Stretton Magna, Burbage, Lutterworth, Houghton on the Hill, Wibtoft. Curates moved from Aston Flamville, Noseley, Sharnford, Elmer, Sheepy, Kimcote, Saddington, Shearsby, Mowsley, Ibstock and North Kilworth. It is sometimes difficult to trace a curate with a usual name.

only twenty-eight received benefices by 1526.[1] Of those who eventually received a benefice, most took about five years after their ordination to do so. Even Christopher Massingberd, who belonged to a very well-known Lincolnshire family, took eight years after ordination to be presented to his first Lincoln living,[2] that of the vicarage of Bourne.[3] Christopher was to collect at least three livings in the diocese and a number of cathedral dignities,[4] and it is interesting that he had some delay, and perhaps difficulty, in collecting his first.

Christopher Massingberd like many of his contemporaries was to become a pluralist, and, clearly, pluralism vitiates all figures based on the number of men ordained and the number of vacancies available for them. The ordinand was not the only one on the market. Licences to hold cures in plurality made it possible for livings to be collected on a large scale. Pluralism spanned the geographical frontiers of the diocese and it is, therefore, impossible to estimate its scope. But, even within the diocese, it was not unusual for a graduate or a royal servant to hold several benefices. The inevitable corollary to pluralism was non-residence:[5] about 25% of all the parishes in the diocese had a non-resident priest between 1514 and 1521 and most non-residents were holding livings in plurality.[6] The competition for livings was, therefore, much greater than the figures for ordinations and vacancies would suggest. It was made greater still for some priests by difficulties of communication and the attitude of patrons to their livings.

There does not seem to have been a central agency of any kind which could have put a would-be incumbent in touch with a patron. In the late fourteenth and early fifteenth centuries, there were brokers in livings who operated through a series of ex-

[1] Register 24, fos. 1 ff.; for a note on this selection see above, p. 62.

[2] *Ibid.* fo. 10v; Christopher was ordained priest in 1497.

[3] Register 23, fo. 97v; his other livings were South Hykeham and Bicker (*ibid.* fos. 117v, 124).

[4] *L.R.S.* 12, p. xii, see also below, p. 164.

[5] See appendix IV for a list of non-residents and their alleged reasons for absenteeism.

[6] For a consideration of what this figure means and how it has been reached, see below, p. 90.

changes.[1] But by the early sixteenth century the number of re-corded exchanges had significantly diminished. For the period 1495–1521, there are only about twenty exchanges recorded and only one of these raises even a suspicion of having been made through a broker.[2] Magister John Egerton exchanged Hattley for Farthingston and Farthingston for Hemel Hempstead.[3] But these exchanges took him four years and the suggestion of brokerage seems improbable. It is possible that the bishop's registrar knew the names of some of those looking for livings and that, on occa-sions, he was able to indicate their need to a patron, but, for the most part, the unknown and unproved would have had consider-able difficulties in finding a patron or a living.

It is obviously quite impossible to construct, in every case, the precise circumstances through which a particular individual was favoured with a living. Biographical details survive for very few clerks and the best that can be done is to indicate the general factors which would incline a patron to favour a man. Obviously there will be many undiscovered exceptions to these general rules but it is unlikely that they will totally change the over-all picture.

A patron was very likely to favour his own family if he could. The same care through which sons destined for the priesthood were sent to school persisted and reached a fitting conclusion if they could then be presented to the family or local living. A family presented one of its own members on at least forty-eight occasions during this period. If family connexions on the female side (which are not identifiable through the name) are allowed for, it is probable that a total of approximately 100 family presentations were made.[4] Sometimes the presentation was to the local living; Richard Thymylby of Poolam presented his son Thomas to the

---

[1] A. H. Thompson, *The English Clergy and Their Organisation in the Later Middle Ages* (Oxford, 1947), pp. 107–9.

[2] Register 23, fos. 44v, 94, 128v, 130, 137, 149v, 243, 278, 293v, 306v[2], 344, 380v, 382. Register 25, fos. 24v, 33v, 39v, 59, 61v, 63.

[3] *Ibid.* fos. 33v, 59, 63. He also held Billing Magna and was said to reside in Lichfield (Cj. 2, fo. 34).

[4] See appendix II; these figures rely on the identity of surname. There will be occasions in which this is a coincidence. Pedigrees do not survive in sufficient number to include such presentations. The total number of presentations made was 2,760, see above, p. 67 n.

rectory of Thimbleby,[1] a rectory to which one of the family had been presented for at least a century. Thomas was lord of the manors of Poolam and Tetford in his own right, and combined his Thimbleby rectory with that of Tetford.[2] Thomas Barnadeston presented his son, John Barnadeston, to the rectory of Coates Magna;[3] the Barnadestons were from Coates and members of the family held the living whenever possible.[4] It was not always easy to find a living which was on the family door-step for a needy son. William Tyrwhit, at one time High Sheriff of Lincoln, presented a relative of his to the rectory of Bigby;[5] Andrew Byllesby, of Bilsby, presented William Byllesby to the rectory of Toft by Newton,[6] which was a few miles away but in which William did not reside, probably because he had a Norfolk living as well.[7] George Henneage, who eventually became dean of Lincoln, was presented by his father and uncle to the rectory of Flixborough,[8] and Edward Grantham, Mayor of Lincoln in 1492 and 1505, presented John Grantham to the rectory of South Hykeham,[9] which was a few miles from Lincoln. A member of the family who went into a religious order was a useful source of patronage. Seth Aturcliff owed his presentations to half South Croxton to the fact that his brother was the abbot of Croxton and the abbey was patron of both these livings.[10] The same kind of relationship probably accounts for the presentation of William Fayrfax to two of the livings in the gift of the prior and convent of Kyme.[11] The abbey and convent of Peterborough presented William Byrde to a canonry of Irthlingburgh; a possible explanation for this presentation is that a Roger Byrd was one of the monks of the house.[12]

[1] Register 23, fo. 103.   [2] *Lincolnshire Pedigrees*, III, 957.
[3] Register 23, fo. 52 v.   [4] *Lincolnshire Pedigrees*, I, 89.
[5] Register 23, fo. 92 v; *Lincolnshire Pedigrees*, III, 1019.
[6] Register 23, fo. 110.
[7] *Lincolnshire Pedigrees*, I, 135; *L.R.S.* 33, p. 88; Emden, *Cambridge*, p. 62.
[8] Register 23, fo. 118 v; *Lincolnshire Pedigrees*, II, 480.
[9] Register 23, fo. 33; *Lincolnshire Pedigrees*, I, 421.
[10] Register 23, fos. 179 v, 227 v.
[11] Register 25, fos. 17 v, 19; *L.R.S.* 35, p. 179.
[12] Register 25, fo. 31; *Peterborough local administration. The Last Days of Peterborough Monastery*, ed. W. T. Mellows (Northants Record Society, XII, 1947) pp. 3, 52.

Colleges and religious orders, like families, tended to present their own members where possible; Balliol College, Oxford, presented its own master, Richard Barnyngham, to the rectory of Brattleby; their other presentations to this living were of members of the college.[1] Pembroke Hall, Cambridge, presented a treasurer of the Hall to the vicarage of Orton Waterville[2] and Clare Hall presented a fellow to the vicarage of Great Gransden.[3] Two fellows of Magdalen College, Oxford, were presented to their rectory of Saltfleetby All Saints.[4] It was rare for colleges to overlook their own *alumni*. Premonstratensian and Austin canons frequently received the privilege of presenting men of their own order to benefices which they had appropriated. A few other religious orders were doing the same.[5] The Benedictine monks of Spalding, for instance, were allowed to serve the churches of Spalding, Pinchbeck, Weston and Moulton.[6] They do not appear to have done so in Moulton and Pinchbeck but they had an ambiguous arrangement at Spalding. There is no record of their making a presentation there, but the prior was said to be providing *presbiteros minus idoneos et indoctos*, and it looks as though the house served the cure.[7] The hospital of St John of Jerusalem had the right to present members of their order to livings and there is a note in the bishop's court book that the rectors of Ludgershall, Withcall, Aspenden, Little Stoughton and Hulcott were members of the order.[8] In the case of the Hospitallers it is very hard to distinguish a brother from a secular priest, but, since they possessed this right of 'self-appointment', it is possible that they availed themselves of it on many more occasions than was noted in the register. Usually it is the canons who are found being presented by their

[1] Register 23, fos. 152, 156v, 157. Emden, *Oxford*, I, 62, 114; II, 1085.
[2] Register 23, fo. 357v; Emden, *Cambridge*, p. 537.
[3] Register 23, fo. 284v; Emden, *Cambridge*, p. 466.
[4] Register 23, fos. 110v, 274v; Emden, *Oxford*, I, 308; II, 767.
[5] D. Knowles, *The Religious Orders in England* (Cambridge, 1957), II, 288–94; see also R. A. R. Hartridge, *A History of Vicarages in the Middle Ages* (Cambridge, 1930), pp. 162 ff.
[6] *Papal Letters 1396–1404*, ed. W. H. Bliss and J. A. Twemlow (Calendar of Papal Registers, V, 1904), p. 199.
[7] *L.R.S.* 33, pp. 60–1.
[8] Register 25, fos. 82v, 83; Cj. 2, fo. 30v.

own houses. A total of seventy-four religious were presented by their own orders to livings in the diocese, of whom thirty-two were Austin canons, twenty-two Premonstratensians, thirteen Gilbertines, three Benedictines, two Cistercians, one was a Bonhomme and one was a Hospitaller.[1] When the abbot himself required presentation, a grant was normally made of the presentation to an intermediary, presumably on the understanding that the recipients would use it to honour the abbot. Thomas Thorpe, prior of Newburgh, was presented to Epworth by Brian Higden and Thomas Dalby, who had been granted the advowson by Newburgh![2] The abbot of Sulby was presented to East Haddon by Nicholas Osborn, again on a grant from the abbot's own house.[3] The Cistercian abbot of Revesby was presented to the rectory of Claxby as a result of a grant made by his own house, as was the abbot of Bardney.[4]

The presentation of canons to parishes had its origin in expediency; they genuinely helped the parishes and regarded the cure of souls as their vocation. As we shall see, by the sixteenth century this help was not always very effective. But there was nothing particularly incongruous in canons holding livings. With the Benedictines, it was different. The communal life is central to their rule and either the parish must suffer or the monk concerned was victimized, since to serve a parish he would have to leave his house. Had there been a severe shortage of secular priests this action would have been excusable and possibly desirable. As it was, it was a part of the tendency displayed by religious and secular patrons and priests to regard a benefice as a piece of property.[5] To the patron, in particular, a benefice was a useful gift which he might bestow to forward his own purposes.

If these purposes were not served by granting the benefice to a relative or, in the case of colleges and religious houses, to a member of the institution concerned, then it was used very frequently either as a reward for services already given to the patron or as an indication that such services were expected.

---

[1] See appendix III.
[2] Register 25, fos. 20v, 26v.
[3] Register 25, fo. 30.
[4] Register 23, fo. 145².
[5] Knowles, *op. cit.* pp. 288–94.

As the best-educated members of society, at least in theory, the graduates were the people most likely to hold high office in church and state and most likely to be in a position to repay kindness. The University of Oxford also recommended the promotion of graduates to benefices on the grounds that their learning would benefit the parish; they suggested that

ut ipse vitali ligno theologice facultatis decenter iam ramificans peramplius frondeat, frondescens germinet, germinansque floreat, et florescens fructificet in catholice doctrine semine quod posterius in animarum campis spargere poterit habundanter.[1]

They were somewhat optimistic in this claim, since many of those who might have benefited the church in this way in fact never resided.[2] But the letter is a useful reminder that benefit to the patron and benefit to the parish might not necessarily be mutually exclusive. Some of the many patrons who presented graduates may have had an eye to one form of benefit rather than another and some may have combined both.

A total of 791 presentations of graduates were made during this period.[3] This figure, though a high one, would not necessarily be significant were it not quite clear that certain patrons favoured graduates more than any other group in bestowing their livings. The Carthusians of Sheen made a total of twenty-five presentations, of which eight were to graduates. The graduates were presented to livings worth £20 or more and only three non-graduates ever received livings of comparable value.[4] The abbot and convent of Ramsey presented a large number of graduates; thirty-one out of forty-four presentations were of them. Here again, the graduate was favoured with the more valuable livings. Twenty-three presentations were made of graduates to livings of £20 and only four to non-graduates, two of whom had an obvious claim

---

[1] *Epistolae Academicae*, ed. Anstey, I, 2, no. 2.
[2] See below, p. 97.
[3] For an analysis of these figures see above, p. 45 n.
[4] Register 23, fos. 164, 171, 212, 216, 227, 240v, 244, 247, 248, 252, 253, 255, 255v, 256, 267v, 272v, 300, 306v; Register 25, fos. 31, 34, 37v, 38v, 39v, 41, 46v. The livings concerned were Byfield, Charlton on Otmoor, Middleton Cheney, Sibstone; for their value, see Salter, pp. 109, 150, 151, 273. Charlton on

to favour:[1] the living of Brington went to Henry Bekensawe; Magister Robert Bekensawe had resigned the living and it was to be held by 1526 by Magister Adam Bekensaw, so it may be assumed that Brington was a family living;[2] there was ample enough incentive to keep it that way as Robert was the queen's almoner and not without influence.[3] John Galion, though not a graduate, was given another of the valuable Ramsey livings, Broughton. John was probably the bishop of Gallipoli and important in his own right.[4] Not surprisingly, Margaret, Countess of Richmond and Derby, favoured graduates in her presentations; she presented graduates to her livings worth over £20 and only two non-graduates received livings from her of comparable value; one of those who did so was a suffragan bishop.[5] It would be wrong to assume that all patrons favoured graduates in this way. The Gilbertines of Chicksands presented no graduates to livings[6] and, though the Augustinians of Osney had close contacts with the University of Oxford, and used half their presentations to help graduates, they did not mark out graduates for particular favour by giving them their most valuable livings.[7] The priory of St John of Jerusalem in England had many livings, but few of them were worth very much; this may account for the fact that of their ninety-three presentations only seventeen were of graduates.[8]

Otmoor went twice to a non-graduate and Sibstone went once (Register 23, fos. 248, 272 v; Register 25, fo. 46 v).

[1] Register 23, fos. 188 v, 353 v[2], 354 v, 355 v, 356 v[2], 358, 358 v[2], 359, 360, 363, 364, 368[2], 369, 369 v, 372 v, 375, 376 v[2], 377 v, 378, 379 v[2], 380[2], 381, 381 v, 382, 382 v[2], 390, 395 v, 397 v, 406 v; Register 25, fos. 6, 28 v, 52 v, 56 v, 57, 57 v, 58 v.

[2] Register 23, fo. 382; Salter p. 184.   [3] Emden, *Cambridge*, p. 51.

[4] Register 23, fo. 358 v; *L. and P.* I, pt. I, no. 5427.

[5] Register 23, fos. 43, 51, 54, 61 v, 71 v, 99 v, 121, 124, 174 v, 201, 213 v.

[6] Register 23, fos. 385 v, 392 v, 395 v, 402, 406 v; Register 25, fos. 61, 62, 63, 63 v.

[7] Register 23, fos. 273 v[2], 276 v, 279, 280 v, 281, 283 v, 288, 289 v, 290[3], 292 v, 295 v, 296[2], 296 v, 298, 301 v, 303, 303 v, 305 v, 307 v; Register 25, fos. 44, 44 v[2].

[8] Register 23, fos. 33 v, 36, 46 v, 58 v, 60, 68 v, 72 v, 79, 84 v, 96, 105, 106, 106 v, 115, 119[2], 120, 121, 130, 132 v, 143[3], 146, 153, 156 v, 158, 160[2], 164, 167, 172, 175, 176, 180 v, 187, 195, 197, 204 v, 207, 217, 218, 220, 222 v, 224, 224 v, 271 v, 279 v, 315 v, 316, 320 v, 327 v, 333, 334, 334 v, 335, 338, 339, 342 v, 345 v, 347 v, 355 v, 381[2], 385 v, 392, 398, 398 v, 399, 400 v[2], 401, 403, 403 v, 404, 405, 407 v; Register 25, fos. 14, 19 v, 22 v, 29 v[2], 32, 35 v, 40[2], 42 v, 54 v, 61, 62 v. These figures are for parish churches and do not include chantries.

Graduates were potentially influential; from their ranks, royal and episcopal administrators were most likely to be drawn. Once a man had actually acquired a position of power and ceased to be merely promising, benefices were showered upon him. William Atkinson, who was chaplain to Princess Mary, was presented to six livings within the diocese.[1] James Whitstones was president of the Council of Margaret, Countess of Richmond, and vicar general of the bishop of Lincoln; he collected six livings.[2] William Barons started his career as a promising graduate; he was a doctor of civil law at Bologna; before his appointment as Master of the Rolls he collected two livings in the diocese and after this he was presented to a further two.[3] Rober Bright, who was presented to two livings, was a chaplain to the king.[4] Philip Morgan, physician to the Countess of Richmond, was presented to the valuable livings of Washingborough and Wheathampstead,[5] and Robert Shorton, who was an executor of her will and a frequent preacher at court, received Kettering.[6] Christopher Plummer, chaplain to Queen Katherine, and George Hamond, chaplain to the Queen of France, each received a living in the diocese,[7] and two ministers of the Chapel Royal each received benefices.[8] It is quite impossible to assess the number of royal administrators of quite lowly status who were favoured in this way, since many of them have left little trace of their activities, but it would be surprising if any were without a benefice for long.

Sometimes patrons presented their own chaplains, and the dependants of a courtier were almost as much in demand as the courtier himself. Robert Burton and Thomas Cade, both chaplains of the Duke of Buckingham, were presented by him to the

---

[1] Register 23, fos. 182, 344v, 372v, 380v; Register 25, fos. 39, 61; L.R.S. 33, p. 110; L. and P. II, pt. II, 4234.

[2] Register 23, fos. 32, 61v, 186v, 197, 271, 353v. Emden, Oxford, III, 2039.

[3] Register 23, fos. 62, 246, 319, 364; Emden, Oxford, I, 115.

[4] Register 23, fo. 194; Register 25, fo. 2v; L. and P. I, pt. I, 4235; II, pt. I, 274.

[5] Register 23, fos. 124, 378; Emden, Cambridge, p. 411.

[6] Register 25, fo. 28v; L. and P. II, pt. II, no. 4183 and p. 1470.

[7] Register 25, fo. 58v; L. and P. II, pt. II, no. 4072; Cj. 2, fo. 34.

[8] Register 25, fo. 54; L. and P. II, pt. II, 876 and no. 3155.

livings of North Luffenham and Burford respectively.[1] Richard Ward and Christopher Cuddeworth were presented to livings by John Dee and Henry VIII—both were chaplains to Sir John Husy.[2] William Burbank was presented to Barnack by the abbot and convent of Peterborough; he was Wolsey's chaplain,[3] and William Clifton was presented to Muston by the prioress and convent of Stixwold—he too was a protégé of Wolsey who later became his vicar general in Durham.[4] Thomas Allen was presented by the abbot and convent of Westminster to Stevenage; he was a close associate of the Earl of Shrewsbury, to whom he signed himself 'your priest'.[5] Richard Cobb was presented by the Duke of Somerset to a living probably simply because he was chaplain to the duke.[6] Peter Beck was twice presented by the Marquis of Dorset, to whom he was chaplain,[7] and Nicholas Metcalf, besides being Master of St John's college, Cambridge, was a chaplain to the bishop of Rochester, by whom he was presented.[8] William Bond received two livings, one from Thomas Hutton, for whose will he was an executor.[9] These men, like the royal servants, treated livings purely as stipends without which they would lack an income to subsidize their other employment.

The bishop, too, was forced to use the livings at his disposal as sources of income. Without them, there was no means by which his own diocesan administrators could achieve an adequate stipend. Bishop's commissaries in particular, as well as the suffragans and vicars general, were without income except for the casual revenue accruing from fees. The bishop and other patrons, especially those within the diocese, both had something to gain from appointing diocesan officials; the bishop needed a loyal staff and could ill afford the discontent that come from bad pay and poor condi-

---

[1] Register 23, fo. 207; Register 25, fo. 44; Emden, *Oxford*, p. 320; *L. and P.* II, pt. II, no. 3173.

[2] Register 25, fos. 15, 29v; *L.R.S.* 33, pp. 56, 66, 76.

[3] Register 25, fo. 34; *L. and P.* II, pt. I, no. 1561.

[4] Register 25, fo. 3v; *L. and P.* II, pt. I, nos. 299, 306.

[5] Register 25, fo. 58v; *L. and P.* II, pt. II, no. 3807.

[6] Cj. 2, fo. 25.   [7] Register 23, fos. 257v, 266.

[8] Register 23, fos. 106v, 303v; Emden, *Cambridge*, p. 403.

[9] Register 23, fos. 47v, 125v; Emden, *Cambridge*, p. 72.

tions; and such was the power of the diocesan official that a layman would be ill advised to fall foul of him. The administrator
was, therefore, an obvious object of patronage. William Mason,
the bishop's commissary in the archdeaconry of Leicester, and a
trusted servant often sent on difficult investigations, received three
livings in this period, only one of which was from the bishop.[1]
John Bell, the suffragan bishop of Mayo, also received three
livings, all of them from different sources.[2] The only person to
receive six livings, besides William Atkinson, was James Whitstones,[3] who combined the advantages of royal service with those
of the bishop's vicar general. Robert Newton appears to have
been a lowly chantry priest with few claims to benefices, but he
was in fact in charge of the court of the dean and chapter
and their *auditor causarum*; he received three livings, only one of
which was in the gift of the dean and chapter.[4] William Wittur,
another of the bishop's commissaries, was presented to three
livings, twice by laymen and once by the bishop himself.[5]

The support of a local family which held an important office in
the shire might be as necessary to the patron as that of the king,
courtier or bishop. The sons of powerful local families were
therefore favoured by both the king and his subjects. The most
obvious example of the king's concern for the good will of the
county is found in Leicestershire, where the prebends and canonries of the Newarke College, Leicester, were nearly always granted
by the king to the sons of local families. The Swillingtons, Wig-
stons and Brokesbys competed for these benefices.[6] But, at the
more mundane level of the parish, a similar process was at work.
George Appleyard was presented by the abbot and convent of
Thornton to both Barrow on Humber and Ulceby; the Appleyards were a well-known Lincolnshire family who are buried at
Ulceby. Thornton Abbey lies nearly mid-way between these

[1] Register 23, fos. 61, 173, 212v, 263v; see also Emden, *Cambridge*, p. 395.
[2] Register 23, fos. 123, 159, 202v; *L.R.S.* 12, p. xv.
[3] See above, p. 80.
[4] Register 23, fo. 205; Register 25, fos. 18, 15v; A. 3. 4, fo. 36v; Robert may
also have held Radnage and East Keal (Register 23, fos. 84v, 327v).
[5] Register 23, fos. 170, 223; Register 25, fos. 4, 53v.
[6] *L.R.S.* 33, p. xxx.

livings, which were not in fact very far from one another, and it is hard to see how in these circumstances Thornton could have presented anyone else. The Appleyards were too near them for ill-feeling to be pleasant for either party.[1] Local loyalty probably lay behind the presentation of George Brudenell by John Cheney of Chesham. George was the son of Drogo Brudenell of Chalfont St Peter, and as such the son of a local worthy; he had the additional advantage of promise. He was at Cambridge and had been allowed to proceed to orders under age.[2] The Burghs were an important Lincolnshire family and this may account for the presentation of Thomas Burgh by William Saye and Henry VIII.[3] Similarly the Massingberds were a notable family of some standing and antiquity: though Christopher Massingberd took some time to get a living, he probably owed his eventual presentation to three livings and various cathedral posts to his family connexions.[4] Thomas Holand was important in the shire and on the commission of the peace; his son's presentation to Thurlby by the prioress and convent of St Michael, Stamford, may well be a reflexion of the father's importance.[5] The Bishops of Geddington appear to have been wealthy, and either friendship or hard bargaining may lie behind the presentation of Henry Bishop to the local living of Geddington.[6] The Pargiturs of Greatworth managed to effect the presentation of one of their number by Roger Lewknor[7] to the local living.

The extent to which any one patron would be influenced by any of these considerations would vary considerably from year to year; on one occasion he might help a friend, and on another he might attempt to make one. Most of the significant patrons in the diocese presented men who belonged to one of the main cate-

[1] Register 23, fos. 105, 108; *Lincolnshire Pedigrees*, I, 35.

[2] Register 23, fos. 239v, 324v; Register 25, fo. 54v; Emden, *Cambridge*, p. 100.

[3] Register 25, fos. 12v, 33v; *Lincolnshire Pedigrees*, I, 207.

[4] Register 23, fos. 97v, 117v, 124; *Lincolnshire Pedigrees*, II, 654; see also above, p. 73.

[5] Register 25, fo. 16v; *Lincolnshire Pedigrees*, II, 506; *L. and P.* II, pt. I, nos. 789, 2733.

[6] Register 23, fo. 220; Longden, II, 109–10.

[7] Register 23, fo. 172v; Longden, X, 169.

gories or combined the advantages of several of them. But many patrons provided a significant number of men to benefices of whom we know nothing at all. We do not know what they may have had in common. They certainly were not distinguished by their birth or education, or, if they were, they have left little trace of it. They appear in fact to lack the very qualities most likely to recommend them for a living. It was perhaps their very mediocrity which proved their good fortune. Had they been better propositions for a patron they would have received a number of livings, at least two, but, instead, most of them are presented with only one living of very small worth, in which they apparently resided and which many of them served devotedly. It is one of the ironies of the sixteenth-century church that those whose income was smallest and who had most need to combine it with another apparently did not do so; it is also ironical that a patron who cared for his parish and wished to see its rector or vicar in residence might be forced to present to it someone who was unlikely to be distinguished for anything more than his mediocrity. Undoubtedly, in at least half of all presentations, the patron was looking for a benefit, that of promise, friendship, power. As we shall see, sometimes this form of patronage would incidentally benefit the parish; sometimes it would not. But the hard fact remains that, when this opportunism in patronage has been admitted, we are still left with something approaching half of all presentations. It is impossible to do more than guess at the importance to be attached to these unknown men. A study of residence and parochial care indicates that they benefited the parish in a direct, if unpretentious, way. There is no reason to suppose that a patron was ignorant of the fact that they lacked other benefices and would therefore reside. It is possible, though incapable of proof, that it was just this factor which accounts for their presentation at all. They may have been appointed simply for the cure of souls.

CHAPTER III

NON-RESIDENCE AND THE CURE OF SOULS

Most of the parishes to which the clergy were presented involved the cure of souls.[1] Where there were parishioners who required the sacraments, and old or sick folk to be visited, the cure obviously required the residence of a priest. The Constitutions of Ottobuono condemned those who held more than one benefice with cure of souls, and who were, by reason of their plurality of livings, unable to reside in one or other of their cures. The church made repeated orders forbidding the holding of cures in plurality, thereby hoping to ensure the residence of rectors and vicars. A second benefice with cure was said to be incompatible with the first, and to involve the resignation of the former cure for the latter.[2] Vicarages, in particular, were held to require residence, and at his institution a vicar had to swear *de continuo residendo et personaliter ministrando*.[3] But orders of this kind were, in the last analysis, doomed to failure. Some dispensations had to be given which allowed for exceptions to the general rule.[4] Scholars had a clear claim to dispensation; the church, in theory, would suffer without their learning, and they could not proceed to university if they were without resources. A benefice which did not require residence was the best means of acquiring such resources. Diocesan officials and royal servants had no adequate stipend for their work and also relied on benefices for a living. Many of these officials were benefiting the church, and it was desirable,

---

[1] A few parishes, Horne and Soutthorpe, for example, were said to have no parishioners (Register 23, fo. 178v; Vj. 5, fo. 101v). For depopulated parishes as a cause of absenteeism see below, p. 98.

[2] A. H. Thompson, 'Pluralism in the Medieval Church', *A.A.S.R.P.* xxxiii (1916–17), pp. 35–73; see also Lyndwood, *Provinciale*, Lib. III, tit. 6: gloss on *beneficia incompatibilia*: *ea quibus imminet cura animarum vel quae requirunt residentiam de consuetudine vel Statuto*...

[3] See, for example, Register 25, fo. 3.

[4] Lyndwood, *loc. cit.*

even necessary, that they be granted a dispensation from residence. But, once dispensations were allowed at all, the way was open to all kinds of abuses: they might be used, as the gift of a benefice might be used, as a source of patronage, a means of making friends of 'the mammon of unrighteousness'. The problem of checking non-residence without forbidding all dispensations was almost insoluble. But few of the critics of the church appreciated quite how complicated the situation was. It was easy to see that dispensations were open to abuse and to declare that all priests should reside, but, where this criticism went hand in hand with complaints of the lack of education of the priesthood, the crux of the problem had been ignored. In transferring the power of dispensation from the pope to the king in 1534, the Commons were transferring a responsibility which the medieval church had failed to discharge satisfactorily, and which it would take the Church of England many centuries to fulfil.

The sixteenth-century church and its critics were at one in thinking that a benefice must be served by a priest and not by someone in minor orders, and that some kind of permanent pastor should be available. But the theory was simpler than the practice. The means by which these demands should be enforced constituted the problem. But, though there were basic defects in the machinery, they did not totally prevent the machine from working. The church did try to prevent men in minor orders holding titles to churches for any length of time, and it did try to see that incumbents resided.

A note was kept in the register of every man who was ordained while already in possession of a living. One hundred and thirty-three men who had held livings as deacons[1] were ordained priest under Bishop Smith; under Bishop Atwater forty-six men were ordained priest having already gained possession of a living.[2] Only about twelve of these did not proceed immediately to priestly orders, and several of the offenders were clerks of the cathedral whose benefice did not involve the cure of souls. There is mention in the visitation returns of parishes which were inadequately served but none through the failure of the incumbent to proceed

[1] Register 24, fos. 1–94.   [2] Register 25, fos. 7–11, 111–36.

to priest's orders.[1] Those who were granted livings while still in minor orders were usually scholars; John Gayton, who received Peakirk in November 1500 while still an acolyte, was a student;[2] he was ordained priest to the title of this living in September 1501.[3] Edmund Cranbroke was a scholar at Oxford and was presented to Brattleby by Balliol College while still an acolyte.[4] He was ordained subdeacon a month after his presentation[5] and in the March and April of the following year was ordained deacon and priest respectively.[6] Nor were they unusual in spacing their orders in this way. The canons forbidding the assumption of major and minor orders in one day appear to have been observed.[7] If men in minor orders were in charge of cures for any length of time, the diocesan records have left little trace of it. Scholars and others in minor orders were not normally given vicarages, which, in theory, required their continuous residence. Some attempt seems to have been made to give them rectories, in which their youth and their absence would not so obviously affect the parish.[8]

Normally the problem of non-residence was more complex and much more difficult to solve. There were considerable difficulties in deciding what constituted non-residence. In general terms an incumbent was required to live in his benefice. But did this mean he could never leave it? Short periods of absence were permitted and, if the parish had many priests, the period could be a longer one. As a result, Lyndwood concluded: *callida tamen interpretatio numquam facienda est.*[9] There can be no doubt that he was right and that churchwardens and scribes were often hard pressed to know what constituted non-residence. Christopher Massingberd, for instance, could have paid no more than an occasional visit to his parish at Bicker; it was visited in 1519 and though Christopher was accused of neglecting his chancel he was

---

[1] See below, p. 104.   [2] Register 23, fo. 174 v.
[3] Register 24, fo. 30 v, see above, p. 42.
[4] Register 23, fo. 154 v.   [5] Register 24, fo. 36 v.
[6] *Ibid.* fos. 38, 39 v.
[7] Lyndwood, *Provinciale*, Lib. V, tit. 11, note x.
[8] See, for example, Register 23, fos. 215 v, 216, 216 v, 219, 223, 324 v, 341 v, 378.
[9] Lyndwood, *Provinciale*, Lib. III, tit. 4, note y.

not accused of non-residence.[1] Yet in that year he was in major residence at the cathedral, acted as master of the works and attended all but one of the nineteen chapter meetings held.[2] Wolsey's suffragan, Thomas Halsey, rector of Drayton-Parslow, was unlikely to have resided for any length of time, though this was not reported.[3] On the other hand, the vicar of Alconbury, though reported as non-resident, officiated at the Easter Communion and irritated his parishioners by communicating them so slowly.[4] The rector of Hamerton was reported in June 1518 as being non-resident since he was on pilgrimage to Santiago de Compostela.[5] He was not away long for he notified the bishop of his return a few months later.[6] Normally an attempt was made to differentiate between the non-residence and the non-existence of an incumbent. At Clee, for instance, it was reported, *non est ibidem vicarius*;[7] there had been no institutions there since the fourteenth century.[8] At Hamerton there had been no institution because the abbey of Colchester had taken such a fat pension out of the living that too little was left to support an incumbent.[9] But here again the churchwardens were not always consistent. There had been no institution to the rectory of Gate Burton since the time of Bishop Chedworth (1452-71),[10] but the rector is simply described as non-resident;[11] it is unlikely that one incumbent held the living for nearly fifty years.

If it was difficult to know what constituted non-residence, it was even harder to know what constituted a legitimate reason for granting of a dispensation. What lay behind the case of the rector of Sawtry who said he dared not reside?

quod ipse ob timorem multacionem [*sic*] membrorum suorum et periculum corporis sui per Edmundum Louth sibi inferendum non est ausus residere in dicto suo beneficio.[12]

Louth had been accused of similar threats of assault before and

[1] *L.R.S.* 33, p. 71.
[2] A. 3. 3, fos. 139 ff.
[3] *L.R.S.* 33, p. 42.
[4] *Ibid.* pp. 1–2.
[5] *Ibid.* p. 2.
[6] Cj. 2, fo. 84.
[7] *L.R.S.* 33, p. 87.
[8] Register 12, fo. 154v.
[9] Vj. 6, fo. 8v.
[10] Register 20, fo. 160.
[11] *L.R.S.* 33, p. 99.
[12] Cj. 2, fo. 26v.

may have been a genuine danger to the rector.[1] The same kind of difficulty surrounded the case of the rector of Swallow who was said to be at Grimsby *ad libitum suum*.[2] He may have held some sort of employment at Grimsby or have been having a good time there; probably no one really knew.

It was against a background of imprecise and often misleading information that the bishop and his officials had to try to enforce the church's canons on residence. It is thanks to their persistence that we have any records about it at all. The bishop's registrar attempted to record the dispensations from residence and licences to hold in plurality shown him by incumbents in the diocese,[3] and he tried to note, in his lists of institutions, the reasons why livings became vacant. Usually a living became vacant because of the death or resignation of the former incumbent. Some of these resignations may in fact have been of priests who had received a second living without having a licence to hold two in plurality; in a few cases the scribe indicated that the resignation had been so caused by using the words *per cessationem* or *per dimissionem*. This formula only occurs occasionally, but in some cases at least it appears to represent an enforced resignation: John Manknell, for instance, was presented to the rectory of Stainton through the dismissal of the last rector, whose living of East Barkwith was incompatible.[4] Similarly the same formula was used for the resignation of Christopher Paynell from Boothby Pagnell; it was noted that Christopher held another incompatible benefice and could show no dispensation for doing so. On this occasion, the vicar general wrote to the archdeacon of Lincoln informing him of the dismissal.[5] But it was chiefly by visitation that the bishop or his deputy discovered non-residents and unlicensed pluralists.

It is from the visitation returns that we can gain some indication of the extent of non-residence and its effect on the parishes concerned. Fragmentary visitation returns survive for the arch-

[1] A John Louth is accused of two cases of disturbance (*L.R.S.* 33, p. 1; Cj. 2, fo. 10); it is probable that the same person is meant.

[2] *L.R.S.* 33, p. 84.

[3] See, for example, Register 24, fos. 212v, 215, 215v, 222, 223v, 224v, 225, 226, 239, 243, 249v, 250, 252, 253, 275, 276.

[4] Register 23, fo. 57v.   [5] *Ibid.* fo. 138.

deaconries of Leicester, Huntingdon, Lincoln and Stow for the period 1495–1510. But a far more comprehensive picture emerges from the episcopal visitations and court books which survive for the period 1514–21. A total of 1,006 parishes were visited by Bishop Atwater or his deputies in that period.[1] There is some difficulty in assessing the total number of parishes in the diocese since there is confusion in all the sources over chapels. Snitterby, for instance, was a chapel though it had a rector. 1,904 parishes are mentioned in the subsidy of 1526 but this figure includes many dependant churches which are more properly described as chapels.[2] If the visitation returns and those for the subsidy are collated, a figure of about 1,700 parishes is reached.[3] From this it would appear that only 58% of the parishes of the diocese were visited. The remaining parishes were from the archdeaconry of Northampton, for which there are few records, and odd deaneries, particularly in the archdeaconry of Stow, which were omitted.[4] To fill this gap in our evidence, there are references in the court book for these areas, but a non-resident probably only appeared before the bishop if there was some reason for supposing that his dispensation was inadequate. The court book, therefore, cannot be said to fill entirely the gap left by the visitation returns. Nearly a quarter of all the parishes visited reported that their incumbent was non-resident. A report of non-residence in this period was made to the bishop, his deputy or to the archdeacon of Leicester in a further forty-eight cases where no such report has survived from the episcopal visitation. We therefore have certain evidence of non-residence

[1] It is sometimes impossible to be very exact with the date of the visitation; that of the archdeaconry of Oxford may have been in June 1517 or in 1520 (*L.R.S.* 33, p. 119 n.).

[2] *L.R.S.* 33, p. 94 n. The figures given differ slightly from those suggested by me in 'Non-Residence in the Lincoln Diocese in the Early Sixteenth Century', *J. Eccl. History*, xv (1964), 40. The chapels and the ambiguity surrounding *capellani* (see below, p. 106 n.) had not then been sufficiently investigated by me.

[3] Hughes gives the total number of parishes as 1,736 and the total number of parishes visited as 1,088; his figure of 247 non-residents is very close to my own; the discrepancy is probably due to his inclusion of chapels (Hughes, *The Reformation in England*, pp. 32, 103).

[4] The deaneries omitted were those of Beltisloe, Ness, Stamford, Grantham, Lovedon, Longoboby, Sleaford, Graffoe and Lincoln.

in a total of 293 parishes in the diocese. Fifty-eight of these were vicarages. But, if the proportion of non-residents in the diocese as a whole is as high as it is among the visited parishes, the real figure must be something approaching 424, with about eighty-five vicarages affected.[1]

It is often very difficult to assess how permanent a problem to the parish non-residence was likely to be. Apart from the episcopal visitation returns for the diocese for 1517–20, there are only fragmentary archidiaconal returns, of varying dates, which can provide an indication of the length of time during which a parish might be without its proper incumbent. It is also likely that, in many parishes, reports of non-residence were made to the bishop's commissary and not to the archdeacon.[2] The archdeaconry visitations cannot, therefore, be taken as giving a complete picture. In consequence, we have no reliable means of knowing whether the problem of absenteeism was getting worse: all that can be shown is that, in some parishes where it *was* reported to the archdeacon and bishop, it lasted twenty years or more.

Table indicating duration of absenteeism[3]

Archdeaconry	Number of parishes and date of first report of absenteeism	State of those parishes and date at second visitation		
		Non-Resident	Resident	Unknown
Lincoln	51 cases in 1500[1]	14(1519)[2]	20(1519)[2]	17(1519)[2]
Huntingdon	19 cases in 1507[3]	8(1518)[4]	5(1518)[4]	6(1518)[4]
Leicester	4 cases in 1489[5]	2(1518–26)[6]	2(1518–26)[6]	
	12 cases in 1498[7]	5(1518–26)[8]	7(1518–26)[8]	
	14 cases in 1509/10[9]	7(1518–26)[10]	7(1518–26)[10]	
	52 cases in 1518[11]	20(1526)[11]	19(1526)[11]	13(1526)[11]
Total	152	56	60	36

[1] A list of all parishes from which non-residence was reported with their appropriate references is contained in appendix IV, see below, p. 193; it is hoped that this list may be the first step towards reaching a more comprehensive picture of pluralism in the country as a whole.

[2] See above, p. 30.

[3] See foot of p. 92 for notes to table.

Only tentative conclusions can be deduced from these figures since the number of parishes from which non-residence was reported on one occasion but which were not visited again is so high. A further difficulty is that the interval between the visitations in the parishes of the different archdeaconries is not consistent. Nevertheless, if all the parishes for which a comparison is possible are added, ignoring the differences in date, it appears that, of 152 parishes, a continuous report of non-residence was given in fifty-six, the incumbent may be presumed resident after the first report in sixty and there is no indication what happened in the remaining thirty-six (p. 91). The chances of a parish having a non-resident incumbent for over ten years, therefore, seem to have been even. If the benefice was a lucrative one and the incumbent important, the chances were that the parish would report continuous non-residence. Church Langton reported non-residence in 1509, 1518

---

[1] Knaith, Broxholme, Sudbrooke, Faldingworth, Fillingham, Flixborough, Waddingham, Massingham, Bigby, South Ferriby, Scarthoe, Thoresby, Barnoldby-le-Beck, Saltfleetby All Saints, Skidbrook, Conisholme, Burwell, Utterby, South Reston, Withern, Theddlethorpe St Helens, Mablethorpe St Mary, Anderby, Sutton, Willoughby, Claxby, Skirbeck, Wyberton Pinchbeck, Newton, Careby, Bitham Parva, Barrowby, Ponton Parva and Magna, Revesby, Wilsthorpe, Claypole, Brant Broughton, Rustington, Quadring, Heckington, Ewerby, Scotton, Graynham, Southorpe, Lissington, Willingham, Hatton, Rand, East Torrington (Vj. 5, *passim*).

[2] *L.R.S.* 33, pp. 55–100.

[3] Woolley, Keyston, Covington, Ellington, Brington, Hemingford Abbots, Southoe, Walkern, Sandon, Caldecote, Kelshall, Aston, Munden Magna, Letchworth, Lilley, Digswell, Hertford St Nicholas, Hertingfordbury, Watton at Stone (Vj. 6, *passim*).

[4] *L.R.S.* 33, pp. 1–8, 100–2, 109–13, 117–19.

[5] Knaptoft, Ibstock, Skeffington, Belgrave (Viv. 2, fos. 7v, 25v, 41[2]).

[6] *L.R.S.* 33, pp. 18, 21; *A.A.S.R.P.* xxviii, pt. i, 210, 217.

[7] Frowlesworth, Sharnford, Sapcote, Aston Flamville, Broughton Astley, Desford, Kimcote, Bruntingthorpe, Stonton Wyvill, Sibson, Drayton, Barwell (Viv. 4, fos. 7, 8, 16, 20).

[8] *L.R.S.* 33, pp. 8–35; *A.A.S.R.P.* xxviii, pt. i, *passim*.

[9] Witherley, Beeby, Cold Overton, Stathern, Loughborough, Ashby la Zouche, Orton on the Hill, Lockington, Kimcote, Church Langton, Lubenham, Kibworth Beauchamp, Bottesford, Witherley (Viv. 5, *passim*).

[10] *L.R.S.* 33, pp. 8–35; *A.A.S.R.P.* xxviii, pt. i, *passim*.

[11] *Ibid. passim.*

and 1526.[1] The reason is apparent. The living was worth a clear
£32[2] and the rector was Polydore Vergil, the papal collector.[3]
Three similar reports of persistent non-residence were made at
Loughborough.[4] The living was worth £26,[5] and was, throughout the period, held by Geoffrey Wren, a clerk in the king's
closet.[6] Stathern was also without a resident incumbent for nearly
twenty years.[7] It was only worth £10[8] but appears to have been
a family living to which Magister William Taylard was presented
by another of the same name.[9] Sapcote reported a non-resident
rector in 1498, 1509 and 1529[10] but it did not have the same incumbent for the whole period. Between 1509 and 1518 it was in
the hands of William Swain, one of the bishop's commissaries;
thereafter it went to James Shorthose, whose claim to a dispensation is obscure.[11] Sapcote was only worth £11 and did not provide as good a sinecure as Knaptoft,[12] from which reports of non-
residence were made in 1489, 1518, 1526,[13] but, since the parish was
depopulated in this period, the absence of the incumbent did not
matter very much.[14] It was hardly surprising that the parishioners
of Great Bowden complained that their rector had never been
there; he was John Chambre, the royal physician.[15] But, if the
desire for gain kept some clerks away from their livings, and
royal or diocesan business kept others, this was not unheeded by
the bishop and his deputies.

Dispensations from the pope or the diocesan bishop were necessary if non-residence was to be allowed at all.[16] The diocesan might

[1] Viv. 5, fo. 89v; L.R.S. 33, p. 9; A.A.S.R.P. xxviii, pt. i, 146.
[2] Salter, p. 117.
[3] Register 23, fo. 248.
[4] Viv. 5, fo. 81; L.R.S. 33, p. 30; A.A.S.R.P. xxviii, pt. i, 211.
[5] Salter, p. 110.   [6] Emden, Oxford, iii, 2093.
[7] Viv. 5, fo. 65; L.R.S. 33, p. 27; A.A.S.R.P. xxviii, pt. i, 164.
[8] Salter, p. 98.   [9] Register 23, fo. 249v.
[10] Viv. 4, fo. 7; Viv. 5, fo. 28; A.A.S.R.P. xxviii, pt. i, 154, 211.
[11] Register 23, fo. 265; Register 25, fo. 39.
[12] Salter, pp. 101, 102.
[13] Viv. 2, fo. 7v; L.R.S. 33, p. 18; A.A.S.R.P. xxviii, pt. i, p. 210.
[14] W. G. Hoskins, Essays in Leicestershire History (Liverpool, 1950), pp. 88, 89 a.
[15] L.R.S. 33, p. 13; Register 23, fo. 260v; Emden, Oxford, i, 285.
[16] Lyndwood, Provinciale, Lib. III, tit. 5, note c.

withold the dispensation, thereby ensuring the presence of the proper incumbent some time within the living memory of the parish. This action was beset with difficulties and might frequently meet with failure. But there is evidence to suggest that some attempt was made to spread the burden of non-residence and severely to limit its duration.[1]

Dispensations usually had a time limit, and for financial reasons, if no other, an attempt was made to see that the limit was not exceeded. Only one non-resident shamelessly paraded a lack of dispensation. Richard Sutton, rector of Odell and Begbroke, showed no appropriate dispensation and failed to get one from the bishop.[2] Of the other known non-residents, nearly one third appeared before the bishop or his chancellor personally or by proctor to show their dispensations. Nearly half of these showed that they had a dispensation, but no note was made of its duration.[3] Details of the time for which the dispensation was valid were given for the remaining forty-six. They were as follows:

Non-residents reported as having a dispensation for 7 years	4
Non-residents reported as having a dispensation for 4 years	1
Non-residents reported as having a dispensation for 3 years	6
Non-residents reported as having a dispensation for 2 years	7
Non-residents reported as having a dispensation for 1 year	11
Non-residents ordered to reside	13
Non-residents who denied being non-residents because they had returned to their parishes	4
Total	46

The sample is a small one and it is possible that only the controversial cases where the validity of the dispensation was in question, or cases in which the claim to a dispensation was a slender one, came before the bishop. It is, however, interesting that, in half of these cases, the bishop either ordered the priest concerned to reside or granted a short-term dispensation. It was a

---

[1] It is interesting that Richard Fox while he was bishop of Durham and Winchester appears to have pursued a policy 'of calling the absentee clergy into residence', see *Register of Richard Fox, Bishop of Durham 1494–1501*, ed. M. P. Howden, p. xlv.

[2] Cj. 2, fo. 34v.   [3] *Ibid. passim.*

common practice in the fifteenth century to keep dispensations short and to oblige the holder frequently to sue for renewal.[1] It was in all probability lucrative. Licences were not to be had for the asking. John Williamson, rector of Barnwell, was ordered to pay 6s. 8d. towards the repair of the Fosse Dyke for his dispensation.[2] Against the entries relating to the rector of Anderby and the vicar of Spelsbury there is a note of *nihil soluit*.[3] Unfortunately no records survive to indicate whether 6s. 8d. was the standard fee and whether non-residence was used as an excuse for episcopal taxation as it was on the continent.[4] But perhaps there was more to it than fees.

There was no apparent financial advantage to be gained from ordering so many priests to reside. Such an order was made with an eye to the cure of souls. The cure of Hawridge could no longer be entrusted to a curate who played football in his shirt, and in Holy week contrived to finish all the offices, including compline, by midday.[5] The curate was suspended and, in the following year, the rector, Christopher Mitchell, was recalled from his cure in London and told to reside. Orders to reside in one parish were often made at the expense of another, presumably to spread the burden. William Redd, for instance, was ordered to serve his cure at Courteenhall in spite of the fact that this would mean he deserted his other cure of Market Bosworth.[6] These orders to reside do not appear to have been made arbitrarily; none were to vicars whose absence was in itself an anomaly; the only explanation for them appears to have been within the parish itself.

Orders to reside did not always meet with success. Following the visitations of Bedford, Buckingham and Huntingdon, 127 citations were served on rectors, vicars and farmers on account of their failure to reside, or the dilapidation of ecclesiastical property. Only forty-seven of those cited appeared. Some of the remainder may have appeared before special commissaries, but against the

---

[1] Thompson, *The English Clergy*, p. 104.
[2] Cj. 2, fo. 34v.   [3] *Ibid.* fos. 34v, 35.
[4] J. Absil, 'L'absentéisme du clergé paroissal au diocèse de Liége au XVe siècle et dans la première moitié du XVIe siècle, *Revue d'Histoire Ecclésiastique*, LVII (Louvain, 1962), 8.
[5] *L.R.S.* 33, p. 44.   [6] Cj. 2, fo. 2.

names of at least half a note of *non comparuit*, or its equivalent, appears.[1] No evidence survives to show whether the offenders were eventually brought to heel, but the repetition of some orders suggests that, even if they were, it was a long process. The rector of Hawridge had been ordered to reside in 1516—three years before the indiscretions of his curate made his presence in the parish imperative.[2] The rector of Fawley had also been ordered to reside in 1516 to no effect;[3] his aggrieved parishioners asserted in 1519 that no rector had resided for thirty years.[4]

A further limit to the power of the diocesan in curtailing non-residence were the long-term dispensations often procured from Rome.[5] If a policy of limitation was to be effective, the active cooperation of the Holy See was necessary. This would involve a financial loss which the papacy could ill afford, and, if the policy was to discriminate at all, a very close liaison with the diocesan would be necessary. But more insuperable than all other obstacles was the vested interest shared by some of the influential clergy and laity in perpetuating the system and frustrating all efforts to reform it.

A financial advantage of one kind or another was the root cause of most absenteeism. It was rare for non-residence to be reported of incumbents whose livings were worth £4 or less. Of sixty-one livings valued at £4 or less, non-residence was reported from only six.[6] Two were in the hands of men who were private chaplains and two were in Oxfordshire and were, therefore, attractive to students in spite of their low value.[7] In contrast, if we take the livings valued at £15 or more, 22% were supporting non-resident priests.[8] Their reasons for absenteeism were very varied. Hamerton, valued at £16, supported the pilgrimage

---

[1] Cj. 2, fos. 77–86 v, see above, p. 20.

[2] *Ibid.* fo. 30.

[3] *Ibid.* fo. 29 v.

[4] *L.R.S.* 33, p. 37.

[5] Cj. 2, fos. 5, 31, 84, 87, 89; Register 25, fos. 13, 15 v, 20 v.

[6] Salter, *passim*; the six livings concerned were Begbroke, Easington, Hungerton, Langton by Partney, Newton Purcell, Pickworth.

[7] See appendix IV.

[8] Salter, *passim*; Northamptonshire is omitted from this figure because of the inadequate evidence of non-residence which it provides.

of Robert Appulby;[1] Croft and Hemswell supported pure pluralists; the valuable living of Brington added to the wealth of the
Beckensaw family.[2] The reasons given by the wealthy for their
absence were as varied as those given by non-residents from the
less wealthy parishes of the diocese. Intrinsic to them all was the
idea that the fruits of the benefice might properly be used to
support some activity other than the actual serving of the cure
concerned. How legitimate in fact were these reasons?

A high percentage of known absentees were graduates, the
people, in fact, most likely to be employed by the king or the
church itself in positions of responsibility. Of all non-residents
$35\frac{1}{2}\%$ were graduates.[2] Considering the range of potential employment open to the graduate, the figure is not exceptionally
high. But only $28\frac{1}{2}\%$ of all presentations to parishes of the diocese
were of graduates. The graduates as a group, therefore, were
likely to display a higher incidence of pluralism than the presentation figure alone would suggest. But they were not alone in
enjoying the privilege of absenteeism.

Many non-residents did not give their reasons for being away,
but, of known non-residents, the principal reasons may be divided
as follows:

Having another benefice (pure pluralists)	97
Studying or at university in an administrative capacity	30
Chaplains to private individuals or in the royal service	21
Canons regular	14
Diocesan administrators	10
On pilgrimage	2
Unknown or with doubtful reasons	119
Total	293
Depopulated parishes[2]	8

Clearly there was little to be said for residing in a parish which
had lost all or most of its parishioners. Fleet Marston was reported
to the bishop as having a non-resident rector in 1519, but it had
been declining throughout the fifteenth century and can have had

---

[1] Salter, p. 184.
[2] See appendix IV.

few inhabitants at this date.[1] Depopulation occurred at Stantonbury between 1487 and 1517, and it was hardly surprising that
by 1519, the vicar was not serving the cure nor residing in it nor
providing for another priest to look after the parish for three days
a week as the bishop had ordered.[2] It took time for the fact of
depopulation to be accepted so that no incumbent was instituted.
But, besides those who were not residing because their parishes
were diminishing, there were others who had a justifiable excuse
for absenteeism. Canon law had always recognized the needs of
the university student, and church leaders and theologians had
often been educated on the fruits of parishes in which they could
not and did not reside. Most of the students who were reported
as being away were at Oxford and Cambridge, but one, John
Fitzherbert, was being supported at Louvain.[3] University administrators and dignitaries were also thought to have a good reason
for being away. Ralph Barnack, the vicar of Adderbury, was the
chancellor's commissary at Oxford; John More, rector of Garsington, was provost of Oriel.[4] Of the nineteen reported non-resident
in Huntingdonshire in 1507, two at least were at the university.[5]

Dispensations were readily forthcoming for diocesan officials
whose reasons for non-residence were clear enough. They were
benefiting the church in a positive way even if the particular
parish which provided their stipend did not directly feel the benefit
of their activities. The rector of Ellington in Huntingdonshire,
reported non-resident in 1507, was in the archbishop's household.[6]
The rector of Kelshall who was reported at the same time was
chaplain to the bishop of Ely.[7] The bishop of Lincoln's vicars
general, James Whitstones and later Henry Wilcocks, had a clear
case for their non-residence at Charlbury and Wootton.[8] The
onerous task of acting as the bishop's *alter ego* left them little
time for their parochial duties. A pilgrimage provided the devout

---

[1] M. Beresford, *The Lost Villages of England* (London, 1954), p. 341; cf.
L.R.S. 33, p. 50. The visitation returns appear to corroborate Beresford's list
of depopulated parishes in this period.
[2] Beresford, *op. cit.* p. 342; cf. *L.R.S.* 33, p. 54.
[3] Cj. 2, fo. 35, see also above, p. 45.   [4] See appendix IV, pp. 193, 200.
[5] Vj. 6, fos. 11, 15.   [6] Vj. 6, fo. 7v.
[7] Vj. 6, fo. 11v.   [8] See appendix IV, pp. 197, 213.

with a good reason for absenteeism. Robert Wright, the vicar of Claxby in Lincolnshire in 1500, gave this as his reason for non-residence.[1] The pilgrim was unlikely to be away from his cure for long, and it was to be hoped that his absence would increase his zeal and eventually that of his parish.

Clerks in the service of the crown or of private but important individuals were in an ambiguous position. In one sense they benefited the church and in another they were parasites upon it. There was something to be said for churchmen putting their talents at the disposal of the state though it was often a source of criticism in the church. By so doing they rendered a clear-cut division between church and state unlikely, if not impossible; they were also in a position to influence policy if they had a mind to do so. But many of the chaplains in the service of private individuals were blatantly using the church as a source of revenue and in lieu of a salary. Wolsey was receiving income enough from the church in 1528, and there was no need at all for his servants to be salaried from benefices in which they did not reside. Yet John Wyllman, the non-resident rector of Morton, Buckinghamshire, in 1528, was his crucifer.[2] The rector of Woolley in Huntingdonshire in 1507 was chaplain to Sir Thomas Lovell;[3] Christopher Plummer, the non-resident rector of Skirbeck in 1500, was chaplain to the queen.[4] The vicar of Sandon, in Huntingdonshire, in 1507 was chaplain to a Mr Foster, with whom he resided in London.[5] The bishop was often in an unenviable position when dealing with non-residents of this type. Their applications for dispensations not to reside and for licences to hold cures in plurality were sometimes made at the request of a powerful layman and could not easily be refused. The rector of Tichmarsh, in Northamptonshire, was called to reside by the bishop (*vocatus ad residenciam*); he said he was domestic chaplain to the king's chamberlain and a three-year dispensation was eventually granted him, at the specific request of the chamberlain himself.[6] Thomas Angell,

---

[1] Vj. 5, fo. 44.
[2] Vj. 6, fo. 137; see also appendix IV for details of similar cases in 1514–21.
[3] *Ibid.* fo. 7. [4] Vj. 5, fo. 48.
[5] Vj. 6, fo. 11. [6] Cj. 2, fo. 25.

rector of Barwell in Leicestershire, had requested the bishop for a dispensation in July 1516 and had been granted one for a single year only. In March 1517 he applied again, but enlisted the help of Humphrey Coningsby, justice of the King's Bench. His request for a dispensation, made at the instance of Coningsby, was granted and this time it was given for three years.[1] George Gray, the dean of Newarke College, Leicester, petitioned for a dispensation for the vicar of Spelsbury and was granted one for three years.[2] It was difficult and it might have been unwise for the bishop to refuse dispensations to the powerful. Fortune might not favour them for ever, but, while it did, the church had to pay for their goodwill even though the price was often a heavy one. As it was, the lay magnate and the crown could reward their servants with benefices and avoid the unpleasant duty of paying them; they also could enjoy the power implicit in the free exercise of their ecclesiastical patronage. Moreover they were unlikely to suffer if the lack of a proper pastor caused harm to the parish; many of those who had their own chaplains had sued for a licence for a private oratory; they could, therefore, pursue their devotions in splendid isolation.[3]

It would appear that the non-residence of regular canons was something of a scandal. It was part of their vocation, in theory, to serve the parishes. There was something paradoxical about their not residing in them. On one occasion at least the paradox was recognized. The canons of Haverholme were supposed to serve Ruskington, in Lincolnshire, but they were reported as being non-resident in 1500.[4] They were immediately ordered to provide a secular priest for the vicarage, though in fact there is no evidence of their having done so.[5] The Hospitallers were particularly bad

---

[1] Cj. 2, fos. 25v, 31.   [2] Cj. 2, fo. 34v.

[3] See for example Register 23, fo. 208: a licence for an oratory was granted to Margaret, Countess of Richmond and Derby, for her manor of Coleweston; similar rights were also granted to William Elmes and William Redhole (Bishop's Accounts, Rentals, 1, fo. 11v). Others had rights of this kind which were of long standing, that, for example, apparently possessed by Richard Atwater of Dinton (L.R.S. 33, p. 39).   [4] Vj. 5, fo. 77.

[5] There was a presentation by the Earl of Oxford to a rectory of 'Ryskynton' (Register 23, fo. 72) but this does not appear to be the relevant one; it would appear that the canons were responsible for only half of the living and the Earl's presentation was to the other half.

offenders; they claimed a right to non-residence in five parishes in the Atwater period[1] and their steward was the non-resident rector of South Ferriby.[2] Like the powerful layman, the religious could use the parishes for their own purpose with little fear of the consequences.

If the desire for financial advantage underlay much non-residence, in one form or another, it was at its most blatant among those who simply combined livings to increase their revenue. They could only be in one place at a time, and only one cure could benefit from their attention, yet they were not satisfied with its revenue. These 'pure pluralists' could argue no mitigating circumstances in their favour; they were not serving the church in a capacity which automatically precluded their residence, as the diocesan and royal officials were. They were benefiting themselves and a single parish at the expense of another. They owed their dispensations to the status which their birth and education gave them. The diocesan bishop could ill afford to alienate the sons of powerful families as the events of the 1530s were to show; so it was that, as the tide of anti-clericalism ran higher, the chances of reform were drowned in fear. If the church attempted to tighten its control over pluralism and non-residence, the laity would feel the pinch. The great families, the Nevilles, the Beckensaws, the Henneages and the Burghs, would find that their clerical sons had an income which was not sufficient for a gentleman.[3] This was a problem which the reforming ardour of the late sixteenth century was not to overcome.

For the financial gains of holding livings in plurality were considerable. Thomas Cade, who held Burford and Buckworth,[4] was assessed in 1526 on a gross income at Burford of £20 and Buckworth of £19 6s. 8d.; the combination probably brought him nearly £27 when all his expenses had been paid.[5] John Clement received a clear £20 from his combination of Haversham and Dalby Parva.[6] The combination of Little Gaddesden and Oakley

---

[1] Cj. 2, fo. 32 v.　　　　　　　　　　　　[2] Vj. 5, fo. 23 a.
[3] Hill, *Economic Problems of the Church*, pp. 208 ff.
[4] For the evidence of non-residence see appendix iv, p. 193.
[5] Salter, pp. 184, 259.　　　　　　　　[6] *Ibid.* pp. 97, 230.

brought John Wyon about £14. 5s. clear profit,[1] and Ralph
Bedyll would have netted a similar sum from Cosgrove and
Gainsborough.[2] Richard Sutton's poor living of Begbroke, which
only brought him £2. 9s. 10d. net, was augmented by his other
living which brought in a clear £13.[3] Stantonbury was only
worth 1s. 10d. to William Foster, presumably because of the loss
of tithe involved in depopulation, and, even when this is added to
his other cure of Bradwell, his profits were under £5, well below
that of most pluralists.[4] Most combinations brought in about £14
when all expenses were paid.

Some pluralists had livings sufficiently close together for a
general supervision to have been extended to the parish in which
the pluralist did not actually reside. Edmund Wingate held the
two cures of Hockliffe and Chalgrave, both of which were in the
same deanery.[5] George Appleyard's two cures of Barrow on
Humber and Ulceby were not far from one another.[6] Two fellows
of Tattershall in 1500 held livings within Lincolnshire and within
range of the college.[7] The vicar of Ewerby, in Lincolnshire, lived
at Evedon but he visited Ewerby occasionally; the worst his
parish could say of him was that he did not reside at Ewerby
continuously.[8] Some of the vicars choral at Lincoln Cathedral
had livings in the county, and, while they must have been away
from them a good deal of the time, a form of supervision would
have been possible.[9] Though William Foster was urged to employ
a curate at Stantonbury both his livings were in the same deanery.[10]
But usually the combinations of livings ignored the dictates of
geography. Livings were combined from Lincoln, London, Somerset or Lichfield, and the chances of a visit from the rector or
vicar must have been slight.[11] It was also harder in these cases to

[1] Salter, pp. 172, 209.   [2] *Ibid.* pp. 33, 161.
[3] *Ibid.* pp. 211, 268.   [4] *Ibid.* p. 235.
[5] See appendix IV; this device was frequently used at the end of the century,
see *The State of the Church in the Reigns of Elizabeth and James I as Illustrated by
Documents Relating to the Diocese of Lincoln*, ed. C. W. Foster (Lincoln Record
Society, 23, 1926), p. 409.
[6] Register 23, fos. 105, 108.   [7] Vj. 5, fos. 38, 66v.
[8] Vj. 5, fo. 81v.   [9] Vj. 5, fos. 8v, 19, 22v, 44, 70, 91.
[10] Salter, p. 235.   [11] See appendix IV, pp. 193 ff.

ensure that the non-resident appeared at visitation either in person or by his proctor. Strenuous efforts were clearly made to see that he did, so that his dispensation was checked, but the long list of fines for non-appearance in the court and visitation books indicate the extent of the problem. The rector of South Ferriby was fined 6s. 8d. for not appearing before the vicar general in 1500, and in August 1501 the fruits of the living had to be sequestered in order to bring the rector to heel.[1] The rector of Thoresby was fined 20s. for his failure to appear on a similar occasion.[2] The fine for the non-appearance of Robert Gilbert, rector of Saltfleetby All Saints, was only 10s. but his contumacy cost him the fruits of his rectory.[3] The rector of Wilden claimed that he did not know anything about the proceedings begun against him and, since he was a scholar and possibly out of the country, he may well have been as innocent as he alleged.[4] If it was hard for the bishop to enforce the appearance of a non-resident, even under threat of sequestration, it was unlikely that a non-resident would pay his church a visit from motives of interest or concern.

The financial repercussions of non-residence were very great. A sizeable amount of money, usually drawn from tithe, went from the parish, which, in its turn, received no form of direct benefit for its outlay. Whatever the over-all benefit to the church of the non-residence of a university student, for example, it was unlikely that the particular parish which bore the financial burden of his activities would have appreciated it. From the point of view of the parish, tithe paid to a non-resident was so much money down the drain.

The curate or priests in charge of livings which supported non-resident incumbents would have felt much the same way. Few of them received more than £5 for doing all the work in the parish; they were often paid less than a quarter of the real value of the living, and there appears to have been very little difference between the stipends of curates who were in charge of a living and those who were not. Responsibility went unrewarded. The curate of Calverton received £4. 13s. 4d. though his rector was

[1] Vj. 5, fo. 23 a.   [2] Ibid. fo. 26.
[3] Ibid. fo. 34.   [4] Cj. 2, fos. 65v, 72, 81, 85v.

away[1] and the curate of Fillingham and Barwell £5[2] each. The
rector of Swepstone was certainly resident in 1518 but he paid his
capellanus, who in the same return is also described as his curate,
£5.[3] Though the vicarage at Wragby was in a bad state of repair,
the vicar appears to have resided in it. He too paid his curate
£4. 13s. 4d.[4] It was inevitable that the unbeneficed clergy should
envy those who could earn more than they, simply by virtue of
their having gained a benefice, and not because they necessarily
did work which in any way differed from that of their less fortunate contemporaries. To add to this grievance, there was the obvious and, for the curate in a parish where the rector was away,
glaring fact, that those whose lot had been set in a 'goodly
heritage' could earn three times their stipend simply because they
possessed the influence to gain a licence to hold cures in plurality.
These curates, as they toiled for years in the same living, had
ample time to ponder their lot. Nor could they look to the bishop
and his officials for an understanding treatment of the problems
of their parishes. The bishops and the higher diocesan clergy had
had, for the most part, no direct experience of the parish.[5] Benefices had come to them while they were at university and when
they were ready to go down from university other appointments,
particularly those in the royal service, lured them away from the
parishes. In these circumstances, the idea of the bishop as father
of his flock can have had little meaning.

The precise effect of non-residence on the life of the parish and
the actual cure of souls is harder to assess. Great care was taken to
see that non-residents left deputies in their parishes, and vicars in
particular had to see that someone served the cures in which they
had promised to reside continuously and to serve personally. Fifty-
eight vicars are known not to have resided[6] and there was obviously a danger of their neglecting their churches. But there is
very little evidence of such neglect in either vicarages or rectories. The rector of Sutton in the Marsh ought to have provided
a vicar in his own absence but had failed to do so;[7] at Linsdale

[1] Salter, p. 238.   [2] *Ibid.* pp. 35, 105.
[3] *L.R.S.* 33, p. 29; Salter, p. 111.   [4] *L.R.S.* 33, p. 64; Salter, p. 29.
[5] See above, p. 15.   [6] See appendix IV.   [7] *L.R.S.* 33, p. 83.

there was no vicar but this was because no vicarage had been ordained;[1] a similar situation appears to have prevailed at Clee[2] and at least five of the parishes visited between 1514 and 1521 had no ordained vicarage.[3] Several parishes only had an itinerant priest, probably because of their poverty,[4] and two were served, on a casual basis, by a religious.[5] Out of a total of thirty-one cases of parishes which were unsatisfactorily served only eight had non-resident incumbents who had failed to provide for them; the rest were either too poor to support an incumbent or no vicarage had been ordained in them.[6]

The effects of non-residence must, therefore, be measured not in terms of the neglect of the cure of souls but in terms of the quality of the deputy. Yet even this line of inquiry is inadequate. The parish which supported a non-resident rector might contrast the quality of the man who was away with that of the curate who was in residence; yet the contrast though real enough to them was meaningless. Had the church enforced residence, and forbidden pluralism, the effect would have been to distribute titles more widely and probably to give the actual title of a living to the men who already possessed the responsibility. To forbid non-residence would have had little effect on the actual quality of the priest-hood, though much on its remuneration.

[1] *Ibid.* p. 42.   [2] *Ibid.* p. 87; see also above, p. 88.
[3] Steeple Aston, North Marston, East Ravendale, Cotes by Stow, Hampton Gay, (*L.R.S.* 33, pp. 48, 86, 96, 123, 130).
[4] See, for example, Barton Hartshorn, Sturton chapel, Twyford, Brill, Boarstall, Dorton, Forest Hill (*L.R.S.* 33, pp. 46, 49, 50, 137).
[5] Wilkesby, Bladon (*L.R.S.* 33, pp. 67, 130).
[6] Other evidence appears to confirm that of the visitation returns; it was unusual for a cure to be left without a priest to serve it. The Muster Roll for Rutland in 1522 (P.R.O. E. 36/55/fos. 35 v ff.) indicates that the following vills were without priests: Greetham, Tickencote, Ingthorpe, Pilton, North and South Luffenham, Thorpe by the Water, Tixover, Preston, Egleton, Oakham with Barleythorpe and Braunceton. Of these, Braunceton and Tixover were chapels (Salter, p. 147[2]); Egleton Ingthorpe, Oakham with Barleythorpe and Thorpe by the Water appear to have been *vills* and not parishes (Salter, pp. 143 ff.) and all the remaining parishes had incumbents in 1526 (Salter, *loc. cit.*). The absence of any priest in some of these parishes in 1522 may be explained by a vacancy within them; Preston and North and South Luffenham became vacant at about this time (Register 27, fos. 107v, 108, 109v); the remaining three parishes may have been temporarily without priests.

The one certain consequence of non-residence was that curates were left in charge of parishes with little or no supervision. Did this result in their behaving any better or worse than they might otherwise have done?[1] As the under-privileged class in the sixteenth-century church, it would not be surprising if the unbeneficed clergy were particularly prone to fall foul of their parishes and of the authorities. If all the visitation returns are taken for the period 1495–1521 lower clergy were reported for misdemeanours of various kinds in only sixty parishes, but in some of these parishes a man was accused of more than one offence. The canon in charge of Stratton Audley did not celebrate mass or the other services at the proper times, and frequented the company of bad women.[2] At Quadring, John Adams, a *capellanus* who had charge of the parish, was accused of being a common farmer and merchant and of living incontinently.[3] The curate of Loughborough in 1518 was a fisherman of strange habits. He allowed his parishioners to die without the sacraments and was averse to 'pricksong', which he said was a chant ordained as a result of pride: *huiusmodi cantus fuit ordinatus tantumodo ex superbia*.[4] A priest of Fleckney allowed his hair to grow too long and wore clothes unsuited to his vocation.[5] At Surfleet, the priest in charge was a merchant and farmer and did not celebrate at the proper times.[6] At Wootton the priest farmed and was with his sheep before mass, and with his horses when his parishioners wanted to make their confessions.[7] Sometimes the complaint against the curate was one of unsociability or a failure to get on with the parish. The parishioners of Loughborough who

---

[1] There is some difficulty in ascertaining who the curate was; the words *curatus* and *capellanus* are used somewhat indiscriminately; at Swepstone a payment is made to a *capellanus* but it is quite clear that the curate is meant, as the one *capellanus* mentioned in the subsidy return of 1526 does not in fact receive the appropriate sum and the curate does (Salter, p. 111). There are many examples of a similar kind in the subsidy returns, and they beg the question whether *curatus* always means 'curate in charge' or 'senior non-beneficed priest'. Similarly *capellanus* may on occasions mean 'curate' or just chantry priest or more generally chaplain (Salter, p. vii). It is, thus, difficult to be sure a man is priest in charge and all faults of *curati* or *capellani* have been noted unless it is stated that the accused was a chantry priest.

[2] L.R.S. 33, p. 125.   [3] *Ibid*. p. 70.
[4] *Ibid*. p. 30.   [5] Cj. 2, fo. 7.
[6] L.R.S. 33, p. 59.   [7] *Ibid*. p. 131.

complained about another curate in 1509 were not specific in their objections. The curate was a graduate and his inadequacies were probably social rather than educational.[1] But on the whole these complaints were the exception, and if all complaints against the lower clergy are examined[2] it is clear that non-residence was not the only cause of many of them. This can be seen in the following table.

Offences of Unbeneficed Clergy

Type of offence	Number of times offence reported, of which offences reported in parishes where the proper incumbent was non-resident are shown in parentheses				
	1500[3] (330 parishes visited)	1507[4] (88 parishes visited)	1509[5] (941 parishes visited)	1514–21[6] (1,006 parishes visited)	1514–21[7] (corrected if all 1,700 parishes visited)
Incontinence	6 (3)	1	3 (1)	12 (5)	20·27 (8·5)
Irregularities in the services, administration of sacraments or services at the wrong times[8]	1	0	0	8 (3)	13·52 (5·1)
Not sleeping in a parish, or away at odd times	1	0	1	5 (2)	8·5 (3·4)
Failure to preach/visit	0	0	0	1 (1)	1·7 (1·7)
Ignorant	0	0	0	1	1·7
Wrong clothes/tonsure	0	0	0	2	3·4
Ill-becoming behaviour not included above	0	0	0	17 (6)	28·7 (10·14)
Inadequate for no stated reason	0	0	0	2	3·4

[1] Viv. 5, fo. 81.

[2] This does not include chantry priests but does include all those designated curates or *capellani*, see above, p. 106 n.

[3] Vj. 5, *passim*; from a total of approximately 330 entries in the archdeaconries of Lincoln and Stow. Few parishes appear to have been visited twice, but it is impossible to be certain of the number which were, since the name of the parish has been torn off some of the entries.

[4] Vj. 6, fos. 1–15v; from a total of approximately 88 entries from the Huntingdon archdeaconry.

The notes to the above table are continued on p. 108.

The one striking fact about these figures is how low they are. In spite of provocation, the lower clergy do not appear to have been falling foul of either the authorities or their own parishes to any marked degree. It is exceedingly difficult to deduce very much from statistics which are so small, and only some tentative inferences may be drawn from them. A certain number of offences amongst the lower clergy were bound to occur in parishes where there was no resident vicar or rector. Non-residence cannot be taken to be the cause unless these offences occur more frequently in the parishes of non-residents than in others. A quarter of all parishes had a non-resident incumbent; if the number of offences reported in parishes where there was no resident incumbent exceeds a quarter of the total number of offences reported, absenteeism may have been a causal factor. It would appear that the curate or unbeneficed priest in a parish where the proper incumbent was non-resident was slightly more likely to be incontinent than a supervised curate. The difficulties of acquiring suitable servants and the strain of loneliness created a presumption that a priest would find the burden of celibacy too great. Many vicars and rectors who had the actual charge of a parish were guilty of

Notes to the table on p. 107 [continued].

[5] Viv. 5, passim; from a total of 941 entries from the Leicester archdeaconry; many of the entries are of the same parish visited both by the archdeacon and by the bishop's commissary.

[6] L.R.S. 33, passim; Cj. 2, passim; 1,006 parishes were visited; more than one offence may occur in each parish, see above, p. 106.

[7] It is estimated that some 600 parishes were not visited or the record of their visitation has not survived between 1514 and 1521. The corrected figure is an estimate of the incidence of the offence if records of an episcopal visitation survived for the 1,700 parishes of the diocese made some time during this period, and if the same incidence of each offence recorded in the smaller sample applied to the larger one.

[8] There is a prima facie case for supposing that the proper incumbent must be non-resident, if the curate, rather than the vicar or rector, is reported as having the responsibility for the services and sacraments; in fact this inference would be incorrect. Several parishes had permanent curates and there was no proper incumbent to be non-resident (Spalding, for example, see L.R.S. 33, p. 61), and some churches were dependent on others (Stratton Audley for example, see L.R.S. 33, p. 125). Where non-residence seems probable from the responsibilities given to the curate, the parish has been included in the non-residence figure (Ingoldmells and Loughborough, for example, see L.R.S. 33, pp. 30, 78).

this offence, and there is some evidence to suggest that it was not only the unbeneficed clergy who were failing to live up to the moral standard required of them.[1] There was a tendency for unsupervised curates to behave irregularly and to take the services at the wrong times or in an unbecoming fashion; they might also sleep out of the parish. But the incidence of these offences in non-resident parishes is only marginally higher than the over-all proportion would lead one to expect. If all offences are considered collectively there was no startling difference between the supervised and unsupervised curate.[2] But this was cold comfort for the parish saddled with a difficult or unpunctual curate. The parish was a unit, and in theory self-sufficient where pastoral matters were concerned. It did not matter to the parishioners of St Michael's Oxford, if they were the only parish in the whole of Christendom which lacked a curate who would preach and visit the sick.[3] To them this was a scandal. They paid tithe in the same way as any other parish and were subject to the judgement of the same God. There was no justification in their eyes why they should receive any less help in the faith than any other parish; for them, there was no reason why they should be singled out to bear the unremunerative financial burden of a non-resident rector. But in fact non-residence was not really the cause of their troubles. If curates in parishes where the proper incumbent was away did not behave any worse than their fellows who were under the surveillance of another priest, neither did they behave any worse than the beneficed clergy themselves. The incidence of immorality among the beneficed priests was as high as it was among the curates in parishes from which non-residence was reported. A curate might well serve a cure better than the proper incumbent, whose powerful friends or influential relations might render him immune from the censures of the ecclesiastical authorities. Resident rectors and vicars were often far from perfect and the parishes over which they presided were frequently dissatisfied.

[1] See below, p. 115.
[2] A χ^2 test ($\chi^2 = 2.46$, using Yates's correction factor; $\frac{1}{2}P$ in range 0·05 to 0·10) failed to establish any statistically acceptable proof of an association between the frequency of offences and non-residence.
[3] L.R.S. 33, p. 139.

CHAPTER IV

THE CARE OF THE CHURCHES

Certain standards were expected of the beneficed parish priest, whether he was a vicar or a rector. Parishioners required special qualities and their respect for their priest was often to be measured by his approximation to their ideal. Most of our knowledge of the sixteenth-century clergy is filtered through the reports of the churchwardens and parishioners at the visitations of the bishop or archdeacon; they reported a priest when he had failed to live up to the standard which they required. That standard received its clearest expression in canon law and the teaching of the moralists and poets. A priest was required to preach at least four times a year, visit sick parishioners,[1] say all the offices daily and, most important of all, to celebrate the mass.[2] He was also to hear the confessions of his parishioners at least once a year and to communicate them at least three times.[3] His life was to be of an exemplary kind; he was not to wear unsuitable clothes, nor frequent inns or brothels, and his associations with the female sex were to be above suspicion.[4] Such were the requirements of the canon law. The moralists of the fourteenth and fifteenth century required still more. A short rhyme written in a late fourteenth-century hand at the beginning of a copy of the *Oculus Sacerdotis* stressed the need for all the social graces:

> In privato sobrietas
> In publico hilaritas
> Inter extraneos affabilitas
> Inter socios et amicos communis benignitas
> In infortunio iocunda liberalitas
> Inter adulantes et magnates discreta dapsilitas.[5]

---

[1] Lyndwood, *Provinciale*, Lib. I, tit. 11, caps i, iii.
[2] *Ibid.* Lib. III, tit. 23, cap i, gloss b on *ab aliquibus*.
[3] *Ibid.* Lib. V, tit. 16, cap xvi.
[4] *Ibid.* Lib. III, tit. 2, cap i.
[5] Bodl. Library, MS. Rawlinson, A. 370.

The same theme underlies a note in a fifteenth-century manuscript in Jesus College, Cambridge:

Sacerdos debet esse vir sanctus, a peccatis segregatus; rector, non raptor; speculator non spiculator; dispensator, non dissipator; pius in judicio, justus in concilio; devotus in choro, castus in thoro; stabilis in ecclesia, sobrius in coena; prudens in laetitia, purus in conscientia; verax in sermone, assiduus in oratione, humilis in congregatione; paciens in adversitate, benignus in prosperitate; dives in virtutibus, mitis in bonitatibus; sapiens in confessione, securus et fidelis in praedicatione; ab vanis operibus separatus, in Christo constans.[1]

Chaucer emphasized the need to visit the sick, and his parson was loath 'to cursen for his tythes'.[2] These requirements express, in a stylized form, the qualities for which the parishioner was looking in a priest; a priest who lacked them might be reported at the visitation of the bishop or archdeacon or both. Reformers may have had higher standards, or different ones, but the parish reports indicate that the village was looking for exactly the qualities described in the *Oculus* and that it had not yet begun to look for others. A failure to administer the sacraments and to visit the sick is reported, as might be expected, but so were the aggressive habits of a vicar who walked round the village armed with shield and sword and talking to a stranger.[3]

In addition to the duties imposed on an incumbent by law or custom, other duties might on occasions be required of him. In October 1500, all clergy in the archdeaconry of Lincoln were ordered to say special prayers and litanies on account of the epidemic of the plague then raging.[4] This duty, and others like it, would tend to crowd an already full day. How busy a priest might be and how much was normally expected of him is shown from a composition between the vicar of High Wycombe and his parishioners. It was agreed that the vicar must have another priest to help him since the cure was so large, and that he must have two

---

[1] Quoted in *Reliquiae Antiquae*, ed. T. Wright and J. O. Halliwell (London, 1843), II, 218.

[2] G. Chaucer, *Canterbury Tales*, Prologue, The Parson, ed. W. W. Skeat (Oxford 1894), p. 15.

[3] *L.R.S.* 33, p. 6.   [4] Register 24, fo. 211.

priests to assist with the parish if he was ever likely to be away. His presence was agreed to be essential at Christmas, Easter and Whitsun when all the parishioners had to be communicated; there were so many confessions to be heard in Lent that the vicar was excused from saying weekday mattins and was not bound to stay in choir for the other offices, provided the assistant clergy were there.[1]

It is clear that at High Wycombe all the offices were being said during the week. This was also true of some small parishes.[2] At Naileston a deacon was required to ring the bells for weekday services[3] and the custodian of the chapel at Harmston was required to make sure the bells were rung before the daily offices.[4] Scant though the evidence is, it suggests that the saying of the daily offices in the church was an accepted norm and that a failure to comply with it would have provoked an outcry. A modicum of preaching also appears to have been expected. Some slight evidence survives to suggest that the clergy were preaching and that those reported for not doing so were the exception rather than the rule.[5] In one parish, a certain Thomas Michael swore that he had heard the rector on Septuagesima Sunday preaching on the seven deadly sins.[6] One priest erred on the side of preaching too much and in places for which he had no licence; he went round the country pretending that he was the queen's chaplain and saying that 'if any man wold lett him to preche eyther to say masse he wold cause him to be thanked by the queene grace and other lordes of the courte'. His reason for this extraordinary behaviour was that 'in bromyard in hereforde[7] sher he named hymself to have xl^{li} a yere of the quene for his exhibition to preche a boute in dyverse places'. For this offence he had been

---

[1] Register 24, fo. 221.

[2] This appears to mark an improvement on the thirteenth century, when there were frequent complaints of a neglect of the daily offices, see J. R. H. Moorman, *Church Life in England in the Thirteenth Century* (Cambridge, 1946), p. 74.

[3] Cj. 2, fo. 58.   [4] Cj. 4, fo. 30v.

[5] For a consideration of the sermons of some of the more erudite priests and of books of sermons, see J. W. Blench, *Preaching in England in the Late Fifteenth and Sixteenth Centuries* (Oxford, 1964).

[6] Cj. 3, fo. 41v.   [7] Bromyard, Herefordshire.

imprisoned once before in the bishop's prison at Banbury and he was warned to abstain from repeating the offence yet again.[1]

There is very little positive evidence to indicate that the parochial clergy were performing the other duties expected of them. The parish reported the faults, but not the diligent care, of its pastor. The vicar of Asthall was said to visit the sick in other parishes as though they were his own,[2] and the devotion of other pastors may perhaps be attested by their witnessing of the wills of their parishioners.[3] But wills were often made *in articulo mortis*, or in circumstances in which the influence of the priest might be especially powerful; they may also indicate a desire on the part of the priest to see that neither he nor his church was forgotten amongst the bequests of his parishioners.

But, if some priests were devoted, there were inevitably others who were not. Some failed to hold services at the proper times or to take the Rogation processions, administer the sacraments, or preach. At Sixhill the vicar was late with the services since he waited for the arrival of one of his parishioners, a certain Mr Moigne.[4] At Willoughton the vicar refused to use the Sarum rite, and process with the Host.[5] In another Lincolnshire parish, the vicar did not go into the pulpit nor did he wear a surplice,[6] and the vicar of Corby would not allow the Asperges in the chapels adjoining the chancel; he was also averse to processions.[7] The pastoral care of the vicar of Minster Lovell was mistimed; he only visited his parishioners when they were dead.[8] No one had preached at Westwell for a year and at Harrington the articles of the faith had not been declared.[9] The vicar of Foston only celebrated mass once a week[10] and the celebrations at Ashby were not at convenient times.[11] Enclosures at Clee interfered with the Roga-

---

[1] Cj. 2, fos. 100, 100 *a*. See also above, pp. 21, 41, for further mention of the same priest.   [2] *L.R.S* 33, p. 133.

[3] See, for example, Longden, I, 75, 109 (John Arras and William Atmere); II, 7, 57 (William Basset, William Beley); V, 165 (Richard Wood); XI, 25 (Thomas Plowright). See also *L.R.S.* 5, *passim*; 10, *passim*.

[4] *L.R.S.* 33, p. 63.   [5] Viv. 5, fo. 10.

[6] *Ibid.* fo. 16 v; the name of the parish is unfortunately not given.

[7] *Ibid.* fo. 67v.   [8] *L.R.S.* 33, p. 132.

[9] *Ibid.* pp. 67, 132.   [10] Viv. 5, fo. 45 v.

[11] Vj. 5, fo. 80.

tion processions,[1] and there had been no processions at Boling-
broke for two years.[2] Vespers had not been said at Great Missenden on the vigil of Corpus Christi day and vespers at Cockthorpe
were over before midday, since the cure was served by a Domini-
can who probably had other duties.[3] Though these cases caused
scandal or alarm in the parishes in which they occurred, they were,
in fact, unusual in the diocese as a whole. The following table
gives some indication of their incidence as reported in the various
visitation returns:

Visitation reports of failure to fulfil pastoral obligations

Fault reported	1500[4] (from 330 parishes)	1507/8[4] (from 88 parishes)	1509/10[4] (from 941 parishes)	1514–21[4] (from 1,006 parishes)	1514–21[4] (corrected for 1,700 parishes)
Services irregular in time or manner of performance	1[5]	0	1[6]	17[7]	28·73
Sacraments or Rogation processions not administered or properly conducted	4[8]	0	1[9]	12[10]	20·27
Failure to preach or visit	1[11]	0	0	7[12]	11·83
Too old or infirm to perform duties	0	0	0	5[13]	8·45

[1] *L.R.S.* 33, p. 87. [2] *Ibid.* p. 76. [3] *Ibid.* pp. 67, 132.
[4] For the basis of correction and notes on number of parishes visited see
above, p. 108. It is not possible to infer from this table that the situation in
the parishes was deteriorating, since the archidiaconal visitation material for 1500,
1507/8, 1509/10 is fragmentary, and it is not clear whether certain offences were
reported, see above, p. 111.
[5] Vj. 5, fo. 67v. [6] Viv. 5, fo. 38.
[7] *L.R.S.* 33, pp. 28, 33, 41, 49, 63², 67, 73, 77, 88, 93², 94, 119, 130, 132, 134.
[8] Vj. 5, fos. 10, 23 v, 67v, 80.
[9] Viv. 5, fo. 45v.
[10] *L.R.S.* 33, pp. 2, 3, 53, 57, 64, 67², 76, 78, 87, 89, 107.
[11] Vj. 5, fo. 16v.
[12] *L.R.S.* 33, pp. 30, 67, 132², 133, 138; Cj. 2, fo. 100.
[13] *L.R.S.* 33, pp. 46², 47, 119; *A.A.S.R.P.* xxviii, part i, 128.

This table indicates that complaints of a failure to administer sacraments or hold the offices at the proper time, or in a seemly fashion, though the most frequent, were, in fact, unusual in the diocese as a whole. If the clergy were neglecting their liturgical duties, the parishioners connived at the offence and did not report them at the visitation. Priests may have preached badly, administered the sacraments irregularly and taken services irreverently but there were few complaints about it. We must conclude either that this was not so: that all was done in a satisfactory way, or that the parish, the laity, were as careless and indifferent as their pastors. Their failure to report an offender could only result in the persistence of his fault, uncorrected by the archdeacon or bishop. But the parishioners were more concerned with the lives of their pastors than with their duties. The actual performance of the liturgical and pastoral duties of the priest were one thing, the spirit in which they were performed was quite another. There is a difference between taking services, and taking them with devotion. Assiduity in prayer and purity of life were rarer qualities. Yet these were needed if the priest was to live the chaste and dedicated life required of him by the moralist. It was all too easy for a priest to appear as just another villager, and make a mistress of his housekeeper, or to cultivate his glebe all day in the same way as his neighbours. Many incumbents did both. Their alleged failures are sometimes hard to classify but the table on p. 116 shows the number of complaints of offences of this kind given in the visitation books.

Notes to the table on p. 116.

[1] For the basis of these figures, see above, p. 108.

[2] Vj. 5, fo. 92.   [3] Vj. 6, fo. 8.   [4] Viv. 5, fo. 32v.

[5] *L.R.S.* 33, pp. 41, 42[2], 43, 45, 46[2], 47, 48, 63, 64, 65[3], 67, 72[3], 73[6], 74[5], 75[2], 76, 78, 79, 80, 82[2], 83[2], 84, 85, 86[3], 87, 88, 89, 90, 92, 93, 94, 97, 98, 99, 119, 120, 121, 122, 124, 125[2], 126, 128, 129[4], 131, 134[2], 136, 137, 138; Cj. 2, fos. 90, 103, 105, 106v.   [6] Vj. 5, fos. 60v, 67v.

[7] *L.R.S.* 33, pp. 40, 46, 49, 63, 67, 71, 72, 76, 82, 94, 99[2], 111, 122, 125, 130, 132; Cj. 2, fo. 56.   [8] Vj. 5, fos. 12, 40v, 44v.

[9] *L.R.S.* 33, pp. 11, 99; Cj. 2, fos. 44v, 59, 62v, 71, 107.

[10] *L.R.S.* 33, pp. 43, 55, 57[2], 76[2], 79, 81[2], 84[3], 88[2], 89[3], 90, 92, 93, 95[2], 97, 105.

[11] Vj. 5, fo. 40v.

[12] *L.R.S.* 33, pp. 2, 6, 77, 108, 126, 138; Cj. 2, fo. 66v.

[13] *L.R.S.* 33, pp. 65, 67, 68.

Fault of incumbent	1500[1] (from 330 parishes)	1507/8[1] (from 88 parishes)	1509/10[1] (from 941 parishes)	1514–21[1] (from 1,006 parishes)	1514–21[1] (corrected for 1,700 parishes)
Having a woman (not known whether suspect or not)	1[2]	1[3]	1[4]	77[5]	130·12
Having a woman (definitely suspect)	2[6]	0	0	18[7]	30·42
Having a woman (proven immoral)	3[8]	0	0	7[9]	11·83
Having a woman (not suspect)	0	0	0	24[10]	40·56
Irregular clothes or untonsured hair	2[11]	0	0	0	0
Behaving in an un-acceptable manner	0	0	0	7[12]	11·83
Farming	0	0	0	3[13]	5·07

Notes to the table will be found on p. 115.

Some of these charges against incumbents could not be sustained in court, and the priest concerned had little difficulty in clearing himself. William Everton, vicar of Wendover, was said to have a woman of doubtful virtue in his house, but he denied the charge when brought before the bishop.[1] There were conflicting reports about Johanna Thakham, who looked after the rector of Thornton. Some of the parishioners did not suspect her of more than verbal indiscretions, while others held that she lived incontinently with the rector, and had made the rectory into an inn. The rector denied all charges of immorality.[2] Sometimes the charge was of a trivial nature and may conceal a village feud or just personal incompatibility. Among those charged with unacceptable behaviour was the rector of Maulden, who was simply accused of not having done any good in the parish.[3] The rectors

[1] *L.R.S.* 33, p. 40; Cj. 2, fo. 103.
[2] *L.R.S.* 33, p. 46; Cj. 2, fo. 106v; unfortunately court proceedings do not survive in sufficient numbers for it to be possible to estimate the number of ill-founded charges or to indicate the proportion likely to have been denied by the rector.   [3] *L.R.S.* 33, p. 108.

of Hanwell and Haseley were discourteous: the former made the old people climb over the cemetery stile instead of opening the gates for them, and the latter would only meet a corpse at the cemetery gate instead of going to the home of the deceased in the customary manner.[1] The rector of East Keal was in the local inn too much, no doubt because his rectory was said to be in a state of collapse, and the inn provided warmth and companionship.[2] At Upton, the rectory displayed an 'ale polle', but the farmer appears to have been responsible for allowing it to become the local tavern.[3] There was sound sense, if flagging devotion, in the activities of the rector of West Barkwith. He augmented his meagre stipend by devoting much of his time to farming his glebe, to the annoyance of his parishioners.[4]

The most frequent charge against the beneficed clergy was that they were incontinent. It was necessary for a parish priest to have a female servant in his house to act as housekeeper and to feed him. This requirement was recognized by the bishop and by the parish. Some chantry priests from Marston Trussell, who had failed to look after their chantries and were suspected of keeping undesirable company, were told by the chancellor in 1526 to find an old and honest woman to look after them.[5] But old and honest women were not easy to come by, and often an incumbent preferred to have his mother or his aunt to look after him. The vicar of Stewkley in Buckinghamshire had his mother with him[6] and the vicar of Aby and the rector of Calcethorpe had female relatives.[7] These women were usually described as being *non suspecte*. Many other incumbents had women in their houses of whom it is not stated whether any suspicion was entertained or not. Of the rector of South Thoresby, for example, it was simply said that he had two women in his house (*habet duas mulieres in domo sua*).[8] Clearly among the seventy-seven so described, there must have been many whose morality was suspect. In eighteen cases there is

[1] *Ibid.* pp. 126, 138.
[2] *Ibid.* p. 77.   [3] *Ibid.* p. 2.
[4] *Ibid.* p. 65; his stipend was only £5. 5s. (Salter, p. 26), significantly below that of other rectors, see below p. 140.
[5] Cj. 3, fo. 24v.   [6] L.R.S. 33, p. 43.
[7] *Ibid.* pp. 72, 82.   [8] *Ibid.* p. 83.

a note that the women in question were *suspecte*.[1] There is some
doubt whether this description had a literal or legalistic meaning.
Continental lawyers used it to describe all women under the age
of forty.[2] It is extremely hard to tell if the term is used in the
visitation returns in this sense. Where a distinction is made between
a woman and a suspect woman, the distinction may not be that of
age. At Burgh, for instance, the question at issue was that of their
way of life and not of their age.[3] The distinction of age is sometimes made, but not necessarily by the word *suspecta*. At East
Barkwith the rector had *duas iuvenculas*; at Langton by Wragby,
he had *duas puellas* and at Panton the rector had *duas mulieres unam
senem aliam iuvenem*.[4] In all these examples the distinction of age
is made but not by the word *suspecta*. The word appears to be
used more broadly to indicate a general suspicion which might
arise from age or from a previous reputation.

Whether or not all the incumbents who had *mulieres suspectas*
were guilty of an actual or a technical fault, it is clear that many
clerks gave ample cause for scandal. The cases which came before
the bishop were probably among the more serious; they indicate
that a few of the clergy were guilty of gross immorality, and it is
likely that some of these cases gained notoriety. The case of the
rector of Addington in Northamptonshire, for instance, was
hardly edifying. He had been presented to the living in 1509/10;[5]
in 1526 he was brought before the bishop for having had two
children by his cook. She was the wife of a certain Mr Byrde and
had a bad reputation, since she had already been in the stocks. The
rector did not wear the usual priestly attire but walked about the
village in chain mail. This served to intimidate his own parishioners, only one of whom testified against him; the rest of the
evidence was given by two men from the next deanery. The
offending incumbent was no *ignoramus*. He was a bachelor in law

---

[1] See above, p. 116.   [2] Hughes, *Reformation in England*, p. 55, n. 2.
[3] *L.R.S.* 33, p. 79. 'habet duas mulieres: dicuntur tamen esse satis honestas
[sic] et bone ac laudabilis conversacionis'.
[4] *Ibid.* p. 63³.
[5] Register 23, fo. 216; there are a number of Addingtons in the diocese but it
is assumed that Great Addington in Northamptonshire is meant, since two of
the witnesses came from the neighbouring deanery of Fleet.

who had received his living from the abbot and convent of Crow-land.[1] Cases of this kind brought with them the usual unhappy and sometimes tragic consequences. The rector of Tighe had given a girl from Ashwell a child; the unfortunate girl begged the chancellor not to let the woman with whom she lodged know of her condition. The rector, who admitted the offence, was ordered, in addition to public penance, to provide for the birth and up-bringing of the child.[2]

There was often some difficulty in bringing offending priests to justice, and still more in ensuring the offence did not recur. The vicar of Saleby in Lincolnshire confessed to the chancellor in 1528 that he had lived with Johanna Raye for the past ten years and had had a number of children by her. He had been brought before the archdeacon of Lincoln for this offence and for another of a similar kind, but the archdeacon's rebukes apparently had little effect. The chancellor ordered him to avoid female company under threat of deprivation. One wonders how effective the order was in the light of the vicar's past record.[3] It was very rare for the bishop or his deputy to deprive a clerk for immorality. One of the few exceptions was the rector of North Kilworth. He was accused in the visitation of July 1518 of having a ruined rectory but of nothing more.[4] But in September of the same year he confessed to incontinence with a girl from Lutterworth, and to attempting adultery with a married woman from a nearby parish; he was imprisoned in the episcopal prison at Banbury and deprived of his living.[5] Others escaped censure by removing all traces of their misdemeanours before the bishop arrived for a visitation. It was said of the rector of Harrington that he had a girl in his house but had removed her just before visitation.[6] There is a note of defeat in the records over this problem. So many of the cases which came before the court of audience were concerned with sexual offences that it was probably not possible to take the matter too seriously.[7] Public penance was invariably ordered and the incum-

[1] Register 23, fo. 216.   [2] Cj. 3, fo. 34 v.
[3] Cj. 4, fo. 10.   [4] *L.R.S.* 33, pp. 18, 19.
[5] Cj. 2, fo. 62 v.   [6] *L.R.S.* 33, p. 67.
[7] About three quarters of all cases brought to the court of audience were concerned with immorality, frequently on the part of the clergy.

bent concerned exhorted to mend his ways. But wholesale deprivation was out of the question if, in fact, all the incumbents
with women in their houses were guilty of immorality. It would
simply result in their replacement by others whose chances of
being any better were not great. The problem is clearly seen in
the case of John Davies of Toynton, who confessed intercourse
with one of his penitents. He was ordered to exchange benefices
presumably to escape from his ill reputation.[1]

Concubinage was not a new problem for the church. The incumbent of an isolated village who found in his cook a com-
panion for his solitude was all too likely to fall a victim to this
kind of fault. But, however excusable the failing, it nevertheless
was a potential danger to the church as a whole and to any particular parish within it. We do not know exactly how widespread
it was since the statistics available are of *complaints* of immorality
and not necessarily of its *incidence*. Similarly there are no comparative figures which would indicate whether it was increasing in
the sixteenth century. But the certain fact behind these figures
was that they would not survive at all had not the parish chosen to
reveal the failing of its incumbent. The churchwardens could connive in the offence or they could report it. In either case there was
likely to be considerable feeling in the parish: the power of gossip
in exaggerating offences was great, and, while the pressures of
secrecy and the threat of exposure may, in some cases, have served
to reinforce self-control, in others they caused an impossible
relationship between priest and parishioner, in which threats of
blackmail were not unknown. An indication of the combination
of intimidation, bribery and gossip engendered by many of these
cases is provided by the case of Robert Becket, a curate. He was
accused of attempting to force himself upon the wife of William
Tailboys saying 'he must nedes have his pleasure of her' and by
putting a gold noble on the bed. He was also accused of having
forcibly assaulted her and, in the attempt, of knocking over some
water and then of having sent her to another woman to ask her
to come to him. As a result of this incident he received 20*d*. from
Mr Tailboys as a bribe to prevent him taking his revenge on Mrs

[1] Cj. 2, fo. 107.

Tailboys by citing her before an ecclesiastical court for the adultery which she had, in fact, refused to commit with him. The churchwardens were aghast at this behaviour, but he merely abused them by calling them 'false perjured churles'. Two maidens from the parish showed their contempt by bringing him a 'babe of clowtes' and asking him to christen it. In these circumstances, the chancellor's order to the curate to avoid feminine society, and to the parish to live charitably together was a trifle optimistic, to say the least.[1] A case of this kind caused scandal and provided the anticlerical with all the evidence he wanted. It was easy to assert that *all* priests were immoral, and it was a short step to argue that, because they failed in this particular, they failed in all. Yet it is interesting to notice that the churchwardens were bound to admit that Robert Becket served the cure well and 'doth his dewty' in saying his offices.[2] The dichotomy between the morality of a priest and his ability to perform the duties of his office, taken with the very extent of moral offences, must have continually raised the question of whether celibacy was absolutely necessary to the priesthood. Indeed the rapidity with which the change came after the break with Rome suggests that the facts had long outgrown the theory.

The shortcomings of the clergy were not confined to those corrected in the ecclesiastical courts. Some were also guilty of offences against the law of the land, and were bound to appear before the appropriate court, usually, in the first instance, before the justices at Quarter Sessions. In all but a few cases a plea of clergy could save them from the consequences of their misdemeanours. Usually, by the late fifteenth century, benefit of clergy was only claimed when the jury had actually found the accused guilty. He was then handed over to the bishop, or his ordinary, and imprisoned until such time as he could purge himself of his guilt with the help of about six others.[3] His sojourn in an episcopal

---

[1] Cj. 4, fo. 44.   [2] *Ibid.* fo. 44.

[3] For a full account of the procedure, see L. C. Gabel, *Benefit of clergy in England in the later middle ages* (Smith College Studies in History, XIV, nos. 1–4 [Northampton, Mass. 1928–9], *passim*). For a certificate that a clerk had been handed over to the bishop, see Register 24, fos. 155, 155v, 165; for an order to the abbot of Peterborough to assume responsibility for transporting clerks from his liberty to the episcopal prison see *ibid.* fo. 179–179v.

prison cannot have been very pleasant. In 1508 it apparently only cost the bishop 7s. 7½d. *per annum* to maintain a clerk in prison, though he claimed it cost him 2s. 4d. per week.[1] At the convenience of the commissary in whose archdeaconry the episcopal prison was, the clerk could proceed to purge himself. Notice of the intended purgation was sent to the parish in which the offence was alleged to have been committed, requesting anyone who wished to contest the purgation to come to a certain place on a certain date. It appears to have been unusual for anyone to contest the purgation since the prison was often far from the place of the offence and the purgation some time after it. In all of the twelve cases of clerical purgation which have survived, the accused succeeded in his purgation and was freed.[2] As a result of claiming benefit, therefore, a clerk could escape with only a short spell in prison, although he had been found guilty by a jury and would probably otherwise have been hanged.

Many of those who availed themselves of this privilege were not in priest's orders at all. None of those who were in the episcopal prisons of Newarke and Banbury in 1509, or later, were priests. All were labourers or yeomen who had been able to read the appropriate psalm, and, for this reason, had claimed benefit of clergy for their first offence.[3] Since no sessions records survive for this date, it is impossible to assess accurately what number of parish priests found their way into the courts accused of 'secular' offences. The only indication of the number of clergy so accused is provided by the records of the court of King's Bench. The normal run of cases would not have got as far as King's Bench, but, of those that did, one in twenty of the defendants in Michaelmas 1490 were clerks.[4] Clergy from the Lincoln diocese were un-

---

[1] Bishops Accounts, Misc. 8. rots 8, 21, cf. P.R.O. C.1/397/26.

[2] Citations Box 81. In this Lincoln was not exceptional; see *Register of Oliver King and Hadrian Castello, Bishops of Bath and Wells*, ed. H. C. Maxwell-Lyte, p. xiii; *Register of Thomas Myllyng*, ed. A. T. Bannister, p. iv.

[3] 4 Henry VII cap. 3; a further limit was made to the plea of clergy for a short time following 4 Henry VIII cap. 2, when the plea could not be entered for certain offences unless the defendant was in higher orders.

[4] M. Blatcher, 'The Working of the Court of King's Bench' (London, Ph.D. thesis, 1936), p. 339n.

likely to be involved in more than one fifth of these cases, and between 1508 and 1521 about four Lincoln clergy a year appeared before the court.[1] Theft was the most frequent offence, often accompanied by assault and even murder.[2] John Wilkinson, who was presented to a church in Grantham in 1511,[3] was accused of attacking a certain John Dickenson, as a result of which Dickenson died. Wilkinson was bailed out of prison by a gentleman of London and a Robert Wilkinson, probably a relative, who was a merchant from Lincolnshire. Like most defendants before the court at this time he said he was not guilty and was acquitted.[4] The affray did him no harm, since he was still in his living in 1526.[5] George Whalley, who had been presented to Carlton Magna in 1506,[6] was accused of breaking and entering the house of William Curtas and taking some of his possessions and sheep and cattle. He too, after a short spell in the king's prison at Lincoln, was granted bail and his case was adjourned *sine die*.[7] William Amswyth, rector of Lowick, was one of a group who broke into the house of Robert Merbury, attacked his servants and took livestock valued at 20 marks. He was acquitted[8] and was still at Lowick in 1526.[9] Another clerk, John Clifton, was killed as a result of an affray for which, it appears, he was largely responsible. It was alleged that he had attacked Ralph Vaux with a pitchfork. Ralph had pleaded with him to leave him alone: 'in the reverence of Godde and in the Kynges name of Englond meddyll not withe me but lett me goo for I am a syke man ande intend not to meddyll withe the.' This entreaty was ineffective and Ralph in self-defence killed John, who had knocked him to the ground twice before meeting any effective opposition.[10]

The exact number of cases of this kind cannot be known unless

[1] See P.R.O., K.B. 29/140–54. The controlment rolls give a guide to the crown cases in the Plea rolls; they are therefore a useful means of ascertaining the number of cases in which clerks were involved, though the references to the Plea rolls are not always very accurate (see Blatcher, *op. cit.*)

[2] Blatcher, *op. cit.* pp. 321 ff.   [3] Register 23, fo. 143.

[4] P.R.O. K.B. 27/1016, rot iii. v.   [5] Salter, p. 69.

[6] Register 23, fo. 115v.

[7] P.R.O. K.B 27/1013 rot xxiv.

[8] P.R.O. K.B. 27/998 rot xvi.   [9] Salter, p. 141.

[10] P.R.O. K.B. 27/1061 rot i. v.

further records are found, but it is clear that they caused much scandal and resentment. Benefit of clergy gave the clerk a privileged position, and it looks as though this was abused; not only were guilty clerks escaping secular punishments but the ecclesiastical authorities were continuing to allow them to proceed to purgation, and thereafter to go free, notwithstanding the verdict of guilty already passed upon them by a lay jury. All those known to have proceeded to purgation succeeded in it and it seems most unlikely that their success was justified.[1] Church and state alike were aware of this unsatisfactory state of affairs. The state attempted to impose limits on benefits of clergy.[2] The church made some attempt to introduce reforms designed to improve the moral standards of clerks and make their claims to privilege less usual. These attempts at reform were largely initiated by Wolsey, and yet it was partly because of him that they were unable to succeed.

In 1518 Wolsey as legate *a latere* had held a council of bishops of both provinces and they agreed to the publication of a series of constitutions for the reform of the church. Many of these reiterated earlier provisions; incumbents were to preach regularly, to hold services at good times, and to preserve the sacrament with due care. The clergy were exhorted to lead better lives and to amend their dress, and to beware of feminine society; greater care was to be taken to examine those acting as deputies for non-residents, and the pious hope was expressed that better men would be chosen as archdeacons and rural deans, and that they would take more care in visiting and correcting clergy and laity and ministering to sick clergy. These constitutions were conservative enough and broke no new ground. Charles Booth, bishop of Hereford, presented them to synods of clergy in his diocese, and they appear to have met with satisfaction.[3] But in the Lincoln diocese things went differently.[4] Synods of Oxford and Northampton clergy assented to the constitutions readily enough, but there was opposition to the proposals at synods of the clergy of

---

[1] See, especially, Citations Box 81; the dozen clerks mentioned all succeeded in their purgation, see above, p. 122.

[2] A. F. Pollard, *Wolsey* (London, 1953), pp. 43 ff.

[3] Wilkins, *Concilia*, III, 681 ff.   [4] *L.R.S.* 33, pp. 148 ff.

Leicester, Huntingdon and Bedford. The clergy of Bedford sought copies of the constitutions before they assented to them; at Huntingdon the opposition was even stronger. One clerk objected that the council of bishops had no power to promulgate constitutions to the prejudice of the clergy without their consent, thereby asserting that a synod of bishops was no substitute for a provincial council even though it was under the presidency of the legate. His words were so persuasive that all the clergy of the archdeaconry protested together *Nos nolumus consentire*. The constitutions had similar rough treatment from the clergy of Leicester. They objected that the constitutions concerned the clergy of all England, of whom the clergy of the archdeaconry were but a small part; they objected, in fact, to being approached individually so that opposition might be too divided to be effective.

On constitutional grounds the objections were sound enough, but it is possible that there was more to it than that. The clergy of Huntingdon appear to have been emphasizing that the legate could not alter accepted practice; their spokesman asserted 'nec legati de latere nec archiepiscopi nec episcopi possunt condere iura sive statuere leges in preiudicium cleri sine ipsius consensu'.[1] It is possible that this may have been a protest against the overweening power of the cardinal, no doubt with an eye to the fact that he was asking of the clergy more than he asked of himself. It is also interesting that the graduate clergy led the opposition in all cases, and that a united front was created. The lower clergy would at worst lose some of their independence and some of their constitutional rights if the provisions were passed; their spokesmen, in several cases, stood to lose much more. One of those leading the opposition at Bedford, a Doctor Sheffeld,[2] was already in trouble with the authorities; he was called before the bishop in December 1518 for being under age while holding a benefice. He refused to accept penance for this offence, was excommunicated, sought absolution and only after several citations came to heel.[3] Another of the leaders of the Bedford clergy was cited to appear before the bishop on account of the ruin of his benefice of

---

[1] *L.R.S.* 33, p. 150. [2] *Ibid.* p. 150.
[3] Cj. 2, fos. 64v, 66v, 67v.

Todington and for his non-residence.[1] He had nothing to gain from a more stringent examination of the deputies of absentees. Nor had John Nevell, another non-resident who acted as spokesman for Leicester.[2] In this opposition to the constitutions, the intertwining of the genuine problem and vested interest is manifest. Sheffeld had a constitutional case, just as there was a case on grounds of expediency for opposing reform of non-residence, but tangled with it were the vested interests of innumerable individuals. The suspicion that, in the early sixteenth-century church, vested interests were the major obstacle to reform, however much they were rationalized, is once again confirmed. But, if the interests of a Sheffeld or a Nevell blocked the successful promulgation of Wolsey's constitutions, that of others stood in the way of an improvement in the economic and social conditions of the parish priest.

The regularity with which the offices appear to have been said, and the application of incumbents and curates, in most parishes, to their duties appears surprising in the light of their social conditions. Celebrations at Humberstone cannot have been very easy, for it was said that the rain came in on to the high altar.[3] It was customary for the vicar of Wrangle in Lincolnshire to reside, but it was hardly surprising that the vicar had ceased to do so by 1519 since the vicarage was described as being in a great state of decay.[4] The rector of Harrington, who was suspected of illicit relations with his serving-woman, had not read the articles of the faith, refused to go on Rogation processions, and had not bidden parishioners to say their beads, may have been sorely provoked. His rectory was said to have fallen down[5] and his net income of about £5 was nothing like enough to rebuild it.[6] A considerable amount of ecclesiastical property was in a neglected state and often the incumbent could do little or nothing about it.

---

[1] Cj. 2, fo. 86 v.   [2] L.R.S. 33, p. 18; he was rector of Knaptoft.
[3] Ibid. p. 31.   [4] Ibid. pp. 71 ff.
[5] Ibid. p. 67.
[6] Salter, p. 9.; the incumbent in 1526 had a gross income of £10 but out of it there was to be deducted the stipend of another priest. It is possible that the rector in 1519 did not have this expense, in which case his stipend ought to have been sufficient for the repair of his rectory.

An indication of the extent of this neglect can be gained from the following table.

Defects in selected deaneries 1517–1520

Deanery and number of churches	Chancel, defect in fabric or furniture	Nave, defect in fabric or furniture including tower	Vicarage or rectory	Cemetery	Vestments, books or sacramental vessels	Chapels	Unspecified repairs
Leightonstone[1]							
20 churches	7[2]	3[3]	3[4]	2[5]	2[6]	0	0
Framland[7]							
37 churches	16[8]	6[9]	0[10]	10[11]	11[12]	0	0
Wendover[13]							
17 churches	6[14]	1[15]	2[16]	10[17]	5[18]	0	0
Grimsby[19]							
31 churches	8[20]	2[21]	7[22]	4[23]	2[24]	0	0
Bicester[25]							
29 churches	14[26]	7[27]	7[28]	14[29]	5[30]	0	0
Fleet[31]							
22 churches	8[32]	1[33]	1[34]	0	1[35]	0	3[36]
Manlake[37]							
19 churches	3[38]	0	0	4[39]	3[40]	2[41]	1[42]
Total of churches: 175							
Total of defects (184 in all)	62	20	23	44	29	2	4

[1] *L.R.S.* 33, pp. 1 ff.
[2] Ellington, Brington, Kimbolton, Thurning, Coppingford, Keyston, Old Weston (chapel to Brington).
[3] Woolley, Coppingford, Swineshead.
[4] Grafham, Alconbury, Upton.
[5] Ellington, Upton.
[6] Kimbolton, Coppingford.
[7] *L.R.S.* 33, pp. 23 ff., 34 ff.
[8] Edmondthorpe, Hose, Barkston by Belvoir, Saltby, Croxton Kyriel, Thorpe Arnold, Garthorpe, Saxby, Stapleford, Scalford, Abkettleby, Coston, Harston, Buckminster, Stathern, Dalby Parva.

Notes continued on p. 128.

Notes to table on p. 127 (continued)

[9] Edmondthorpe, Brentingby, Plungar, Buckminster, Eastwell, Hareby.

[10] None.

[11] Barkston by Belvoir, Eaton, Saltby, Melton Mowbray, Coston, Knipton, Kirkby Bellars, Burrough on the Hill, Waltham on the Wolds, Dalby Parva.

[12] Wymondham, Wyfordby, Croxton Kyriel, Sproxton, Saxby, Barkston by Belvoir, Freeby, Welby, Harston, Eastwell, Hareby.

[13] *L.R.S.* 33, pp. 39 ff.

[14] Hampden Magna, Cuddington, Ellesborough, Hampden Parva, Weston Turville, Haddenham.

[15] Kimble Parva.

[16] Hampden Magna, Ellesborough.

[17] Princes Risborough, Hampden Magna, Cuddington, Stone, Hartwell, Missenden Parva, Ellesborough, Hampden Parva, Weston Turville, Wendover.

[18] Aston Clinton, Cuddington, Hulcott, Missenden Magna, Haddenham.

[19] *L.R.S.* 33, pp. 83 ff.

[20] Holton-le-Clay, Barnoldby-le-Beck, Tetney, Grimsby St James, Beelsby, Waltham, Hawerby, Tealby.

[21] Grimsby St James, Ashby with Fenby.

[22] Hatcliffe, Laceby, Hawerby, Rothwell, Clee, Tealby, Riby.

[23] Beelsby, Irby on Humber, Cuxwold, West Rasen.

[24] Holton-le-Clay, Humberstone.

[25] *L.R.S.* 33, pp. 121 ff.

[26] Finmere, Weston on the Green, Islip, Hampton Gay, Oddington, Chesterton, Charlton on Otmoor, Fritwell, Bucknell, Heyford Warren, Kirtlington, Launton, Middleton Stoney, Stratton Audley.

[27] Hampton Poyle, Weston on the Green, Ardley, Chesterton, Charlton on Otmoor, Noke, Heyford Warren.

[28] Lillingstone Lovell, Mixbury, Oddington, Wendlebury, Charlton on Otmoor, Fritwell, Heyford Warren.

[29] Fringford, Finmere, Newton Purcell, Ardley, Mixbury, Merton by Ambrosden, Oddington, Souldern, Chesterton, Charlton on Otmoor, Noke, Launton, Bletchingdon, Hethe.

[30] Newton Purcell, Lillingstone Lovell, Souldern, Kirtlington, Stratton Audley.

[31] *L.R.S.* 33, pp. 107 ff.

[32] Flitwick, Ampthill, Gravenhurst, Tingrith, Cranfield, Haynes, Pulloxhill, Ridgmont.

[33] Cranfield.

[34] Marston Moretaine, Westoning, Maulden, Haynes.

[35] Eversholt.

[36] Westoning, Millbrook, Gravenhurst.

[37] *L.R.S.* 33, pp. 92 ff.

[38] Redbourne, Hibaldstow, Whitton.

[39] Luddington, Waddingham St Mary, Crowle, Whitton.

[40] Luddington, Redbourne, Winteringham.

[41] Althorpe, Winterton.

[42] Luddington.

It is clear that, in these deaneries, the chancel was the most likely part of the church to require repairs. In five of the seven deaneries considered, defects in the chancel were more numerous than faults of any other kind. Sometimes it was said that: *Cancellus est ruinosus*. This sounds more serious than it probably was. *Ruinosus* is an adjective used, apparently without discrimination, of windows and books as well as chancels and naves. It is often hard to know how serious the defect was to warrant the term. It appears to cover the important and the trivial; it seems to mean little more than that the church concerned needed some attention. More important than the extent of the damage was the responsibility for doing something about it. The chancel was the rector's responsibility. In appropriated churches, which constituted one third of the total number of parishes in the diocese, the responsibility lay with the appropriator, which, in most cases, was a religious order. In the deanery of Leightonstone, the chancel repairs needed at Ellington, Thurning, Coppingford, Keyston and Old Weston were the responsibility of single rectors, while those of Brington and Kimbolton were the responsibility of the abbot of Ramsey and the prior of Stonely respectively.[1] In the deanery of Wendover, the prior and convent of Rochester were to blame for the chancel defects at Cuddington and Haddenham[2] while the remaining four defects were the fault of single rectors.[3] In the deanery of Bicester, eight faulty chancels were the responsibility of single rectors[4] and a further six that of religious orders: Osney should have done the necessary repairs at Weston on the Green, Hampton Gay and Chesterton; St Frideswide's were responsible for Fritwell, and the London Charterhouse and the prior and convent of Bicester for Kirtlington and Stratton Audley respectively.[5] In the deanery of Manlake two out of three of the chancel repairs were the responsibility of religious houses, and in that of Fleet at least half should have been repaired by monastic appro-

[1] *Valor Ecclesiasticus*, IV, 258; V.C.H. *Huntingdonshire*, I, 360n.
[2] *Valor Ecclesiasticus*, IV, 248.
[3] Viz. Hampden Magna, Ellesborough, Hampden Parva, Weston Turville.
[4] Viz. Finmere, Islip, Oddington, Charlton on Otmoor, Bucknell, Heyford Warren, Launton, Middleton Stoney.
[5] *Valor Ecclesiasticus*, II, 159 ff.

priators.[1] In the deanery of Framland corporate rectors were responsible for as many as ten of the sixteen repairs.[2] This figure is
a high one. Since only one third of all the parishes in the diocese
were appropriated, the religious orders should not have been liable
for more than a third of the chancel repairs necessary in any
particular deanery.[3] But there was a tendency throughout the
diocese for this figure to be exceeded: religious were apt to
be guilty of the neglect of as many as half of the total number
of chancels reported as being in need of repair. In such cases,
the incumbent had simply to wait until the house concerned
acted.

The parishioners themselves were not so negligent about their
duties in repairing the church fabric as they were in enclosing
churchyards. It is not always at all clear whose responsibility the
churchyard was. Lyndwood stated that the parish should be responsible for the enclosure *propter porcos et animalia alia quae possunt illud deturpare*.[4] At Althorpe the cemetery of St James's chapel
was said to be in ruins *incuria rectoris*[5] and at Enstone in Oxfordshire the parishioners could hardly be blamed when the cemetery
was fouled by the vicar's horse.[6] When legal action was taken, it
was usually the churchwardens who assumed responsibility. The
wardens of Amersham had no defence against the accusation that
the cemetery was not properly enclosed and that animals grazed
there *ut in aliis pasturis*.[7] They agreed to enclose it or pay a fine of
40s.[8] The cemetery at Iver was reported by the wardens as being
enclosed by January 1520;[9] the wardens of Great Hampden promised to enclose their cemetery,[10] but it was the farmer of the
rectory of Wing who was warned about the cemetery there.[11]

[1] *L.R.S.* 33, pp. 92, 107.
[2] Viz. Hose, Barkston by Belvoir, Croxton Kyriel, Thorpe Arnold, Garthorpe, Stapleford, Scalford, Abkettleby, Buckminster, Dalby Parva, see *Valor
Ecclesiasticus*, IV, 154.
[3] Hartridge, *A History of Vicarages in the Middle Ages*, p. 204.
[4] Lyndwood, *Provinciale*, Lib. III, tit. 27, cap. ii, gloss on *clausarum coemeterii*.
[5] *L.R.S.* 33, p. 92.
[6] *Ibid.* p. 136.
[7] *Ibid.* p. 38.
[8] Cj. 2, fo. 107v.
[9] *Ibid.* fo. 105v.
[10] *Ibid.* fo. 103v.
[11] *Ibid.* fo. 89.

Here again the trouble was due to his animals fouling it and not to the inadequate enclosure provided by the parish. Probably the parish was responsible for the enclosure, and it was up to the incumbent or farmer to see that animals did not foul it. Where the rectory was let to a layman, and the vicar was responsible for the spiritual well-being of the parish, the two might be incompatible. The farmer would use the cemetery for his livestock, which might seriously impede the vicar in taking funerals and processions. But the vicar who bore the inconvenience was impotent to do anything to remedy it. At Little Steeping the rector let his rectory to farm and the farmer's horse fouled the cemetery. The curate had to manage as best he could in this situation, but a number of parishioners were dissatisfied and did not come to church.[1]

If the parishioners were normally responsible for the cemetery, then they were neglecting this duty more frequently than their other more important one of caring for the nave. If the nave roof was leaking then the parish was both responsible and inconvenienced. There was more incentive to mend a roof when its repair would bring the positive benefit of dry and warm services! Dilapidated books would inconvenience few, and the church ornaments probably deteriorated more through carelessness than the positive neglect of the parish. From time to time churchwardens were ordered to do something about both, but the impression is that the offence was not a very serious one.[2]

A temporary defect was unlikely to have the demoralizing effect which might result from long-standing neglect and the apparent impotence of the ecclesiastical authorities to force the responsible party to remedy it. Yet this was the lot of many incumbents. Ten churches in the archdeaconry of Buckingham reported some fabric deficiency in 1491.[3] The same report was made in five of these churches when the bishop visited them nearly thirty years later.[4] The chancel at Mursley was still defective, and, though many of the faults were small, their persistence was irksome. Of

[1] *L.R.S.* 33, p. 77.   [2] Cj. 2, fos. 105-7.
[3] Aylesbury Record Office, D/A/V. 1, *passim.*
[4] Viz. Hillesden, Little Hampden, Cuddington, Stone, Mursley, see *L.R.S.* 33, pp. 35-55.

sixty-seven faults reported to the archdeacon or his official in Leicestershire parishes in 1509,[1] twenty-seven were reported again about ten years later.[2] Sometimes the fault went uncorrected for thirty years. The church roof at Queniborough needed attention in 1489; it was still needing repairs in 1518.[3] Rain came in on the high altar at Foston in 1489;[4] it still did so twenty years later. Nor were episcopal visitations any more successful in achieving improvement than those of the archdeacon. Of 172 churches visited by the bishop in 1518/19 and by the archdeacon in 1526, at least twenty-three reported the same fabric faults. At Church Langton nothing had been done about the windows, the cemetery had not been enclosed at Shangton, the prior and convent of Lenton had still done nothing to prevent the rain coming in at Wigston, and the rectory at North Kilworth apparently remained unrepaired even though it was reported in 1516, 1518, and 1526.[5]

The responsibility for remedying some of these long-term defects was fairly equally divided. Of the chancels reported as being in need of repair in 1509, and reported again subsequently, seven were the responsibility of monastic rectors and four of single rectors. The parish was responsible for failing to do something

[1] Vj. 5, *passim*.
[2] Viz. Sapcote, Enderby, Cotesbach, Nailstone, Prestwold, Hoby, Queniborough, Lowesby, Gumley, Kibworth Beauchamp, Wistow, Welham, Foston, Eaton, Edmondthorpe, Oadby, Medbourne, Holt, Market Harborough, Markfield, Bottesford, Wymondham, Ratcliffe-on-Wreak, Normanton, Market Bosworth, Lockington, Claybrooke; see *L.R.S.* 33, pp. 8–35.
[3] Viv. 2, fo. 41; cf. *L.R.S.* 33, p. 33.
[4] Viv. 2, fo. 19; cf. Viv. 5, fo. 7v.
[5] *L.R.S.* 33, pp. 8–35; cf. *A.A.S.R.P.* xxviii, 145 ff. The churches in which no progress had been made were Church Langton, Shangton, Houghton on the Hill, Kibworth Beauchamp, Lubenham, Cosby, Wigston, Thurlaston, Dunton Bassett, North Kilworth, Saxelby, Bottesford, Wymondham, Eastwell, Edmondthorpe, Saltby, Eaton, Little Dalby, Coston, Harston, Market Bosworth, Thurmaston, Shepshed. It should be noted that all these figures are minimal since there is some doubt whether the same questions asked at each of the visitations. The archdeacon appears to have been more concerned with ornaments, and sometimes a church reports one fault one year and another in the next; subsequent visitations reveal that neither was corrected though both faults were not mentioned together, see, for example, the visitations at Enderby, Foston, and Donington in 1509 and 1510 (Viv. 5, fos. 7v, 8, 17, 43,• 44v, 52).

about some thirteen cemeteries and the remaining faults were distributed between parish and incumbent.[1]

Many incumbents found it very difficult to fulfil their obligations in repairing the fabric. If the single rector was to avoid paying for all the necessary repairs, he had to see that his predecessor paid his share in the form of dilapidations.[2] Theoretically this was easy enough but, from the evidence we have of it in practice, it looks as though the main burden of the expense fell on the rector actually ordered to make the repairs. On 14 June 1514, for instance, the vicar general ordered William Sharp, rector of Careby, to spend dilapidation money to the value of £4, inherited from his predecessor, on the repair of the rectory; he was ordered to contribute £2 annually from his own stipend for three years towards the repairs, bringing his total contributions for the period to £6.[3] The total income from this benefice was £10, of which £5. 6s. 8d. went to a chaplain, 7s. went in a pension and 10s. 2d. went in procurations and synodals. His profit cannot, therefore, have been more than £3. 16s. 2d. and, if £2 were to go on repairs, his net stipend would have been negligible.[4] It is, of course, possible that Careby church had had extensive repairs a few years earlier, and that all the dilapidation money had been absorbed. But it is difficult to see how the money could have been accumulated and successfully transmitted from one incumbent to another over a period of time when such relatively small sums were involved. It looks as though a rector accepted a church in need of repair at his own risk. Even someone with a substantial stipend might find himself in trouble. Magister Thomas Topcliff, the rector of Hougham, complained to the bishop in 1529 that he had spent £20 in two years on the repair of a chapel attached to the church.[5] He was a wealthy incumbent who received about £38 from this living and a further £20 (gross) from his other main living of Gainsborough. But his commitments were also heavy, and he was unwilling to acquiesce in this steady drain on his income.[6] A further obstacle to his cooperation was the know-

---

[1] Viv. 5, *passim*; for the parishes see above, p. 132, note 2.
[2] Lyndwood, *Provinciale*, Lib. III, tit. 27, cap. i.   [3] Cj. 2, fo. 8.
[4] Salter, p. 56.   [5] Cj. 4, fo. 62v.   [6] Salter, pp. 33, 73.

ledge that other rectors were disregarding their obligations with impunity. It was unlikely that the ecclesiastical authorities would force the papal collector, Polydore Vergil, to repair the church windows at Church Langton; it was still more unlikely that they would, with any speed, compel monastic appropriators, particularly if they were outside the diocese, to remedy defects in the chancels of their appropriated churches. Yet financially some of the religious orders were doing so well out of their appropriated churches that it ought to have been possible for them to give a lead in the repair and rebuilding of the chancels of their churches. Hemel Hempstead, for instance, was valued as being worth £42. 3s. to the rector and fellows of Ashridge;[1] from this the vicar's stipend of £13. 6s. 8d. was not deducted.[2] The abbot and convent of Peterborough received £54. 6s. 8d. from the church at Oundle and when the vicar's stipend had been paid they had a clear profit of £40.[3] The prior and convent of Newnham received £24 clear, from their church of Cardington; their only expense was apparently 1s. 6d. for a lamp.[4] The knights of St John of Jerusalem received £16 from their church of Langford[5] while the abbey of Elstow in Bedfordshire received £66. 13s. 4d.[6] from their church at Hitchin. The priory of St Katherine by Lincoln was receiving £106 in spirituals in 1500; of this only £2. 6s. was spent on the churches themselves.[7] Not all monastic appropriators could afford repairs even if they had been willing to do them. Claxby, for instance, was valued at nothing for the abbot and convent of Crowland 'quia vicarius ejusdem habet omnes et singulas decimas in augmentacione vicarie sue ut per declaracionem'.[8] Chicksands received only £2. 13s. 4d. from its church of Haynes in Bedfordshire.[9] The revenues of the churches of Roxton, Bromham and Arnesby appropriated to the priory of Caldwell yielded £14, £11 and £13. 6s. 8d. respectively.[10] The priory of Kyme did not

---

[1] *Valor Ecclesiasticus*, IV, 225; the sum is stated, at that time, as being in the hands of the incumbent.   [2] Salter, p. 171.

[3] *Valor Ecclesiasticus*, IV, 280.   [4] *Ibid*. pp. 187–8.   [5] *Ibid*. I, 405.

[6] *Ibid*. IV, 188; a pension of £2. 13s. 4d. paid by the vicar to the convent was due in addition to this.

[7] Religious Houses, 6.   [8] *Valor Ecclesiasticus*, IV, 85.

[9] *Ibid*. p. 194.   [10] *Ibid*. p. 189.

do so well from their numerous rectories. They received a total of £48. 1s. 8d. from nine rectories[1] in contrast to the £74 received from seven rectories and a chapel by the monastery of Launde.[2]

Taken over a period of years even an annual profit of £5 would add up to a sufficiently large sum to enable a house to meet its parochial responsibilities. Yet it is striking that it is not always the poorest houses which proved to be the worst rectors. There were no complaints against the prior and convent of Elsham, whose poverty was such as to exempt them from the payment of a tenth in 1491.[3] Conversely the prior and convent of Dunstable, who were not exempt and received a sizeable revenue from their churches, had one of the worst records of any proprietor. The chancel or church roof needed repair in their churches at Flitwick, Pulloxhill, Harlington, Westoning and Ridgmont.[4] The priory of Chicksand was too poor to do much for their churches; they were completely exempt from payment of the subsidy of one tenth in 1491[5] and were unable to repair their chancels at Haynes and Keysoe.[6] In contrast the poverty of the priory of Markyate proved no obstacle to its repair of all the churches for which it was responsible.[7] But the wealthy houses of St Alban's, Ashridge, Leicester, and the pervasive knights of St John of Jerusalem did little or nothing in this period to help their churches. Ashridge neglected the chancels of two of their churches.[8] Six churches made complaints against the abbot of St Alban's;[9] at least five complaints were made against the knights of St John.[10] The abbot and convent of Leicester had neglected the chancel at Fleckney, Enderby and Thorp Arnold, and at Fleckney the curate's house needed repairs for which the abbey was responsible.[11] The curate at Fleckney was brought before the bishop for his improper clerical dress, his long hair and his disobedience to his vicar;[12] but it

[1] Ibid. p. 117.   [2] Ibid. p. 163.
[3] Subsid. 1, 4; cf. L.R.S. 33, p. 91.   [4] L.R.S. 33, pp. 107, 108³, 109.
[5] Subsid. 1, 4.   [6] L.R.S. 33, pp. 109, 115.
[7] Subsid. 1, 4; cf. L.R.S. 33, pp. 102–4.
[8] Viz. Hemel Hempstead and Chesterton, L.R.S. 33, pp. 101, 123.
[9] L.R.S. 33, pp. 43, 52, 101, 102, 106.
[10] Ibid. pp. 51, 60, 96, 111, 113.   [11] Ibid. pp. 13, 16, 24.   [12] Cj. 2, fo. 7.

would take a strong man indeed to fulfil all his obligations when some of the mightiest religious houses in the land were flagrantly ignoring them, in his very parish, and to his personal inconvenience.

The demoralizing effects of the neglect of church property which was a characteristic of so many parishes within the diocese were balanced by the opposite effect in other parishes. Where Fleckney exhibited signs of neglect and decay, Louth was a hive of activity. After the enormous expense of building the spire of the church in the beginning of the sixteenth century, the parish settled down to a regular contribution to its maintenance and to that of the church as a whole. The bells received constant attention as did the organ. 26s. 8d. was paid to a mason for repairing the church walls and contributions were made to the mending of the church porch. The windows received the periodic attention of a glazier, and there were regular payments for the cleaning of the church, the washing of the linen and the cleaning of the candlesticks.[1] These expenses were annual, and careful accounts were kept of them. Such accounts have not survived from other churches, and it is hard to know how many other parishes were as zealous in their rebuilding and maintenance schemes as Louth. But the large number of cases of neglect, in particular of chancels, suggest that Louth was unusual.

The pictures of neglect and decay which confronted some incumbents would not have been so convincing or so serious had it not been for a similar decline in the personal fortunes of the incumbent himself. A leaking roof or a crumbling chancel were but the outward symbols of an economic crisis which many parish priests were in no position to withstand. The treasurer of Lincoln Cathedral wrote to one of his colleagues, 'ye know right well our liflode mendes not but decayes every day more and

---

[1] *The First Churchwardens' Book of Louth*, ed. R. C. Dudding (Oxford, 1941), pp. 188 ff.; these accounts do not vary very greatly from year to year; the examples are from the accounts for 1517–18. For a discussion of church-building and the fate of some other churches, see A. H. Thompson, *The English Clergy*, pp. 128 ff. Where churches were restored or rebuilt in the fifteenth century, it is often hard to be sure of the exact date of the work unless accounts survive, for example, see *idem*, *L.R.S.* 14, p. xxiv.

more.'[1] He was expressing the fate of many incumbents in the two decades before the break with Rome.

The financial pressures to which the clergy were subject were increasing markedly by the second decade of the sixteenth century. There are no reasons for supposing that the outlay of a sixteenth-century incumbent on such basic commodities as wheat or its equivalent, meat, fish, butter, cheese, drink, fuel and textiles varied very much from that of William Savernak of Bridport in Dorset, whose account book survives. The need for these basic household requirements varied very little between the centuries,[2] and only complete self-sufficiency or exceptional good fortune would protect an incumbent from a rise in the price of these commodities. Within the diocese, there were several different agricultural regions which produced varying harvests and a surplus or dearth of different goods in any particular year. Lincolnshire and Leicestershire were nearer to the coal-producing areas of the north and in consequence likely to obtain fuel at a cheaper price than that which obtained in other parts of the diocese.[3] Within Lincolnshire itself there were distinct regions, and, while there were great similarities in the cultivation of each, one region reared sheep for mutton and another for wool.[4] Prices therefore varied considerably between regions, and, from time to time, prices in certain areas would have differed from the national average. But the regional differences of outlay over a period of years tended to balance each other, and the average national price-level can be taken as a rough guide to the expenses of a parish priest.[5] Between 1300 and 1500 there were short-term rises in prices but the general

---

[1] A. 3. 2, fo. 145 v, see below, p. 168.

[2] E. H. Phelps Brown and S. V. Hopkins, 'Seven Centuries of the Prices of Consumables, compared with Builders' Wage-Rates', *Essays in Economic History*, ed. E. M. Carus-Wilson (London, 1962), vol II, 180.

[3] W. G. Hoskins, *Essays in Leicestershire History* (Liverpool, 1950), p. 2; even within Leicestershire there were variations in fuel supply, and there would tend to be a greater shortage in the east.

[4] J. Thirsk, *English Peasant Farming* (London, 1957), pp. 6–108.

[5] The accounts from which the average was calculated tend to come from areas outside the diocese or from the accounts of Eton College or Oxford Colleges. Lincolnshire would probably have exhibited a marked difference from either area.

trend is towards stability. From 1500 to 1510 there was a tendency for prices to increase, though they fell back to the pre-1500 level in 1509, 1510 and were to fall back again in 1511. After 1511, however, prices steadily rose so that in 1520 they were nearly 50% higher than they had been in 1495 when Bishop Smith was translated to the see of Lincoln.[1] This rise in prices would greatly affect all incumbents in the diocese who were on fixed incomes and who could not provide for their normal household requirements by farming their glebe land.

Prices were not the only pressure to which the clergy were being subjected. Direct taxation became increasingly stringent at exactly the time at which prices were rising so markedly. A tenth was granted from the clergy in the convocation of 1495[2] and a further £40,000 was granted in 1497, of which the king pardoned £10,000 of the second instalment of £20,000 due in November;[3] grants of £12,500 were made in 1502 for the crusade;[4] four tenths were granted in 1512[5] and a further two tenths in 1514–15.[6] Within these grants charitable subsidies to the archbishop of Canterbury were included. These 'charitable subsidies', so called because they were, theoretically, gifts of grace, and not formal taxes requiring consent, extended the range of taxation from the actual benefice itself to all the individuals receiving a stipend within it. In 1489, chaplains earning between £5 and 10 marks were liable to pay 6s. 8d., those earning between 10 marks and £10 were liable for 13s. 4d., while those with over £10 were liable for £1.[7] In 1496, the charitable subsidy was extended to those with incomes of £2; they were liable to pay 3s. 4d. and those earning

[1] Phelps Brown and Hopkins, op. cit. pp. 184, 194. The Agrarian History of England and Wales, IV, ed. J. Thirsk (Cambridge, 1967), 847.
[2] Calendar of Fine Rolls, Henry VII, p. 555.
[3] Register 24, fo. 270.
[4] A. F. Pollard, The Reign of Henry VII from Contemporary Sources (London, 1913), III, 181; W. E. Lunt, Financial Relations of the Papacy with England 1327–1534 (Cambridge, Mass., 1962), p. 158.
[5] F. C. Dietz, English Public Finance 1485–1641 (Cass reprint 1964), p. 93 n.
[6] Guildhall Library, Register Fitzjames, fo. 119.
[7] F. R. H. du Boulay, 'Charitable Subsidies Granted to the Archbishop of Canterbury 1300–1489', B.I.H.R. XXIII, 157–9.

between 4 marks and 10 marks were liable for 6s. 8d.; the remaining assessments were the same as they had been in 1489.[1] As a result of the extension in the range of the subsidy, the lower clergy were subject to an increase in taxation at just the time when an increase in prices was about to be felt. How able were they to withstand this pressure?

If the stipends of all priests in charge of parishes, or dependent chapels are averaged, it would appear that their average was £10. 8s. 11½d.[2] But the average conceals wide variations. It includes men like the archdeacon of Oxford, who was assessed for the 1526 subsidy on an income of £131. 7s. 4d.[3] Further, all attempts at reckoning an average income are apt to overlook the difference between a fixed income and a variable one.[4] There was a great deal of difference between a vicar who had no glebe and no fees, and a rector who had both; the vicar would immediately feel a rise in prices; the rector might be protected from it. The clergy were not all likely to suffer equally from the increasing pressures of the early sixteenth century. Rectors were in a much more favourable position than most vicars and curates.

If the incomes of incumbents are distributed it is also clear that many rectors were earning more than vicars (table on p. 140).

The average gross rectorial stipend in 1526 was £12. 13s. 8½d.

[1] Register 24, fo. 270.
[2] Salter, *passim*; a total of 1,958 incomes were averaged. I am grateful to the Cambridge Department of Applied Economics for the use of their calculating machines for all the statistics which follow.
[3] Salter, pp. 277, 278.
[4] See F. W. Brooks, 'The Social Position of the Parson in the Sixteenth Century', *Journal of the Archaeological Association*, 3rd Series, x (1945–7), for a somewhat unsatisfactory attempt to assess the real value of a parson's stipend in comparison with that of an agricultural labourer. Not only does Mr Brooks overlook the importance of glebe, his statistics are also based mainly on the *Valor* and he is, therefore, calculating from the gross value of a benefice and not on the basis of the actual amount which any individual beneficed within it might receive. It is also hard to see how he has assessed the income of a labourer; his calculations are based on a labourer's daily wages, yet he has not produced any evidence to show how many days' work in a year a labourer did in fact do. It is also difficult to place much weight on the inventories of the goods of parish priests as a means of assessing their income from any particular parish; the deceased may have been a pluralist, and have made his money through a combination of a number of livings.

Distribution of income table

Gross income[1]			Net income[1]	
Rectors	Vicars		Rectors	Vicars
41	44	Up to £4. 19s. 11d.	20	14
279	336	£5–£9. 19s. 11d.	63	26
297	119	£10–£14. 19s. 11d.	46	17
87	25	£15–£19. 19s. 11d.	24	5
129	21	Over £20	21	4

and the average net rectorial stipend was £9. 9s. 6¾d.[2] Though a rector's expenses were considerable, since he was responsible for all the visitation fees from the benefice, and had to keep his own rectory and the chancel of the church in a state of repair, he also received all the fees for the conducting of services, for mortuary and for saying the bead roll and for conducting odd requiems when asked. More important, he was protected to some extent from the price rise by his own self-sufficiency. Rectories had land, and the rector farmed it himself or let it to one of his parishioners to farm for him. In any event, he would be able to obtain his food either through his own labour or that of a servant. Matthew Knightley, presented to Cossington in 1508, grew corn and hay quite apart from rearing poultry, geese, pigs, sheep and cows.[3] The rector of Harston grew rye, barley, corn, oats and hay as well as possessing pigs, heifers and cows on a modest scale.[4] John Greves, rector of Waddington, whose living was valued at £18 in 1526,[5] had sheep, cows and barley.[6] In addition the rector was often

[1] These figures are based on Salter, *passim*; some incumbents were assessed on their net income, and some on their gross income, and they have been kept apart accordingly. In nearly 100 parishes, the incumbent was either not assessed, or his assessment was not given, or there is some doubt about his status.

[2] Salter, *passim*; these figures are calculated from rectorial incomes and expenses in certain selected deaneries, viz. those of Aston, Gartree, Manlake, Lawres, Goscote, Peterborough, Baldock, St Ives, Dunstable, Mursley, Higham Ferrers.

[3] Hoskins, *Essays in Leicestershire History*, pp. 9–10; Register 23, fo. 261.

[4] Hoskins, *op. cit.* p. 3.   [5] Salter, p. 74.

[6] *L.R.S.* 5, p. 162.

allowed to trim the trees in the churchyard, a useful source of fuel. The rector received all tithe; this meant that his prosperity kept in step with that of the area in which he lived. When the local farmers were doing well then their tithe would increase accordingly. If a rector managed to produce a surplus of food-stuffs on the glebe, he might even be doing better as a result of rising prices than he had before their increase. In times of bad harvest, the rector felt the pinch in much the same way as his parishioners: his own crops failed and the tithe due on those of his parishioners was equally scant. But repeated bad harvests were rare in this period, and it was unusual for there to be a run of four bad ones as there were between 1500 and 1504.[1] But, if rectors experienced difficulties at these times, the lot of the vicar and the curate was worse.

The gross average stipend of a vicar in 1526 was £9. 9s. 1¾d., while his net stipend was usually £6. 13s. 1½d.[2] Sometimes this stipend was a flat payment, and the vicar concerned could boast no other assets besides his vicarage and perhaps a small garden. The exact arrangements depended on the form of agreement made by the appropriator at the time the vicarage was ordained. Some of the vicarages ordained in the thirteenth century derived their income from lesser tithe. The vicar of Keddington in Lincolnshire received all the lesser tithe except tithes of wood; the same arrangement obtained at Haynes, while at Middle Rasen the vicar received all the lesser tithe except that due on sheep and wool.[3] Sometimes the vicar was expected to subsist on the dues and voluntary offerings paid to the actual servitor of an altar, but there was a tendency to add to it the smaller tithe.[4] Some of the vicarages ordained in the thirteenth century had some land. The vicar of North Aston had six acres, but the vicars of Husborne Crawley and Pattishall had a field and three virgates respectively.[5]

[1] W. G. Hoskins, 'Harvest Fluctuations and English Economic History, 1480–1619', *The Agricultural History Review*, XII (1964), 28–46.

[2] Salter, *passim*.

[3] *Liber Antiquus of Hugh of Wells*, ed. A. Gibbons (Lincoln, 1888), pp. 20, 60, 64.

[4] Hartridge, *Vicarages in the Middle Ages*, 36–7.

[5] Gibbons, *op. cit.* pp. 3, 20, 35.

Appropriators ordaining vicarages in the late fifteenth and early sixteenth century generally had to be more generous. The vicar of Great Marlow, appropriated by Tewkesbury Abbey in 1494, was to receive 20 marks per annum payable at four times of the year, and in addition to his house was to have a small garden and half an acre of land.[1] The vicar of Taynton received 12 marks and had a garden[2] and the vicar of Swineshead received 20 marks in addition to his house, garden and orchard; he was expected to provide for a curate at his own expense.[3] The subsidy recorded his living as being worth exactly 20 marks.[4] On occasions, the vicar received all the fees and the Easter offering, but this was not invariably the case: a marginal note to the agreement concerning the appropriation of Biddenham by Denney Abbey records that the vicar might have only the emoluments arising from the commemoration of the departed 'commonly called the bead roll', and from espousals and masses; he could also have the grass growing in the churchyard and the produce of the trees there, though the trees themselves belonged to the proprietors.[5] Probably the vicar of North Aston was one of few able to provide for all his household needs from his land; none of the vicars with only a house and a garden had a chance of doing so. Yet the vicar of Swineshead appeared better off than the vicar of North Aston and he was assessed at a higher rate for the subsidy.[6] But in fact he was likely to be badly hit by the increasing stringency of taxation and by the price rise, in a way his colleague was not. Taxation assessments would take some time to adjust to the increase in the value of land and the falling purchasing power of money. A vicar's stipend was assessed on the face value of his monetary income; that of the rector or landed vicar on the rentable value of his land and the face value of his monetary income of tithe and fees. But rents did not rise as steeply as prices, or as quickly, with the result that the rector was unlikely to be as hard hit by taxation as the vicar with no land. By 1520 certain vicars in the diocese were

[1] Religious Houses, 7a.
[2] Register 24, fo. 132v.   [3] Ibid. fo. 128v.
[4] Salter, p. 65.   [5] Religious Houses, 7d.
[6] Salter, p. 267; the vicar of Aston was reckoned as having a gross stipend of £8.

likely to be approaching extreme poverty. Others relied on private sources of income to weather the storm. John Beke, vicar of Aby, had a certain amount of land in his own right;[1] the vicar of Whitchurch, who appears to have died a wealthy man since his goods were valued at £11. 0s. 4½d.,[2] in fact held this vicarage in plurality and resided (and no doubt made his money) at Abingdon.[3] The vicar of Chicheley had lands in Newbury, and probably relied on them for the bulk of his income.[4] There may have been cases where the vicar managed to obtain the farm of the rector's land or to acquire other land of his own. The vicar of South Elkington had managed to acquire two temporal farms,[5] and there was good sense in the vicar of Leake who teamed up with a parishioner to hold the farmer of the rectory in custody, presumably in order to lay a hand on the profits of the farm.[6] Cases of hardship would normally have been heard in the consistory court, for which there are no records; some were brought to the bishop's attention in his audience court. The vicar of Scalford, for example, told the bishop that he had received nothing from the fruits of his vicarage; they had been wrongly confiscated owing to the decay of the chancel which it was the duty of the proprietors to repair.[7] The vicar of Catesby complained that he had an inadequate stipend. He pointed out that the living had originally been a rich one, bringing in enough tithe for both the rectors and the vicar, but that its agricultural wealth had disappeared. The bishop ordered that the vicar and his successors were to receive £8 per annum, the money from mortuary and the other devotions, as well as the candles from the Candlemas celebrations. A vicarage was to be built with a hall and several rooms including a kitchen, and there had to be adequate stabling and a garden provided. The vicar had to keep the vicarage in a good state of repair and to provide candles and bread for the church.[8] The improvement of the vicar's stipend was the mini-

[1] L.R.S. 5, p. 162.
[2] Aylesbury Record Office, D/A/We. 1, fos. 14v–16 (number 36).
[3] L.R.S. 33, p. 45.
[4] Aylesbury Record Office, D/A/We. 1, fo. 167 (number 128).
[5] L.R.S. 33, p. 73.   [6] Ibid. p. 72.
[7] Ibid. p. 34.   [8] Register 25, fo. 97v.

mum which the rectors, the prioress and convent of Catesby, could do. They were reported for the depopulation of the village and the eviction of some sixty of its inhabitants in 1517 and 1518;[1] no other case is recorded of a vicar claiming that he had been impoverished by the depopulation of his parish, and the consequent loss of tithe, but, since the diocese included many of the counties worst hit by depopulation, his case was certainly not unique.[2] The reason for the impoverishment of the vicarage of Peterborough was not recorded. In 1518 the vicar complained that his stipend was inadequate, and a new agreement was reached with the appropriators, the abbot and convent of Peterborough, by which the vicar should receive £13. 6s. 8d. from them instead of tithe, and should receive all the offerings of the faithful for bead roll and all the money from exequies and burials. He was also to have his food at the abbot's table and his servant was to eat with the servants of the house.[3] The generosity of the provision suggests an awareness of the vicar's needs, either on the part of the house, or on the part of the bishop. But, if generosity went too far, the appropriated church would cease to be of value to the appropriator; at Claxby, for instance, it was said that the rectory was valued at nothing to the abbot and convent of Crowland since all the tithe and profits of the rectory had had to go to the vicar in augmentation of his vicarage.[4] It lay with the religious houses to improve the lot of the vicar, but few of them had the will to do so. The laity shared their greed; after the dissolution of the monasteries, the plight of the vicar remained much as it had been before, and the opportunity of putting stipends on a permanently sound footing was lost.[5]

If the vicar was apt to be poor, the curate was poorer still. His income was, on average, a mere £5. 3s. 2d., and very few curates received any more than this.[6] Little evidence survives of their living conditions, but, in bigger churches, they probably lived together with someone to look after them. This was the arrange-

[1] Beresford, *The Lost Villages of England*, p. 116.
[2] *Ibid.* pp. 337 ff.
[3] Register 25, fo. 84; for an agreement for Winchendon, see fo. 83 v.
[4] *Valor Ecclesiasticus*, IV, 85.
[5] See Hill, *Economic Problems of the Church*, pp. 77 ff.   [6] Salter, *passim*.

ment envisaged for the chantry priests of Marston Trussell who were causing the bishop so much trouble.[1] If the curate had a house of his own it might be sparsely furnished. The curate at Leckhampstead who acted as deputy for the rector[2] had few possessions. His stipend was valued at £6;[3] when he died intestate in 1521, he left property valued at £2. 17s. 9d. Little of it was much use. The furnishings were an old sheet and bed valued at 7d. together, and another pair of sheets and a bed cover valued at 1s. 4d. and 1s. 8d. respectively. His only furniture, apart from this, was a 'broken coffer' valued at 6d. His most valuable possession was his best gown valued at 18s., and three mares valued together at £1. He clearly was not a man of wealth, and if he had a house to himself he was very short of cooking utensils.[4] Probably he lived in the rector's house in his absence, and managed to make a little on farming the glebe for him. A few others may have been more fortunate in that they had land of their own. A chantry priest at Algarkirk had three acres of land at Pinchbeck,[5] and others may have inherited just enough to see them through hard times. But for the curate, as for some of the vicars, the increasing stringency of clerical taxation and the growing menace of inflation must have stretched their resources to the uttermost.

The prospect might be grim indeed if, in addition to these problems, a further one was added. A few parishes had to bear an additional burden in this period: they had to finance a previous incumbent with a pension. Between 1495 and 1514, 178 pensions were granted from livings in the diocese; between 1514 and 1520/1, a further seventy-two were sanctioned.[6] All pensions had to have the bishop's consent, and some were clearly justified. Edmund Lichfield, rector of Tring, was an old man; he resigned the living to a younger man on the condition that a pension be assigned to him. He was granted a pension of £40[7] from the living, which was valued at £69 gross.[8] But, although it is impossible to estimate how many pensions were granted for similar reasons, it is clear

---

[1] Cj. 3, fo. 24v; see above, p. 145.
[2] *L.R.S.* 33, p. 46.   [3] Salter, p. 241.
[4] Aylesbury Record Office, D/A/We. 1, fo. 13v.
[5] *L.R.S.* 5, p. 41.   [6] Registers 23 and 25, *passim.*
[7] Register 24, fo. 167v.   [8] Salter, p. 172.

that for some they were becoming just another means of re-
warding royal servants. Houghton Conquest, for instance, was
valued at £13. 13s. 4d. gross.¹ In 1509 the bishop ordered it to
pay Magister John Underhill a pension of £10 until he received a
living valued at £100.² In the following year, the pension was
reduced to £4 but the reason for it was clear enough.³ Underhill
was a graduate who held many livings and canonries; his claim
to a pension was that he was a promising young man who was
likely to rise high in the royal service. He became chaplain to the
king in 1526.⁴ William Knight, another royal servant and dip-
lomat,⁵ received a pension of £4 from the living of Ramsey,⁶ which
was valued at £7.⁷ High diocesan officials also took their share of
the spoil. John Cutler was a resident canon and special commissary
in the diocese;⁸ he received a pension of £16 from Surfleet,⁹ which
was valued at £19.¹⁰ Augustine Church, a suffragan in the diocese,¹¹
was granted a pension of £8 for the living of Maulden,¹² valued at
£10,¹³ until such time as he might receive another benefice valued
at 20 marks. In sanctioning these pensions, the bishop was caught
in the same cross-currents which made action on non-residence
so difficult. Diocesan servants and scholars who were eventually
to hold office in church or state might genuinely need the money
from pluralism, or from pensions, to finance their work. If this
loophole were allowed, and a pension could be given to someone
other than the old and the sick, the way was open to abuse. The
church could not offend the crown and the powerful men at
court or in the shire; she was therefore unable to gainsay their
protégés when they came to ask for benefices or pensions. If the
church was to avoid the rigours of *praemunire*, if she was to avoid
the risk of being unmercifully taxed, and if she was to avoid the
loss of her cherished privilege of benefit of clergy, then she must
avoid alienating those who held positions of power in the state,

¹ Salter, p. 206.
³ *Ibid*. fo. 407.
⁵ *D.N.B.*
⁷ Salter, p. 191.
⁹ Register 23, fo. 131.
¹¹ Register 24, *passim*.
¹³ Salter, p. 200.

² Register 23, fo. 405 v.
⁴ Emden, *Cambridge*, p. 604.
⁶ Register 23, fo. 380.
⁸ Register 23, fo. 35.
¹⁰ Salter, p. 64.
¹² Register 23, fo. 407 v.

be they laymen or ecclesiastics. The church was at the mercy of the state.

The immediate effect of sanctioning a pension was to render the rector or vicar from whose living it had been granted a great deal poorer than he would otherwise have been. Normally a pension was of one third the total gross value of the stipend. Under Bishop Smith, there were only eighteen exceptions to this, mostly exceptions made for royal servants and diocesan officials. Fortunately most of those who had a claim to a pension were in profitable livings in any case, and under one third of the incumbents were left with a living worth less than £6 gross.

All curates and vicars who had no land, and many of those whose livings were subject to a pension, were liable to feel the effects of rising prices in the second decade of the sixteenth century. Rectors found the purchasing power of their stipends falling, though often protected from the need to purchase foodstuffs by owning land. For many of the clergy it was absolutely necessary to wring as much tithe as possible from their parishes, and there could be no question at all of allowing anyone to escape the payment of fees.

Disputes over tithes and fees figure prominently in the diocesan records. There are tithe disputes between patrons, tithe disputes between parishioners and incumbents, and tithe disputes between vicars and patrons. In the commissary's court of the archdeaconry of Buckinghamshire alone, 8% of the cases brought concerned fees or ecclesiastical dues of some kind.[1] The remaining cases were nearly all concerned with the morality of the laity. Sometimes apparently paltry sums appear to be involved. The abbot of Gloucester and Brasenose Hall, Oxford, came before the bishop's court of audience in 1518 over a dispute about the tithe of Chipping Norton. It was agreed that the Hall had a right to all tithe but that they should pay the abbot 10s. annually.[2] The rectors of Aldwincle St Peter and Aldwincle All Saints had a long-drawn-out argument. Certain land lying between their two

---

[1] Aylesbury Record Office, D/A/V. 1, fos. 1v–21v. This constitutes the largest group of cases with the exception of immorality cases.
[2] Register 25, fo. 95v.

parishes was in dispute, and in 1515 their case was deferred until either side could bring sufficient evidence to prove his right.[1] In 1528 they came before the bishop again and agreed to submit to arbitration.[2] On other occasions it was the vicar who was contesting the case. John Clement, the vicar of Little Dalby, whose vicarage was assessed at a paltry £8,[3] sued the farmer of the rectory in 1518 for tithe on the grain from sixty acres of glebe land which the rector was no doubt farming for a good profit.[4] The vicar of Mumby contested with the bishop his right to the tithe from sheep and pelts due from those owning more than five sheep. The vicar proved his case that tithe was only due to the bishop from those owning more than *ten* sheep.[5] As tithe payers, it was the parishioners who were most frequently contesting their claims to tithe; Thomas Whichcote refused to pay tithe to the prior of Nocton for the wood he had cut down at Flaxmoor in the parish of Dunston: he was ordered to pay within two weeks.[6] Richard Samwell owed wool tithe to the prior of Daventry to the value of £6. 10s., and various parishioners at Legbourne were bound to pay the prior and convent for the trees they had cut down in the parish.[7] There was a complicated dispute at Sleaford. The vicar of Sleaford had, according to some, refused to provide the stipend for a chaplain to celebrate in the hamlet of Holdingham. To add insult to injury, he had also demanded from the inhabitants of the hamlet, tithe on cows at a rate to which they were not accustomed. The inhabitants claimed that the usual rate was 3d. for a milk cow with calf, and 1½d. for a 'bare Cowe'. The vicar agreed only to take tithe at this rate and to provide the required chaplain.[8] At Tilbrook the villagers successfully asserted that they were not bound to pay tithe on apples or any other fruits, especially those dug with the spade; they claimed that they had provided the rector with a house instead of the tithe.[9] Tithe on brushwood was unpaid by one parishioner at Dowsby; the rector was not resident and the rectory was in ruins;[10] one wonders

---

[1] Cj. 2, fo. 9.
[2] Cj. 4, fo. 30v.
[3] Salter, p. 79.
[4] *L.R.S.* 33, p. 154.
[5] Cj. 4, fo. 23v.
[6] Cj. 2, fo. 38v.
[7] *Ibid.* fos. 52v, 70.
[8] *Ibid.* fo. 44.
[9] Cj. 3, fo. 30v.
[10] *L.R.S.* 33, p. 56.

whether the witholding of the payment was a protest against the rector or a cause of the state of his rectory.

Fees were another source of irritation. At Haseley a parishioner owed mortuary for the burial of her husband;[1] at Pyrton there was a similar debt,[2] and great bitterness was created at Ridlington when the rector refused to allow the curate to hear confessions or communicate his parishioners unless they paid oblations at Easter at the rate of 2d. for each unmarried communicant. The villagers claimed that the usual rate was 1d. The rector asserted that he had asked the previous incumbent what the rate was and had been told that it was the same at Ridlington as elsewhere; the bishop did not accept the rector's interpretation of this ambiguous directive, and ordered that oblations be paid at the rate of 1d. for the unmarried.[3] Probate and mortuary fees were the most frequent bone of contention. Most of the cases before the commissary for Buckinghamshire were the result of a failure to pay mortuary. Mortuary rather than probate fees appear to have provided a legitimate cause for resentment.

Accounts were kept, at least during vacancies in archdeaconries, for mortuaries and there is some evidence of the fees charged for the probate of wills. A Lincoln archdeaconry account book survives for the vacancy in the archdeanery caused by the death of Thomas Hutton, the previous incumbent.[4] The book gives a list of probate charges; unfortunately few inventories survive for the exact period in question (1505–6), and none is in good enough condition for the total value of the deceased's goods to be legible.[5] There are therefore no criteria for assessing whether fees are excessive or not, except that provided at a later date by legislation. In 1529 it was enacted that those with goods or debts valued at £5 or less should pay no probate fee at all, but should pay a small fee to the scribe for making a record of the probate grant itself. Goods and debts valued at between £5 and £40 were liable to a fine of 3s. 6d., and those exceeding £40 were liable for 5s.[6] The com-

---

[1] *Ibid.* p. 138.　　　[2] *Ibid.* p. 121.　　　[3] Cj. 3, fo. 45.

[4] Rev/L/1, 3.　　　[5] Inventories, Boxes 2 and 3.

[6] J. R. Tanner, *Tudor Constitutional Documents 1485–1603* (Cambridge, 1930), p. 13.

parison of this scale with the actual fees charged is illuminating. Nine out of nineteen of those granted probate by the commissary for Buckinghamshire paid no fee at all in 1522;[1] those not charged are obviously not included in the 1505–6 account book, but the records of probate of the dean and chapter of Lincoln indicate that a number of wills were exempt *in forma pauperis*.[2] The idea of exemption was therefore not a new one; the novelty could only lie in the levels at which exemption was granted. But, higher up the scale, things were different. Of the 412 probate charges[3] noted in the 1505–6 account book, 118 were of payments of 5s. or more, and 55 were of over 10s., double the maximum envisaged by the later legislation. The remaining charges (over 50%) were of less than 5s. Of those charged over 10s., Edward Browne paid as much as £4, but his will was that of a rich man;[4] the same could be said for Simon Leverett, who paid £10.[5] It looks very much as though the resentment against probate fees could really only have come from the rich and the moderately wealthy; the poor were not subjected to them. The objection was one of scale and not of principle.

It was quite different with mortuary and the other fees for which the executors might be charged. Mortuary was due to the church in which the deceased, while alive, received the sacrament. It could only be pardoned when the deceased had so little property that, by giving one of his beasts to the church and another to his lord, he would leave his wife and family with nothing.[6] And mortuary could be expensive. No mortuary is recorded at less than 6s. and that of the rector of Welby was assessed at as much as 24s. when his probate fee had been 13s. 4d.[7] The prior of North Witham paid a mortuary of 13s. 4d. and a probate fee of £1.[8] The vicar of Kirkby Green paid a mortuary of 6s. and a probate fee of 9s.[9] Mortuary was on a flat rate; the variations in the amount

[1] Aylesbury Record Office, D/A/C. 1, fo. 2v.
[2] A. 3, 2, 3, 4, *passim.*   [3] Rev/L/1, 3, *passim.*
[4] Rev/L/1, 3, fo. 14v; cf. *L.R.S.* 5, pp. 24 ff.
[5] *Ibid.* fo. 16v; cf. *L.R.S.* 5, p. 26.
[6] Lyndwood, *Provinciale*, Lib. I, tit. 3, gloss on *de mansuetudine.*
[7] Rev/L/1, 3, fos. 17, 19.   [8] *Ibid.*
[9] *Ibid.* fos. 14v, 19.

of recorded payment were the result of variations in the value of the deceased's best animal or item of clothing with which mortuary was paid. The scribe's fee was also a flat payment. The estate of the curate of Leckhampstead, whose goods totalled 57s. 9d. in value, was liable to a scribe's fee of 2s. 4d., as were the estates of the wealthy.[1] These fees pressed hard on 'the meaner sort', especially when the poverty of the incumbent or recipient of the fee made it likely that he would ask for his pound of flesh.

Only one episcopal account book survives which indicates the scale of other fees, but it is corroborated by the churchwardens' accounts for Louth. The marriage of Katherine Ward cost 1s. 2d. in 1500, and purification cost Emma Bocher 1d. and Johanna Tybby 1½d.[2] Oblations at a funeral brought in between 9d. and 1s. Most burials in church cost 6s. 8d. and one in Louth porch cost 3s. 4d. with the tolling of the bells costing a further 1s. The Easter offering at Louth totalled about 3s. *per annum*, and the average Sunday collection was about the same.[3] But, if these fees and dues did not actually occasion any of the disputes of which we have a record, they played their part in creating such bitterness as existed between priest and people. They were the cause of innumerable debts which were recorded at the bishop's visitation, and which it was hard to settle without recourse to the ecclesiastical courts. Debts were owed at Cold Brayfield, at Dowsby, at Fringford, and Garsington;[4] at Heyford Warren, Richard Butcher owed 12s., Richard Markhill another 7s. and a Paul Markhill a further 6s. 8d.; the rector, possibly as a retaliatory measure, had in his turn refused to provide a measure of ale and a baptismal robe for his parishioners.[5] There may be a connexion between the withholding of mortuary at Pyrton and the refusal of the curate there to bury a body on Maundy Thursday.[6]

An *impasse* of this kind was an ingredient of the growing anti-

[1] Aylesbury Record Office, D/A/We. 1, fo. 14.
[2] Bishop's Accounts, Misc., 7, fos. 17–18.
[3] *The First Churchwardens' Accounts of Louth*, ed. Dudding, p. 189.
[4] L.R.S. 33, pp. 53, 56, 121, 137.
[5] *Ibid.* p. 124.
[6] *Ibid.* p. 121.

clerical feeling which was a marked characteristic of London in the sixteenth century. The outbursts of anticlericalism were not as dramatic in the Lincoln diocese as they were in the city.[1] In Lincoln a few parishioners attacked priests[2] and some called them abusive names. Johanna Goodriche had defamed Alice Goodriche by calling her a 'prestes hoore'.[3] The rector of Ridlington, whose action over fees had caused such an outburst, had hit an apparitor over the head when called a 'bawdy priest' by him.[4] But, though there were ample ingredients to feed it, anticlericalism was a smouldering rather than a blazing fire. The resentment was apparent in some parishes but in others it lay dormant until such time as Parliament and a ruthless king chose to fan it. The bitterness caused by the ecclesiastical courts, by non-residence, concubinage, the neglect of churches and the taking of fees was not obvious. The powerful received some benefit from an unreformed church and the parishioner was often impotent to reform it even if he had a mind to do so. Yet the time would come when the impotence would be changed into a force strong enough to sweep away the pope, the monasteries and the mass, but not, ironically enough, many of the real causes of local grievance.[5] Until that time came, the effect of the combination of devotion and corruption which was the lot of many parishes remained largely hidden.

There is no reason to suppose that there was no genuine devotion mingled with the resentment and bewilderment at the strange ways of a God who could allow his churches to fall down and his priests to live in sin but who, through his ministers, visited his wrath on a widow refusing to pay mortuary. The devotion of the parish and the quality of the faith of the individual parish priest are both by their very nature hidden. Faith at any time is largely

[1] See especially A. Ogle, *The Tragedy of the Lollards Tower; the case of Richard Hunne with its Aftermath in the Reformation Parliament 1529–32* (Oxford, 1949).
[2] See, for example, Cj. 2, fos. 10v, 36v, 37v, 68.
[3] Cj. 4, fo. 22v.   [4] *Ibid.* fo. 20v.
[5] Non-residence, the neglect of the fabric and the abuses of the ecclesiastical courts were to persist throughout the century: see Hill, *Economic Problems of the Church*, and F. D. Price, 'The Abuses of Excommunication and the Decline of Ecclesiastical Discipline under Queen Elizabeth', *English Historical Review*, 57 (1942), 106 ff.

an unknown quantity unless forced into the open by a crisis. For many the crisis was acutely personal, and only the few had to give an account of their beliefs before the bishop or the king, usually because they were suspected of heresy. The very fact that they were suspected makes them exceptional, and yet it is only the faith of these few that we know anything about. No priest in this period was brought before the bishop accused of heresy but several laymen were suspected. The evidence about heresy in the diocese in this period is fragmentary and the depositions of the accused often reveal little of the convictions which the accused shared with his neighbours. Central to the lives of orthodox and heretic, to priests and laymen, was the mass. For the heretic this was the great cause of stumbling: Robert Scarlet of Whaplod said he had 'as lever to see the sacreng of a podyng as to see the sacreng of a masse'.[1] Another heretic found transubstantiation so vivid a concept that he asserted that there must be around the Host 'veraie white breade the thikness off A small twyne threde, for, he saith, that when A man or woman shalbe howseled the edge off the hoste may happen to hyt upon a mans' tothe, And then iff the circle off breade were not there to keep in the bloode, the blod wold peradventure fall down without his lyppys'.[2] Another confessed that he received the sacrament not 'as god but under god'.[3] The orthodox priest and his parishioner probably received the clearest expression of their belief in Mirk's sermon for Corpus Christi day: 'that is the feste of goddes owne body whiche is offird every day in the aultre to the fader in heven in remyssyon of our synnes to al that lyven in parfyte charyte and grete socour'.[4] The priest's special role is that given by Christ to all his apostles on Maundy Thursday, to exercise the power and dignity given him 'to make His own body of brede and wyne on theaulter'. Mirk went on to assert that each priest had the gift and power to 'make the sacraments to be good or evyl' by the use to which he put its grace. No doubt he shared the preoccupation of his age with the precise effects which the mass, and, more generally, intercession

[1] Vj. 5, fo. 54 v.   [2] Cj. 3, fo. 21 v.   [3] Cj. 3, fo. 33.
[4] Bodl. Library, S. Seldon d. 8, fo. 33 v; cf. the more sophisticated views of the mass quoted by Hughes, *Reformation in England*, pp. 91–2.

and the invocation of the saints could have.[1] Thomas Wattes of Grafton was accused of saying that there were no saints in heaven and that 'o' lady nor noo sacte [sic] doeth enny miracle'.[2] But devotional literature was usually explicit about the advantages which attendance at mass might bring, and the church penalized all those who stayed away from Sunday services and did not avail themselves of those advantages.[3] The convictions of priest and people met in the confessional. There a priest could most easily be found wanting, but there his influence for good or ill was at its greatest. Obviously no evidence survives about the priest's attitude to this sacrament or of the way in which he administered it. His faults and those of his parishioners remain lost for ever, and with it the convictions, the devotions and the simple piety which may have characterized some incumbents in this period. Such qualities were not examined at visitations, nor were they the material for a court case, yet they clearly provided comfort to priests like Thomas Crosby. He was poorly paid additional priest at Loughborough at the time when the curate distinguished himself by fishing instead of visiting sick parishioners and by objecting to Pricksong;[4] yet when Crosby died 'be holding the mysere and the wretchynes of this worlde' he called to mind the book of Job 'and also the wordes of thys holy man Jobe saing that men born of women ther dayes bene weray schorte in lewing'.[5] Even those who were caught up in the worst abuses of the church were still able to reflect upon the issues which faced all men and which most men found at the heart of their religion—the issues of life and death.

[1] Bodl. Library, S. Seldon, d. 8, fo. 34. See also Maynard Smith, *Pre-Reformation England*, pp. 91 ff.
[2] Cj. 3, fo. 33.
[3] Bodl. Library, S. Seldon d. 8, fo. 34.
[4] *L.R.S.* 33, p. 30.   [5] *L.R.S.* 5, p. 118.

CHAPTER V

THE COLLEGIATE CHURCHES

The majority of the secular clergy in the diocese in the early six-teenth century served a parish, in theory, if not in practice. But there was a small group of clerks whose work lay in the collegiate churches and consisted primarily of liturgical rather than pastoral duties.[1] The most important collegiate church in the diocese was the cathedral church of St Mary, Lincoln. The cathedral had fifty-eight canons, each of whom held a prebend: the distinctive fea-ture of a canonry was that its recipient was assigned a stall in the choir of the cathedral and a place in the chapter house.[2] The pre-bend was the pecuniary recompense for the canon's duties, and it brought with it the rectorship of a church and ordinary juris-diction over the prebendal parish.[3] One of the canons held the senior position as dean, and others the offices of precentor, chan-cellor, treasurer and subdean; there were also eight archdeacons, most of whom held canonries in addition to their archdeaconries.[4] Originally most of the canons were resident, but from the thir-teenth century the practice of non-residence had become so wide-spread that it was eventually legalized.[5] A few canons resided and the rest employed deputies, vicars choral, who occupied their stalls in choir. By the sixteenth century, the chief feature of this type of collegiate church was its high proportion of non-resident canons; it was rare for more than five to reside,[6] and the rest had

[1] Throughout this chapter I have taken Professor Hamilton Thompson's definition of a collegiate church as being that in which 'the college itself was the governing body' (*L.R.S.* 33, p. xc); Oxford colleges and Eton College have been omitted.

[2] Lyndwood, *Provinciale*, Lib. III, tit. 7, caps. iii, gloss on *praebendas*.

[3] *Ibid.* 'Praebenda vero est jus spirituale recipiendi certos Proventus pro meritis in Ecclesia competentes percipienti ex Divino officio cui insistit; et nascitur ex Canonia tamquam filia a matre'.

[4] Richard Rawlins did not combine a canonry and prebend with the arch-deaconry of Huntingdon.

[5] K. Edwards, *The English Secular Cathedrals in the Later Middle Ages* (Man-chester, 1949), p. 20.   [6] See below, p. 157.

little connexion with the cathedral except as a source of income.
Prebends became the best means of providing royal or episcopal
servants with an income, and, as such, their recipients were usually
those whose distinction earned them the privilege of non-residence
and the reward of a lucrative benefice.[1]

In contrast to the cathedral, there were other collegiate churches
in the diocese in which the clergy were supposed to reside and
were not, therefore, canonically able to hold further benefices.
The purpose of most of these foundations was intercession for the
souls of the founders. The Northamptonshire foundations of Cotterstock and Wappenham were of that type, as was the Leicestershire college of Noseley.[2] Five other collegiate churches were
neither exclusively chantry foundations nor exactly modelled on
the cathedral church of Lincoln; they were Fotheringhay, Higham
Ferrers, Irthlingborough, Tattershall[3] and the Newarke college,
Leicester. In these colleges the members were statutorily resident
but they were allowed to hold other benefices. The largest of
these collegiate churches was the Newarke college, which had a
dean, twelve canons and thirteen vicars; the purpose of the foundation was twofold: the canons were to intercede for their
founder, the earl of Lancaster and his kin, but they were also to
supervise a hospital for poor folk.[4] The later foundation of Tattershall was on much the same lines. The seven chantry priests celebrated for the founder, Humphrey Bourchier, Lord Cromwell,
and his family, but the college (which was not complete until
1510) also sustained thirteen alms men and women. Some of the
colleges existed uneasily beside the parish church: at Higham
Ferrers the college and its chapel were separate from the parish

[1] For a discussion of the recipients of canonries see below, pp. 157 ff.
[2] *L.R.S.* 33, p. lxxxix.
[3] Anon, *History of Fotheringhay* (Society of Antiquaries, 1786): this college
was endowed with the lands from alien priories and consisted of a master,
twelve chaplains, eight clerks and thirteen choristers. For Higham Ferrers, see
The Register of Henry Chichele, Archbishop of Canterbury 1414–1443, ed. E. F. Jacob
(Oxford, 1937), I, li. For Irthlingborough, see A. H. Thompson, 'An Early
History of the College of Irthlingborough', *A.A.S.R.P.* xxxv (1919–20). For
Tattershall, see *idem, The Manor, Castle and Church of Tattershall* (Lincoln, 1928).
[4] A. H. Thompson, *The Hospital and New College of the Annunciation of St
Mary in the Newarke, Leicester* (Leicester, 1937), pp. 1–103.

church, but a few of the college masses were said within the church.[1] Very careful instructions were drawn up to govern relations between the collegiate foundation of Noseley and the parish church: the college was not to enjoy the parochial rights of hearing confessions and giving communion.[2]

The duties of the collegiate clergy were primarily intercessory, and in that way they closely resembled the religious orders. But the duties laid upon them by their statutes were clearer in theory than in practice. The canons of the Newarke college, Leicester, like the canons of Lincoln, were ceasing to reside;[3] in consequence the canonries of both churches were apt to be regarded as sine-cures and were highly prized. The canonries of the Newarke were in the gift of the king; those of the cathedral were in the gift of the bishop. The close relationship in which the bishop stood to the king made it unlikely that a particularly lucrative prebend would be granted without some consultation, or perhaps even positive royal assent.[4] Only those whose claims to patronage were great could hope to aspire to canonries. Nearly all who did so fall into the categories from which, as we have seen, the parish clergy were most likely to be drawn. But, whereas, in considering the gift of parishes, half were found to have gone to men whose recommendations are unknown, in the case of cathedral canon-ries, the qualifications of the majority of recipients are abundantly clear.[5]

Between 1495 and 1520, the bishop collated to canonries and prebends of Lincoln a total of 125 clerks who never resided at all. Of these 105 were graduates, seventy-four of whom had been to Oxford and thirty-one of whom had been to Cambridge. Nearly three-quarters of the graduates held higher degrees; only thirteen canons had unknown qualifications for preferment and only seven

[1] *L.R.S.* 33, p. xii.
[2] A. H. Thompson, 'The Manor of Noseley with some account of the free chapel of St Mary', *Transactions of the Leicestershire Archaeological Society*, XII (1921–2), 214 ff.
[3] *L.R.S.* 37, p. 5; Robert Boone, Thomas Wigston and Gilbert Becensaw were reported as being non-resident.   [4] See above, p. 82.
[5] For a consideration of the patronage of parochial benefices, see above, pp. 74 ff.

can be shown not to have been graduates.[1] Nor were their educational attainments their only claim to preferment. Thirty-eight
were in the royal service, and twenty-four had served a bishop as
chaplain or vicar general or in an administrative capacity. Some
like Thomas Hutton combined the virtues of learning and loyal
service: he was archdeacon of Lincoln (1494–1506), and had, no
doubt, gained the post because of his services to the king as
master in chancery, and to the bishop of Lincoln as his official.[2]
Robert Sherbourne, who was archdeacon of Buckingham for a
period, had served Cardinal Morton as secretary and had spent
some time in Rome and in the royal service. He was later to
become a bishop.[3] The archdeaconry of Huntingdon usually went
to a man marked out for special preferment, often in the form of
a bishopric. It was held successively by Christopher Urswick,
William Warham, John Forster, William Atwater and Richard
Rawlyns. Urswick was prominent for his service to the Tudors,
and was appointed almoner to Henry VII in 1485, and was to be
an executor of his will: he never became a bishop but received a
large number of benefices.[4] Richard Rawlyns was also king's
almoner, and he became bishop of St Davids in 1523.[5] Warham
became archbishop of Canterbury in 1503, but he held the archdeaconry until his promotion to the archbishopric.[6] John Forster
probably obtained the archdeaconry as a reward for his services to
the university of Oxford during a time in which William Smith
was closely associated with it.[7] The prebend of Sutton with Buckingham, valued at £123 *per annum*, was easily the most profitable

---

[1] The figures are as follows: non-resident canons 125; unknown qualifications 13; known not to be graduates 7; graduates 105, of whom 31 held a
degree in theology, 16 held a degree in canon law, 17 held a degree in civil
law, 16 held degrees in both laws, 5 held degrees in medicine, 20 held degrees
in arts with no other degree. These figures are based on John Le Neve, *Fasti
Ecclesiae Anglicanae 1300–1541, I, Lincoln Diocese*, ed. H. P. F. King, *passim*.
Further details of the canons were obtained from Emden, *Oxford*, I–III, and
Emden, *Cambridge*. Those canons who held office for a few months only at the
end of the period have been omitted. For a consideration of canons who were
resident, see below, p. 162.

[2] Emden, *Oxford*, II, 991.   [3] *Ibid.* III, 1685.
[4] *Ibid.* 1935.   [5] *Ibid.* 1551.
[6] *Ibid.* 1988.   [7] *Ibid.* II, 709.

in the bishop's gift. Between 1486 and 1502, and 1504 to 1507, it went to two resident canons,[1] but, thereafter, there is some confusion about who held it. Sometimes a clerk worked his way up from a comparatively unremunerative prebend to a really good one: Thomas Swain, who served bishop Atwater as a household clerk, and was occasionally used by him as a special commissary, received from him in 1516 the prebend of Stow in Lindsey, which was valued at £9. 13s. 4d. *per annum*. From this prebend he moved rapidly to those of Haydor and Corringham, and finally, in 1518, he succeeded in obtaining that of Aylesbury, which was valued at about £46.[2] The interest which each successive bishop of Lincoln displayed in learning may account for the promotion of some scholars. William Grocyn received the prebend of South Scarle, and a headmaster of Magdalen school and author of a treatise against Luther, Thomas Brinknell, was prebendary of Marston St Lawrence. John Stanbridge, the grammarian, was prebendary of St Botolph, and Edward Powell, a theologian and author of several treatises, was given that of Carlton with Thurlby. There were a few exceptional appointments. A religious, Peter Caversham, abbot of Notley, received the prebend of Asgarby and two foreigners were appointed to prebends: Polydore Vergil, the papal collector, held the prebend of Scamblesby, and Adrian de Bardis, another Italian, held that of Thame.[3]

No other collegiate church in the diocese sustained so large a body of non-residents. For this reason, no other collegiate church had so large a number of *sublimes* and *litterati* as the cathedral. But canons were beginning not to reside at the Newarke college, Leicester.[4] The possibility of a dispensation from residence, and the fact that canons might hold other benefices tended to make the college an attractive proposition. The deanery of the Newarke, in particular, was the perquisite of royal servants or those with high family connexions. The statute ordering the election of the dean from among the existing canons was ignored and the deanery

[1] Viz. John Cutler and Edmund Hanson; see below for a consideration of the resident canons, p. 163.

[2] See above, p. 37; for the valuation of prebends, see R. E. G. Cole, *Chapter Acts of the Cathedral Church of Lincoln* (L.R.S. 12, 1915), pp. 201 ff.

[3] Le Neve, *Fasti, ad loc.*   [4] See above, p. 157 n.

simply became a direct royal appointment.[1] In 1500 James Whitstones was appointed. He was at that time acting as vicar general
to Bishop Smith, and was a trusted servant of Margaret, Countess
of Richmond and Derby.[2] He was succeeded in 1512 by John
Yong, who had gone on a number of diplomatic missions for the
king.[3] In 1515, William Knight was appointed; he was subsequently translated to the bishopric of Bath and Wells but at this
time was chaplain to the king.[4] In 1517, George Gray, the younger
son of the Marquis of Dorset, was appointed.[5] He was the only
one of the early sixteenth-century deans who does not appear to
have been a graduate, and whose merits were those of birth rather
than education and service. The other canons of the Newarke
were similar to their colleagues at Lincoln but a little less distinguished; of thirty-two clerks holding prebends of the college
in this period, twenty were graduates, but only seven held degrees
higher than that of M.A.[6] Of the remaining twelve, three at least
were related to prominent local families,[7] and two others were of
gentry stock.[8] None had been in the royal service, and only two
had served the bishop in an administrative capacity. The canonries of the Newarke were attractive enough to the graduate
who had no ambitions beyond that of getting benefices, but they
were not attractive enough to the royal servant or diocesan administrator, who could hope for something more lucrative. The
stipend of canons was £13. 6s. 8d. each;[9] this compared favourably
with that of most parish churches[10] but it did not compare so well
with the prebends of Lincoln, nearly half of which were worth
more.

The other collegiate churches of the diocese could not boast so

[1] A. H. Thompson, *The History of the Hospital and the New College of the
Annunciation of St Mary in the Newarke, Leicester*, p. 139.
[2] See above, p. 28.   [3] Emden, *Oxford*, III, 2136.
[4] *Ibid.* II, 1063.
[5] A. H. Thompson, *History of the Hospital and the New College of the Annunciation of St Mary in the Newarke, Leicester*, pp. 139, 140.
[6] *Ibid.* pp. 231 ff.; see also Emden, *Oxford*, I–III; *Cambridge, passim.*
[7] Viz. Roger Pisford, Richard Brokesby, Peter Swillington.
[8] Viz. Peter Gerrard and Gilbert Beckensaw; the brother of the latter was a
resident canon of Lincoln, see below, p. 163.
[9] A. H. Thompson, *op. cit.* p. 206.   [10] See above, p. 140.

many graduates; either the patron was reluctant to appoint them, or the graduates disdained the appointment. Two successive deans of Irthlingborough were graduates but none of their clergy had university qualifications.[1] There were no graduates appointed to Noseley at this time, and Higham Ferrers and Cotterstock only had two.[2] At Tattershall, the dean of Lincoln was the non-resident warden, and there were two graduate fellows and four others.[3]

Unlike the resident canons of the other collegiate churches, the resident canons of Lincoln cathedral were men of some standing. Like the non-resident canons of Lincoln they were from well-known families or they had risen from obscurity by obtaining a degree, usually a higher one. But, unlike the absentees, they had chosen to devote their time and energies to the cathedral, with the consequence that, although they might become eminent in the county or diocese, they were less likely to attract the attention of the court. From 1500 to 1520, fifteen canons chose to reside for varying periods of time, and a further four resided for a few months. The number of residents in the close in any one year was apt to vary: in 1506 there were only three or four in residence,[4] with the result that one complained to the bishop that for three days the whole weight of affairs had fallen upon him since his colleagues were either sick or away on business.[5] Between 1510 and 1511, there were only three canons attending chapter meetings.[6] Usually there were five, and on occasions there could be as many as seven.[7] Very stringent rules governed the residence of canons. A canon who wanted to reside began by undertaking 'major residence', which meant that he was committed to residing for two thirds of the year.[8] He paid an initial sum of £40 to

[1] Register 23, fos. 171, 179v[2], 180, 210, 215, 215v, 224v; Register 25, fos. 33, 34.

[2] For presentations to Noseley, see Register 23, fos. 239v, 247v, 263, 268, 268v; Register 25, fo. 40v. For Higham Ferrers, see Register 23, fo. 200v; Register 25, fo. 41. For Cotterstock, see Register 23, fos. 170, 219.

[3] Register 25, fo. 17v; Salter, p. 6.   [4] A. 3. 2, fos. 130 ff.

[5] Vj. 6, fo. 2v.   [6] A. 3. 4, fos. 34 ff.

[7] A. 3. 3, fo. 1.

[8] H. Bradshaw and C. Wordsworth, *Statutes of Lincoln Cathedral Arranged by the Late Henry Bradshaw* (Cambridge, 1892–7), III, 163.

the common fund on commencing residence, but thereafter he was entitled to a share of the common income and of any other perquisites; he was also assigned a house. After a period in major residence, a canon could proceed to minor residence, and was required to reside within the close for seventeen weeks and three days. Whether in major or minor residence, a canon needed the dean's permission to be away from the city even for a single night.[1] From time to time, questions about residence were brought to the chapter for their discussion and ruling. In 1507, there was some debate about whether Lent should be included in the residence period; canons might be away in Lent in order to visit their parish churches, and, perhaps, hear the confessions of their parishioners, but it was ordered that, if they were absent from the close in Lent, they must make up their residence during the rest of the year.[2] The remuneration of the resident canons varied considerably: the non-residents paid septisms, theoretically a seventh of the value of their prebends, to the common fund, and when all the chapter expenses had been paid the remainder was distributed among the resident canons. In practice, the income of the residents was swollen by the stipends which they received from their other benefices, and by the legacies which they sometimes received: the dean of Lincoln was assessed for as much as £396. 6s. 1¾d. for the subsidy of 1526, but it is not clear how many benefices he held.[3] Usually a resident canon received a little over £20 *per annum* from the common fund, but, in a year of heavy taxation or exceptional expenditure, he might receive as little as £6.[4]

The qualifications of the fifteen canons who undertook major and minor residence were chiefly educational.[5] Only two do not appear to have held degrees.[6] One canon, in contrast, held the degrees of doctor of medicine, civil law and theology, and he was also an illegitimate member of the Talbot family.[7] Most of the

---

[1] A. 3. 2, fo. 68v.   [2] *Ibid.* fo. 145.   [3] *L.R.S.* 12, pp. 207–8.
[4] Bj. 3. 3, see under the years 1514–20 (no foliation).
[5] Thomas Hill, John Wallys, John Cowland and Geoffrey Symeon, who resided for only a few months, have been omitted from this figure.
[6] Henry Apjohn and John Cutler.
[7] John Talbot, see Emden, *Oxford*, III, 1845.

remaining canons held higher degrees. Five were canon lawyers,[1] four theologians,[2] one was a civil lawyer,[3] and two held only an arts degree.[4] The subdean, Simon Stalworth, who resided between 1502 and 1507, was also a clerk of the hanaper,[5] and William Smith, archdeacon of Lincoln, who spent twelve years in the close, was a nephew of the bishop.[6] Another resident, Christopher Massingberd, was from a local family,[7] and Simon Grene, *alias* Fotherby, who became precentor in 1510, was probably born in Fotherby near Louth.[8] It was not necessarily the officers of the cathedral who resided: after his appointment as dean in May 1514, John Constable resided,[9] and successive precentors and treasurers resided for most of the period,[10] but there was no resident chancellor until 1512,[11] and the subdean, after a considerable period of residence, ceased to reside in 1509.[12] Edward Darby, the archdeacon of Stow, resided for thirteen years, and the treasurer and subsequent dean, John Constable, had resided twelve years by the time Bishop Atwater died. But they were unusually devoted, and most of their colleagues ceased residence after about 7 years. Occasionally a resident was allowed to be away for a period. Nicholas Bradbridge, who was appointed chancellor in November 1512, asked to be allowed to go on pilgrimage to Rome in July 1516; he pointed out that this had been his 'fervent desire' since his student days, and the chapter allowed him to go with no loss of income.[13] He was apparently only away for about six months since he was on his way back by January 1516/17.[14] Sometimes a canon ceased to reside when he was offered another post: the period of residence within the close might be a probationary period for a spell of diocesan service, or for higher office within the cathedral itself.

[1] Richard Roston, John Grantham, William Smith, William Fitzherbert, John Constable.
[2] Edmund Hanson, Simon Grene, Nicholas Bradbridge, Robert Becensaw.
[3] Christopher Massingberd.
[4] Simon Stalworth and Edward Darby.
[5] Emden, *Oxford*, III, 1753.   [6] *Ibid.* 1722.
[7] See above, p. 73.   [8] *L.R.S.* 12, p. x.
[9] A. 3. 3, fos. 64 ff.   [10] A. 3. 2, A. 3. 3, A. 3. 4, *passim.*
[11] A. 3. 4, fos. 48 v ff.
[12] A. 3. 4, *passim*; A. 3. 3, fos. 53 ff.
[13] A. 3. 3, fo. 88.   [14] *L. and P.* II, pt. II, no. 2776.

Richard Roston, who, as we have seen, became vicar general to Bishop Atwater, had protested major residence in the close in September 1504;[1] He continued to reside until 1511;[2] four years later he had become the bishop's most trusted servant.[3] The experience of the chapter had no doubt given him some training in administration, and had shown his ability. He had held the post of provost with the duty of *cognoscendi procedendi[que] in causis et in negociis capituli*:[4] he was also used as a proctor for the dean and chapter in negotiations with Wolsey.[5] The case may have been the turning-point in his career; it was shortly after it that he left the close. John Constable, Nicholas Bradbridge and Christopher Massingberd all resided for a period before being promoted to a higher office in the cathedral.[6]

The resident canons were confined to the close by their own choice. They had decided to protest residence, and to spend some time in the cathedral rather than pursuing a number of other opportunities which were apt to come the way of the graduate. Their qualifications were such that they could expect promotion eventually, and, even if residence in the close marked the sum of their achievement, they could congratulate themselves on a good stipend and a position of some standing in the shire. Their subordinates in the cathedral, like the curates in the parishes, were often not so fortunate. They lacked the qualifications which gave the higher clergy mobility, and some of them spent their entire lives in the cathedral in positions which brought them little financial remuneration and probably little interest.

The lower clergy in the cathedral were divided into three groups: the vicars choral, the poor clerks and the chantry priests; these groups were not absolutely distinct because there was some overlap in personnel. The poor clerks had the duty of keeping the altars, attending the offices and assisting at mass. The vicars choral were the deputies for the non-resident canons, with a primary duty, as their name suggests, of participating in the offices.[7] But

[1] A. 3. 2, fo. 100.   [2] A. 3. 4, fo. 31 v.
[3] See above, p. 27.   [4] A. 3. 3, fo. 101.   [5] A. 3. 4, fo. 16 v.
[6] A. 3. 3; A. 3. 4, *passim*; for their promotions, see Le Neve, *Fasti*.
[7] A. R. Maddison, *A Short Account of the Vicars Choral, Poor Clerks, Organists and Choristers of Lincoln Cathedral* (London, 1878), pp. 1–42.

they also tried to augment their stipends by obtaining a chantry. Some of them had worked their way up to the rank of vicar choral from being choristers and poor clerks. John Dockett, who was a chorister in 1501, was a vicar choral in 1506 and was still holding the same post in 1514. Thomas Ellys became a vicar in 1506 from being a chorister in 1501 and Thomas Flowre had been a chorister and poor clerk before his appointment as vicar.[1] A quarter of the vicars choral in 1514 had been promoted from being poor clerks.[2] One of those appointed after 1514 had also served in the cathedral for some time. John Barnes, admitted as a vicar choral in June 1514, had been a chorister in 1506 and a janitor of the close in 1514.[3] Many were appointed as vicars choral before they had been ordained priest. A third of all vicars choral in 1514 were not in priest's orders.[4] It looks as though the prospects of promotion from poor clerk to vicar choral were good, even though a candidate lacked full orders. But there promotion could stop. Vicars choral were apt to remain as such for a very long time. Of twenty-five vicars choral in 1501, seventeen were still vicars in 1506, and nine were still there in 1514,[5] and three of these, Richard Bailey, Thomas Clay and William Freeman, were still vicars choral in 1526.[6] Those who remained vicars choral for longest usually managed to obtain a chantry about ten years after their initial appointment, and about five years after their ordination as priest. Only two out of the nine vicars who had been appointed by 1501 and were still holding their posts in 1514 had not received a chantry.[7] Those who were fortunate enough to do so kept them. Of the thirty chantry priests doing homage to the dean in May 1514 only five resigned their chantries completely.[8] The records of resignations were not very carefully kept, and a

[1] Maddison, *op. cit.* pp. 70–1, 93; A. 3. 3, fos. 63 ff.
[2] A. 3. 3, fo. 63; cf. Maddison, *op. cit.* p. 77, viz. Richard Smith, John Dockett, Thomas Ellys, Henry Sherwyn, Thomas Flowre.
[3] A. 3. 3, fo. 64; Maddison, *op. cit.* p. 94; Bj. 3, 3, 1514–15.
[4] Richard Smith, Richard Bailey, John Dockett, Thomas Ellys, Thomas Hiege, Nicholas Hanson, Thomas Barrett, Robert Ryche, Thomas Flowre, William Hawkon, see Maddison, *op. cit.* pp. 76 ff.
[5] *Ibid.* pp. 70–1; cf. A. 3. 3, fo. 63.   [6] Salter, p. 82.
[7] Viz. William Selby, Thomas Wright.
[8] A. 3. 3, fos. 64v, 75², 129, 148.

few more may in fact have resigned, but, of the remaining twenty-five, three are known to have died in office and eleven were certainly still holding a chantry twelve years later.[1]

There are too few records for the other collegiate churches to be able to ascertain how long vicars stayed in the same post.[2] Similarly their scant visitation returns only allow glimpses of how the resident clergy, both canons and vicars, worked together, and very little can be reconstructed from them of the life of a collegiate church in the early sixteenth century. For a picture of this kind, we are forced to rely very heavily on the records of the cathedral church, supplementing them, where possible, with the incomplete records of the other collegiate churches.

Affairs were conducted at Lincoln by the resident canons in chapter. Actually, the canons shared out amongst themselves certain offices which brought with them specific duties. The most important office was that of provost, who had the duty of supervising the churches and estates belonging to the common fund, and of acting for the chapter in any business or legal transactions which might arise. This office was held for a year and went in turn by seniority to each of the resident canons. The other offices were less onerous; one canon was appointed annually to be master of the choristers, another to supervise the fabric and another had charge of the shrine of St Hugh; two canons audited the chapter accounts and another was master of the Burghersh chantry.[3] The resident canons met in chapter at irregular intervals; a full chapter meeting was usually held on a Saturday morning, but on occasions an informal meeting was convened after vespers or compline. The number of meetings held in any one year varied considerably. In part the variations were due to the conscientiousness or otherwise of the scribe in reporting meetings, but some differences were likely, from year to year, depending on the amount of business. Only

---

[1] The three who died were Thomas Retford, John Castell, John Sargiant (A. 3. 3, fos. 83 v, 107, 153 v). For the others compare A. 3. 3, fo. 63, with Salter, p. 83.

[2] Full visitation material survives for the Newarke college but the names of vicars were only given at the visitations of 1525 and 1528 (*L.R.S.* 37, pp. 6, 147).

[3] The change-over from one office to another was at the beginning of September (A. 3. 2; A. 3. 3; A. 3. 4, *passim*).

nine meetings are recorded in 1504, but forty-eight are noted in 1506; in 1508 there were as many as fifty-six, but, thereafter, about twenty are recorded as being held each year.[1]

Most of the canons attended about two thirds of the meetings held during their term of residence. Christopher Massingberd attended more meetings than any of his colleagues; one hundred and fifty were held, which potentially he could have attended, between 1512 and 1520; in fact he is recorded as being present at one hundred and twenty-four of them.[2]

The business which came to the chapter was varied, and it reflected both the power and the influence which the cathedral church enjoyed. The close was not under the jurisdiction of the city; the sheriffs and justices of the city had no power to arrest within it, nor had they the right to licence ale houses or billet soldiers there.[3] The dean and chapter enjoyed these powers, which continued unchanged until the civil war. It was, no doubt, for this reason that, at a chapter meeting in May 1517, the chapter reasserted its right of entry 'ad prisonam vocatam Downgion'.[4] The dean and chapter were also the ordinaries for the exercise of ecclesiastical jurisdiction within the close and over the churches appropriated to the common fund.[5] A large number of chapter meetings resulted from the most onerous part of this obligation, the granting of probate to wills. There is no indication that a conflict ever arose between the bishop and the dean and chapter about their respective powers. Episcopal visitations were conducted apparently without incident,[6] and the only sign of any difficulties between them is a mention in the common account book of a payment to Henry Wilcocks, the bishop's chancellor, of £4 *pro benevolentia*.[7] Relationships amongst the cathedral dignitaries, and the discipline of the lower clergy were more difficult than those between the chapter and the city or the bishop.

[1] *Ibid, passim.*   [2] A. 3. 3, *passim.*
[3] J. W. F. Hill, *Medieval Lincoln* (Cambridge, 1948), p. 124.
[4] A. 3. 3, fo. 107v.
[5] Bottesford, Orston, Glentham, Wellingore, Hambledon, Searby in 1514 (Bj. 3. 3, 1514–15); the farms varied a little from year to year.
[6] Vj. 6, fos. 1 ff.; Register 24, fo. 230.
[7] Bj. 3. 3, 1514–15.

Some chapter meetings were devoted to an attempt to solve the disputes which were inevitable in a collegiate church. They were not conducted with the acrimony which had characterized the quarrels amongst the canons in the fifteenth century but important questions were raised. Trouble started when the treasurer disputed whether it was necessary for the canons in residence to ask the dean's permission before leaving the town, but that question was settled in two days in favour of the dean by the intervention of the bishop.[1] More serious was the question, again raised by the treasurer a month later, about the election of a provost; the treasurer wanted to depart from the usual practice of electing the canons in rotation according to seniority.[2] On the face of it this seemed a paltry dispute on a mere matter of precedence, but three days later another quarrel broke out with the treasurer at its centre, which may well have been connected with the question of the provostship. On 21 October 1503, at a chapter meeting, the treasurer was ordered to provide wine for the chantry priests celebrating within the cathedral. He told the dean: 'By god I wil fynde noe wyne to any of them for nothing, that I know, yet they gete noone of me. Do what ye wille.'[3] This outburst may have been prompted by some unscrupulous intimidation on the part of the dean since the treasurer went on to say: 'Ye shall not be my Juge I appele fro you, ye be parciall and ye have put me in jeopardy of my life 8 or 9 tymes both within your house and without.'[4] But the treasurer, John Cutler, was clearly a difficult colleague: he was reported in 1507 as having been constantly arguing with Richard Roston.[5] Behind the difficulties of personal relationships, however, and exacerbating them, there appears to have been a genuine problem. The statutes and customs of the cathedral clearly stated that it was the treasurer's duty to provide for the expenses of the sacristy, look after the bells, repair the ornaments of the church, and provide the sacramental bread and wine, as well as the water, coal, incense, bell ropes, rushes, cruets and other utensils used in choir.[6] Cutler could not hope to make a case on grounds

---

[1] A. 3. 2, fo. 68 v.   [2] *Ibid.* fo. 67 v.   [3] *Ibid.* fo. 78.
[4] *Ibid.* fo. 78.   [5] Vj. 6, fo. 4 v.
[6] Bradshaw and Wordsworth, *Lincoln Cathedral Statutes,* I, 285.

of precedent. But in 1526 his income from which he was supposed to meet these obligations was less than any other member of the chapter.[1] In 1502, a year before the dispute, the price of consumables had begun to rise to a level rarely reached before that date, and was maintained at that level for a few years thereafter[2]. Whether the prices of incense and wax in 1502 rose as steeply, we do not know, since the treasurer did not keep personal accounts which have survived, but by 1526, when the price of consumables was only marginally higher than it had been in 1502, the treasurer's expenses on repairs, wax, incense, coal and sacramental bread and wine was £13. 16s. 8d.[3] His normal share of the common fund was £20. As a result his expenses on these items were taking a large portion of his income. In 1526, he was also paying the stipend of the bell ringers; he paid for feeding the choir, and the wages of the sacrist and verger, with the result that his over-all expenses totalled £37. 2s.—significantly more than he was receiving from the common fund.[4] In 1526, therefore, he was subsidizing his necessary expenses at the cathedral from the stipend he was receiving from his other benefices. It is possible that this was happening, to some extent, in 1502, and that the treasurer was feeling the pinch of a rise in prices. At least this interpretation would explain the next dispute which rocked the chapter and in which he participated.

It concerned the altar of St Peter. In June 1507, the question arose whether the custodian of the altar, who had the duty of celebrating for the souls of past bishops and who heard the cases which came before the chapter court, ought to be paid at a flat rate of £8 per annum, or whether he should receive commons, wine and incidental benefits ut canonicus. The question dragged on for several months, and the treasurer refused to entertain the idea of paying the custodian more than £8.[5] A clue to his intransigence is to be found in a letter he received from another canon, and which he read out to the other residentiaries in support of his case. It read:

[1] L.R.S. 12, p. 209.
[2] E. H. Phelps Brown and S. V. Hopkins, 'Seven Centuries of the Prices of Consumables', Essays in Economic History, ed. E. Carus Wilson, II, 194; Agrarian History of England and Wales, IV, ed. Thirsk, 847.
[3] L.R.S. 12, p. 209.   [4] Ibid.   [5] A. 3. 2, fos. 145 v ff.

Will I never consent to gif more while I am in the churche of Lincoln.
God knoweth we have more nede to help our selfe than other men;
ye know right wel our liflode mendes not but decayes every day more
and more. We ought in conscience to love our selfe furste and then
other. And if it were so that I could not luffe my self firste, other men
teche me how I shulde begyn.[1]

The writer of the letter and the treasurer clearly recognized that,
if the custodian received commons *ut canonicus*, there would be a
corresponding loss of income for themselves from the common
fund; it would be less expensive to pay £8 than to pay commons
when food prices were rising. No one else saw their point, and
the dean ruled that the custodian should receive commons *ut
canonicus*.[2] The decision was almost immediately reversed by the
bishop, who decreed that the custodian should be paid £8 and
asserted that his predecessor had ordered this arrangement.[3] As
the income to be distributed to the residentiaries dwindled, no
doubt they had cause to be grateful for the decision.[4]

Apart from a question about the proper places in procession
which the archdeacon of Stow and the subdean should occupy,[5]
chapter meetings were free of disputes until 1516. In October of
that year, Robert Becansaw resigned the treasurership, and, on the
authority of episcopal letters, Christopher Massingberd was admitted.[6] But in February 1516/17 John Burges was appointed as
treasurer, and admitted to the office, and Massingberd contested
the appointment. The case was referred to the archbishop of Canterbury,[7] and in October 1517 Burges was formally admitted as
treasurer. Massingberd appears to have accepted the decision, for
he assumed his former role of resident canon without appointment.[8] His treatment appears unjust since he is recorded as acting
as treasurer between October 1516 and February 1516/17, and
clearly some confusion arose subsequent to his admittance as
treasurer. John Burges was in a position to push his own claims,
irrespective of those of others, because he was in close attendance

[1] A. 3. 2, fo. 145 v.   [2] A. 3. 3, fo. 8.
[3] Vj. 6, fo. 2.   [4] See above, p. 12.
[5] A. 3. 4, fos. 22v, 25v, 34.   [6] A. 3. 3, fo. 101 v.
[7] *Ibid*. fos. 104v, 106v.   [8] *Ibid*. fos. 120–1v.

on the bishop.[1] But probably Massingberd came out of the encounter better than his adversary. Burges had to pay his predecessor as treasurer a pension of £20, and if, as we have seen, the treasurer was finding his expenses too heavy, the pension would have been a crippling burden.[2]

The other collegiate churches of the diocese also had their share of discord. At Fotheringhay, Richard Plummer provoked trouble among his colleagues, though we are not told why.[3] At the Newarke, the aristocratic dean, George Gray, proved something of a liability. He was trying to gain the exclusive right to the patronage of benefices which were supposed to be in the gift of the whole chapter. He also tried to keep the custody of the chapter seal, in spite of the fact that he was often away. He forced an unwilling canon to act as his deputy without any remuneration at all. This was the situation when the bishop visited Newarke in 1518.[4] It was to deteriorate. By 1525 and 1528 when further visitations were made, the canons had begun to hold meetings to organize resistance to the dean.[5] The life of the college was completely disrupted by the fights that broke out between the dean's supporters and those of his adversaries, and the canons were soliciting the help of the vicars by entertaining them in their own houses. Canons and vicars were neglecting the offices, and the presence of Sir Richard Sacheverell and his wife, the Lady Hungerford, in the precincts of the college exacerbated the whole situation. As aristocratic patrons of the college, they were in a good position to flout the dean's authority, and to organize resistance to him; they could also organize blood sports of a more conventional kind for the canons, and their hounds pervaded the college.[6] In these circumstances the devotional life of the residents must have been severely disrupted. Life at Lincoln was peaceful in comparison.

All the collegiate canons had problems in controlling their lower clergy. The chapter at Lincoln devoted considerable time to them with remarkably little success. It appears to have been difficult to force the poor clerks and vicars choral to attend the

---

[1] See above, pp. 168–9.
[3] L.R.S. 35, pp. 146 ff.
[5] Ibid. p. 125.

[2] A. 3. 3, fo. 101 v.
[4] L.R.S. 37, pp. 2 ff.
[6] Ibid. p. 123.

offices. In 1503, four poor clerks were brought before the chapter for not observing the offices;[1] in 1505 the vicars choral were accused of not bothering to get up for mattins, which were at 2.0 a.m.,[2] and in 1508 they were again accused of neglecting the night offices—this time because they had been frequenting ale houses and were presumably too inebriated to attend in choir.[3] In 1509 the negligence of the vicars and poor clerks was discussed and new orders were issued. Vicars were to make sure that they were in choir and not merely wandering about the nave during divine service. Each vicar absenting himself from mattins was to be fined 1d., and the same fine was payable by vicars and chantry priests who were absent from mass, vespers or from processions. All the fines were to be paid to the shrine of St Hugh.[4] In 1511 Thomas Clay, a vicar choral, was warned that he must come to mattins,[5] and in 1512 the provost of the senior vicars promised to see that his charges attended the offices.[6] In other collegiate churches, the problem of attendance at the offices was great. At the Newarke the canons were offending, even to the extent of missing high mass, while vicars were neglecting their quota of masses for the departed.[7] At Fotheringhay, the vicars were misbehaving in choir and one canon neglected to celebrate.[8]

Part of the problem with the lower clergy was the other attractions with which the neighbourhood provided them. The poor clerks were up before the chapter in 1507 accused of fighting and arguing together, and of frequenting brothels;[9] in 1508, one of them had spent several nights outside the close without permission,[10] and, in 1516, five of them had gone up the cathedral tower with torches, hoping to catch the pigeons which then, as now, plagued the cathedral. Their torches started a small fire, and it was the merest good fortune that the tower was not burned down. They were suspended from office for a period.[11] The vicars confined their indiscretions to drinking and to calling the archdeacon

---

[1] A. 3. 2, fo. 66.
[2] Ibid. fo. 108v.
[3] A. 3. 3, fos. 12v, 25.
[4] A. 3. 4, fo. 4.
[5] A. 3. 4, fo. 36.
[6] Ibid. fo. 48v.
[7] L.R.S. 37, pp. 1, 3–4.
[8] L.R.S. 35, p. 147.
[9] A. 3. 3, fo. 4.
[10] Ibid. fo. 43.
[11] Ibid. fo. 85.

of Stow rude names (*verba opprobriosa sive vilipendiosa*), but there was some difficulty in forcing them and the chantry priests to have their meals together.[1] In 1505, the vicars were ordered to live together in the house provided for them, and the chantry priests were forbidden to eat with the canons or the choristers but were enjoined to take commons together.[2] There was doubt about the adequacy of the education of the lower cathedral clergy. In 1503 the poor clerks had been accused of neglecting to go to school, and the same charge was made against them a year later.[3] Richard Roston reported to the bishop at his visitation in 1507 that:

pauperes clerici...sunt indocti et inhabiles nec bene docentur per instructorem in gramatica quia nec instructor est ydoneus nec ipsi clerici suam adhibent diligenciam.[4]

The same accusation had been made in 1501, and there were complaints that the choir boys did not know grammar or how to chant.[5] But things may have improved after the visitation of 1507. No more complaints were made about the education of the poor clerks, and provision was made for the instruction of the choristers. In 1508 Henry Alcock was admitted as a teacher of grammar to the choristers,[6] and in 1511 the newly appointed choirmaster promised to teach 'plainsong, priksong, discaunt and counter-poynt' and to observe all the day and night offices.[7] The singing in the cathedral was good enough, or the patronage of Wolsey was strong enough, for the king to forbid the removal of any of the 'singing men' from the cathedral unless to serve in the Chapel Royal.[8]

The vicars at the Newarke college were not above reproach. One was reported as living with a married woman in the town, and many of the others were frequently away; they often neglected to wear their habits, and the choristers did not take commons together.[9] At Fotheringhay, the vicars were bad-mannered,

[1] A. 3. 3, fos. 25, 126v.
[2] A. 3. 2, fos. 72v, 73v, 105v, 110v.
[3] A. 3. 2, fos. 66, 96v.
[4] Vj. 6, fo. 2v.
[5] Register 24, fo. 234.
[6] A. 3. 3, fo. 15.
[7] A. 3. 4, fo. 30.
[8] A. 3. 3, fo. 65v.
[9] *L.R.S.* 37, pp. 3, 5, 127.

insubordinate and given to gossiping through the services. Furthermore, they neglected to wear their habits.[1] At both Fotheringhay and Tattershall, there seems to have been dissatisfaction at the educational standard of the clergy,[2] and, at Higham Ferrers, the fellows were ordered to use Latin at meals.[3]

There are a number of reasons which may explain why the collegiate clergy appear to have been less conscientious and more unruly than their counterparts in the parishes. In the first place, we know significantly more about the lower cathedral clergy than we know about the parochial clergy. The offences of the parochial clergy only came to light at a visitation, and were only reported if the parish saw fit to tell tales. The records of chapter meetings in the cathedral give a much fuller picture, and when the bishop visited he was not relying on parishioners for his information, but on canons who might be anxious to gain his notice and favour. The discord which prevailed in some of the collegiate churches, for which there are no records of chapter meetings, was apt to encourage informing. The factions at the Newarke college reported against each other, and it is clear that at Fotheringhay there would have been less said about Richard Plummer had he not also been responsible for quarrelling with his fellows.[4] But, when all allowances have been made, the difference between the standards of the collegiate and parochial clergy cannot be explained wholly in terms of the quality of the surviving evidence. In collegiate churches, like Higham Ferrers, for which visitation records alone have survived, the picture is significantly worse than that given of all but a very few parishes. The explanation for the discrepancy probably lies in a combination of causes. The vicars in the collegiate churches were poorly paid. In 1514, eleven poor clerks of the cathedral collectively received £11. 18s. 4d. to be shared out between them;[5] the vicars choral did a little better. The archdeacon of Lincoln paid his vicar £2 annually[6] but in 1526 the vicars choral were assessed at £3. 13s. 4d. each, probably because their commons was included in this sum.[7] The basic

---

[1] L.R.S. 35, p. 151. [2] Ibid. p. 148; L.R.S. 37, p. 111.
[3] L.R.S. 35, p. 166. [4] See above, p. 171.
[5] Bj. 3. 3, 1514. [6] Rev/L/1.   [7] Salter, p. 82.

stipend of the vicars and poor clerks was lower than that of the curates, though they were protected from inflation because the provision of commons made it unnecessary for them to purchase their own food. The vicars at the Newarke received £4. 13s. 4d. each, but that does not appear to have included their commons which they received in addition.[1] For the lower clergy at Lincoln, the poor pay was allied with difficult prospects of promotion. We have noticed that many of them stayed as vicars for a considerable time. They were also dependent for promotion on the whim of the canons. The patronage of the cathedral offices, especially those of poor clerk and vicar choral, belonged to the resident canons. It was a highly prized perquisite. Presentation to the parish churches belonging to the cathedral was by each canon in turn in order of seniority, and the same order governed appointments of vicars choral.[2] As a result, the lower clergy were very much at the mercy of the canons, and might be tempted to court their favour to gain promotion. In 1501 there was a complaint that the traditional safeguards against admitting unsuitable clerks as vicars choral were being overlooked. It was said that vicars were not being examined in chant and in reading, as the cathedral statutes had ordered.[3] This combination of poor prospects and low pay may go far to explain the negligence of the lower cathedral clergy.

In the other collegiate churches, the explanation may lie deeper in the attitude of both canons and vicars to their vocations. At the Newarke, Fotheringhay and Higham Ferrers, the canons were as irresponsible as the lower collegiate clergy. In 1525, the canons of the Newarke were receiving women into their houses, and one at least was accused of adultery.[4] The fellows of Fotheringhay were apt to sleep away from the college, and one was noted for incontinence.[5] At Higham Ferrers there was a suspicion that women were in the college too often and the cook's wife actually fed in the college hall with the warden's servants.[6] The taverns of the

---

[1] A. H. Thompson, *The History of the Hospital and the New College of the Annunciation of St Mary in the Newarke, Leicester*, p. 206.

[2] A. 3. 4, fo. 11.   [3] Register 24, fo. 231 v.

[4] *L.R.S.* 37, pp. 123–4.   [5] *L.R.S.* 35, pp. 145 ff.   [6] *Ibid.* p. 166.

city were frequented by the canons of the Newarke in 1518,[1] and it was probably the desire for ale and female company which enticed the canons of Higham Ferrers into the town without the warden's permission.[2] Like some of the religious orders, the collegiate clergy appear to have lost their sense of purpose; they were no longer observing their statutes, and they were no longer observing the offices which were fundamental to the existence of a chantry foundation. There is no evidence to suggest they did not believe in the efficacy of intercession for the departed, but they do seem to have lost interest in their duty of continuing it. In consequence the collegiate churches were resembling acrimonious country clubs rather than centres of Christian charity and devotion.[3]

In the parishes, and, to some extent, in the cathedral, the demands of the parish and of the secular world kept alive a sense of duty. The cathedral had a position to maintain in the city and in the diocese. The shrine of St Hugh was a centre of pilgrimage, and the duties of maintaining it and instructing the laity may have served to prevent the canons drifting into an aimless and seemingly purposeless existence. The accounts of the cathedral indicate something of its importance and centrality in the life of the city and the diocese. Men were employed to look after the cathedral and even to keep it open at meal times; others had the daily duty of lighting and extinguishing the candles which were at the door of the choir and round the shrine of St Hugh.[4] The bells had to be rung before all the offices, just as they were rung in the parish churches, but at the cathedral a number of ringers were needed, and the work was onerous enough for the chapter to make provision for the bell ringers to have access to the fountain in Christopher Thompson's house at all necessary times.[5]

---

[1] L.R.S. 37, p. 1.   [2] L.R.S. 35, p. 166.
[3] For the religious see, particularly, The Register or Chronicle of Butley Priory, Suffolk, ed. A. G. Dickens (Winchester, 1951), pp. 12, 22–3. 'Nevertheless, when all...necessary qualifications have been made, the weaknesses of late monasticism stand revealed nowhere more clearly than in these less sensational visitation records, in the ill-success of decent individuals trying to operate a system which needed not merely organisational reform but a vast new influx of spiritual inspiration' (p. 12).
[4] Bj. 3. 3, 1514–15.   [5] A. 3. 4, fo. 4v.

There were so many chantry masses to be said that special arrangements had to be made to fit them all in. The first masses were said just before 6.0 a.m. and they went on until 11.0. a.m. It was probably because the cathedral required organization on a large scale that its canons were conscientious and its accounts were kept; chaos could ensue if they were not.[1]

But the cathedral was more than a very large church. It was also a centre for instruction and a centre for entertainment. Sermons were preached before the visitation of the bishop,[2] and special arrangements were made in 1505 for Lent sermons to be preached in the nave, and Advent sermons to be preached in the chapter house.[3] Books were left to the cathedral to be chained to its library,[4] and, for those who could not benefit from these, there were the cathedral plays performed on feast days.[5] John Barnes, a vicar and janitor of the close, was the stage manager and he was paid 13s. 4d. regularly for his work;[6] so appreciative was the chapter of his efforts that it was agreed that he had earned an annual pension of 20s. *per annum* by 1509.[7] Little is known about the exact form of these plays but the accounts contain an annual entry of 6d. for gloves for Mary and the angels, and 3s. 6d. was spent on shoes; the feast of St Anne was celebrated with a play which demanded a clock and a crown for Mary which cost the chapter as much as 10s.[8] The stage management of the play at the feast of the Assumption was difficult enough to earn Barnes an additional 2s.[9] These activities had the effect of keeping the cathedral clergy busy and of giving them a pastoral function as well as a liturgical one. It was not always recognized by the lower clergy, but it may have helped to prevent the canons from behaving like their counterparts at the Newarke and elsewhere.

The failings of the collegiate clergy would affect the parishes

---

[1] A. 3. 2, fo. 132v; for regular auditing of the accounts, see A. 3. 2; A. 3. 3, *passim*; cf. *L.R.S.* 35, pp. 146, 165.

[2] Register 24, fo. 230. [3] A. 3. 2, fo. 109.

[4] *Ibid.* fo. 12v.

[5] V. Shull, 'Clerical Drama in Lincoln Cathedral 1318–1561', *Modern Languages Association of America*, LII (1937), *passim*.

[6] Bj. 3. 3. [7] A. 3. 4, fo. 6v.

[8] Bj. 3. 3, 1514. [9] A. 3. 3, fo. 87.

slightly, if at all, because few of them had any close connexion with the parish church. But they did affect the church as a whole. They lent colour to the criticism of the clergy voiced by the anti-clericals, and they brought the clergy into disrepute. If Simon Fish had wanted evidence of the misdemeanours of the clergy for his *Supplication for the Beggars*, he could find ample in the collegiate churches. If justification had been sought for the dissolution of the chantries and of chantry foundations, it could easily be found at the Newarke, Fotheringhay or Higham Ferrers. The failings of the few were too easily ascribed to the many.

CONCLUSION

The picture of the sixteenth-century clergy which emerges from the diocesan material is complex, and cannot be fully assessed until other diocesan studies are undertaken for the same and for an earlier period. The Lincoln diocese appears to have presented peculiar problems and may not prove to be typical. Its bishops had succeeded in defining closely its relationship with the archbishop of Canterbury and the papal legate and in limiting to some extent their interference in diocesan affairs. But the interference of the monarch could not be limited; the diocese was subject to heavy royal taxation and the see itself was largely in the gift of the king. Its bishops and their most important administrative assistants were usually royal servants. There is some slight evidence of a conflict in loyalty between the duty of a diocesan towards his see, and his duty to his monarch. In theory the diocesan *in remotis* administered the diocese by the appointment of deputies, but in practice this expedient was open to limitations; a deputy was not inefficient, but he lacked sufficient status to deal with the powerful, and he did not have the wide area of discretion enjoyed by a bishop. More damaging to the satisfactory conduct of diocesan affairs was the total lack of parochial experience of the bishop and his assistants. The way to promotion in the diocese did not lie by way of the parish, but through the universities to royal service or to a period of residence in the cathedral. Confronted with erring priests and parishioners, the bishop could have little personal insight into their problems. Yet, in spite of these limitations to the satisfactory administration of the diocese, there are some signs that it was effective in preventing abuses. Ordination was not indiscriminate, and, though some mystery surrounds the titles which monastic houses were giving to ordinands, there is little evidence to suggest that the canonical requirements about age, education and suitability were ignored. The education of an ordinand by the early sixteenth century was better than it had been in the early fifteenth, though it was still haphazard. The period between ordination and the acquisition of a benefice was a difficult one, and many priests do not seem to have acquired a cure at all. Their failure to proceed to a benefice was not always due to a lack of education; the gift of a benefice lay with patrons whose ideas of suitable qualifications were not necessarily those most in keeping with the needs of the parish. Royal service, family connexions and early signs of a promising career in church or state were the qualities which many patrons looked for in bestowing their favour. But they were also the qualities needed to gain the clerk a dispensation from residence and a licence to hold cures in plurality. The clerk most likely to catch the eye of a patron was least likely to reside in the parish. But parishes were not neglected. The rectors, vicars and curates who served them appear to have exhibited few of the enormities described by Simon Fish. Clerks were apt to find celibacy irksome, and some were becoming increasingly impoverished by inflation and stringent taxation; few neglected their pastoral and liturgical duties despite the fact that the fabric of their churches was often allowed to fall into decay. In their devotion to duty they differed from the collegiate clergy. The collegiate clergy in this period had lost a sense of vocation. They rarely had any pastoral functions to fulfil, and their *raison d'être* lay in intercession which they frequently neglected.

The failings of the few were seized upon by the critics of the church, particularly by Simon Fish. Fish was not concerned with statistics; he was relaying gossip, and in that respect he shows how important to the church as a whole the immorality of even one of its priests might be. But few Tudor parishioners were as anticlerical as Simon Fish. The laity were not attacking the parochial clergy with his venom. The visitation returns of the diocese suggest that they either found little to complain about in their pastor or they were sufficiently sympathetic to his offences to connive at them. Hostility to the church only appeared on certain issues. The large number of complaints about the decay of the fabric suggest that there was some resentment that rectors, whether religious houses or single clerks, were not using tithe for one of its main purposes. The number of court cases concerning fees also suggests that the financial ties between the priest and his parish were often strained. The difficulty which the ecclesiastical courts experienced in trying to enforce attendance may well indicate a hostility to their function, exacerbated by the number of ill-founded charges which were made before them.

It is impossible, at present, to estimate the extent to which the sixteenth-century church differed from the fifteenth; but it is clear that, even in the first two and a half decades of the sixteenth century, rapid changes were taking place. There was an abrupt change in the economic fortunes of some clerks and a gradual change in the methods of education. The printed book not only made possible a new standard of education amongst the priesthood, it also created the possibility that the priest would have to defend his faith to a better-informed laity.

It is a fascinating though fruitless task to speculate what effect the interaction of these changes and signs of hostility would have had without the king's divorce. The break with Rome was not caused by changes within the church. It was the royal will which determined whether the changes would take place in a church in communion with the see of Rome or in schism from it. But, once the break with Rome had come, the points of stress in the parishes, the changes in economic fortune of the priests and the increased educational media all played their part in determining the reaction of the country to it, and the speed at which reform could take place as a result of it. The complexity of some problems, as they had emerged in the early sixteenth century, rendered them incorrigible; the interaction, for instance, of the vested interests of both clerks and laymen made it difficult to alter the structure of clerical stipends by ordering that tithe be paid only to the priest in charge, or to limit non-residence by forbidding absenteeism for any reason whatsoever. The hostility to, mingled with envy of, the religious houses who used tithe for their own purposes and did not use it to improve the parish church may explain the ease with which they were dissolved. Gossip about the failings of the collegiate churches had also created the impression that foundations with a purpose of intercession for the departed had ceased to serve a useful function. Until these matters became controversial, they were not openly defended and justified, nor was the case for their existence understood. But, when they did come under attack, it was too late to defend them against an accumulated prejudice. The storm was too sudden for exponents of orthodoxy to utilize the printing press and rouse the country into defending what it had long taken for granted. In the confusion of the 1530s, old hostilities could be turned to a new purpose. Few were like Fisher and More and could fully understand the issues at stake; some were not trained in the rationalia of the old faith and others had served the king too long to oppose him. It is beyond the scope of this study to show how the parochial clergy reacted to the changes which followed the break with Rome. But in the complaints of the Puritans, particularly those against ecclesiastical courts, there lingered the grievances of an earlier generation.[1] Some of the problems facing Elizabeth were left to her by her father.

---

[1] See especially *The State of the Church in the Reigns of Elizabeth and James I*, ed. C. W. Foster, appendix II, 469.

APPENDICES

BISHOP'S COMMISSARIES IN THE ARCHDEACONRIES

Note: It is not usually possible to be sure when a man became a commissary and when he ceased to hold the office; the dates at which he is known to have been acting as commissary are given with the reference. Asterisks indicate that the commissary is also known to have acted as the archdeacon's official.

Lincoln

Henry Apjohn	1495	Register 24, fo. 98; Vj. 5, *passim*
Richard Roston	1500	Bishop's Accounts, 7, fo. 13 v
William Smith	1505, 1506, 1507	*L.R.S.* 5, pp. 26, 28, 30
Brian Higden	1508, 1509	*Ibid.* pp. 37, 40
William Clifton	1511, 1514	*Ibid.* pp. 45, 57, 62, 63, 65
*Robert Halam	1515, 1518, 1519	*Ibid.* pp. 68, 76, 77, 83
William Wittur	1520, 1521	*Ibid.* pp. 83, 87, 88, 89; Proxies, Box 71

Stow

Henry Apjohn	1495, 1500	Register 24, fo. 98; Vj. 5, *passim*
Richard Stooks	1499, 1500	Bishop's Accounts Misc. 6, fo. 3; Bishop's Accounts 7, fo. 13 v
William Clifton	1513, 1514	*L.R.S.* 5, pp. 52, 55, 59, 60, 67
John Smith	1519	Cj. 2, fo. 69

Bedford

Henry Rudyng	1495–7	Register 24, fo. 98
Richard Roston	1500	Bishop's Accounts 7, fo. 13 v

Buckingham

Roger Horde	1495, 1499, 1501	Register 24, fo. 98; Bishop's Accounts, 7, fo. 13 v

William Cumberford	1504	Aylesbury Record Office, D/A/We, fo. 197
*John Cocks	1519	Aylesbury Record Office, D/A/We, fo. 94; Bodleian Library, Browne Willis MS. 14, fo. 12
John Haget	1520	Aylesbury Record Office, D/A/We, fo. 1
Thomas Jackson	1521	Cj. 2, fo. 103

Huntingdon

Edward Shuldham	1492	Bishop's Accounts, Misc. 6
William Stevyns	1495	Register 24, fo. 98
Richard Roston	1500	Bishop's Accounts, 7, fo. 13 v
Henry Wilcocks	1515?	Vj. 6, fo. 28 v
John Grene	1518	Cj. 2, fos. 63, 84

Northampton

Thomas Knight	1495, 1500, 1502–4	Register 23, fos. 183 v, 198; Register 24, fo. 98; Bishop's Accounts, 7, fo. 13 v
William Wittur	1512	Register 23, fo. 223
*Robert Gostwick	1519	Register 25, fo. 31; Visitation Monitions, 1500–1739, June 1519

Oxford

John Veysey	1495	Register 24, fo. 98
Henry Wilcocks	1499–1500	Bishop's Accounts, 7, fo. 13 v
Edmund Horde	1517	Cj. 2, fos. 48, 50 v
John London	1521	Cj. 2, fo. 107

Leicester

John Edmunds	1495–1502	Register 24, fo. 98; Register 23, fo. 229 v; Bishop's Accounts, 7, fo. 13 v; Additional Register 7, fo. 146
*William Mason	1509–11	Viv. 5, *passim*; Additional Register 7, fo. 5
*John Silvester	1518	Cj. 2, fos. 58, 59, 78, 84; L.R.S. 33, p. 153

APPENDIX II

FAMILY PRESENTATIONS
TO BENEFICES

Note: A family did not *always* present one of its members every time. So the total number of presentations of any kind are given; e.g. the Waynewrights presented twice to Anderby but only one of their presentations was of a member of the family.

Parish	Total number of presentations	Family	Register
Anderby	2	Waynewright	23 fo. 90
Appleby	3	Grymeston	23 fo. 154v
Bedford St Leonards	1	Bray	23 fo. 408
Belton in Axholme	1	Asheton	25 fo. 26v
Bigby	5	Tyrwhit	23 fo. 92v
Boothby Pagnell	2	Paynell	23 fo. 79
Braybrooke	3	Gryffyn	23 fo. 213
Brington	3	Litton	23 fo. 183
Broughton	2	Broughton	23 fo. 317v
Buckden	3	Coren	25 fo. 56
Buckingham	3	Smyth	23 fo. 364v
Calceby	1	Fairfax	25 fo. 17v
Clothall	1	Dalyson	25 fo. 58
Dowsby	3	Marmyon	25 fo. 20v
East Barkwith	1	Kéld	23 fo. 53
Ewerby	3	Fairfax	25 fo. 17v
Finedon (Thingden)	4	Atturcliff	23 fo. 179v
Flixborough	1	Henneage	23 fo. 118v
Frodingham	1	Miller	23 fo. 142
Garsington	3	Fishwick	23 fo. 286
Gilmorton	1	Hasilryg	25 fo. 39
Grantham	4	Dey	23 fo. 157
Grayingham	1	Thompson	23 fo. 157v
Great Coates	1	Barnardeston	23 fo. 52v
Great Staughton	3	Thwaits	23 fo. 354

[187]

Parish	Total number of presentations	Family	Register
Kimcote	1	Maw	23 fo. 260
Kingerby	2	Doughty	25 fo. 16
Laceby	3	Grymston	25 fo. 80 v
Luton	2	Sheffield	23 fo. 393 v
Nettleton	2	Spenser	23 fo. 48 v
Ownby	2	Salter	23 fo. 98
Pilton	4	Basset	23 fo. 168 v
Rothwell	2	Bolles	23 fo. 126
Ryhall	1	Netelham	23 fo. 189 v
Seal	1	Vernon	23 fo. 266 v
South Croxton	2	Atturcliff	23 fo. 243
South Willingham	1	Compton	25 fo. 21
Spridlington	2	Lacy	23 fo. 153
Stathern	1	Tailard	23 fo. 249 v
Swayfield	1	Newton	25 fo. 18
Thimbleby	1	Thimbleby	23 fo. 103
Thurlaston	1	Turwile	23 fo. 260 v
Tighe	3	Sherard	23 fo. 213
Toft next Newton	1	Billesby	23 fo. 110
Welby	1	Day	23 fo. 109 v
West Rasen	2	Mane	23 fo. 81 v
Willoughby	2	Willoughby	23 fo. 67 v
Wington	1	Ambrose	25 fo. 63 v

RELIGIOUS PRESENTED TO BENEFICES

Parishes to which religious were presented by their own order or by an intermediary on a grant from their own order

Parish	Order*	Pre-sentations of this kind	Total pre-sentations to this parish	Reference
Allington	Newbo P	1	1	Reg. 23, fo. 143 v
Anwick	Haverholme G	1	1	Reg. 25, fo. 20 v
Appleby	Thornholme A	1	3	Reg. 23, fo. 124 v
Aynho	Walden B	1	3	*Ibid.* fo. 169
Blyton	Thornholme A	3	3	*Ibid.* fos. 148, 156, 160 v
Bracebridge	St Katherine by Lincoln G	1	3	*Ibid.* fo. 88 v
Brocklesby	Newsham P	3	3	*Ibid.* fos. 42, 132, 146
Burton Stather	Norton A	1	2	*Ibid.* fo. 159 v
Canwick	St Katherine by Lincoln G	1	1	*Ibid.* fo. 68
Chacombe	Chacombe A	1	3	*Ibid.* fo. 219 v
Churchill	St Frideswide A	1	3	Reg. 25, fo. 49 v
Claxby	Revesby C	1	2	Reg. 23, fo. 145
Cotes by Stow	Welbeck P	1	3	*Ibid.* fo. 155 v
East Haddon	Sulby P	1	3	Reg. 25, fo. 30
Elsham	Elsham A	1	1	*Ibid.* fo. 12
Elsfield	St Frideswide A	1	1	Reg. 23, fo. 290 v
Epworth	Newburgh A	4	4	*Ibid.* fos. 152, 156 v, 159; Reg. 25, fo. 20 v
Finedon (Thingden)	Croxton P	1	1	Reg. 23, fo. 172 v
Fritwell	St Frideswide A	1	4	Reg. 25, fo. 48 v
Great Ludford	Sixhills G	1	2	*Ibid.* fo. 80 v

* A = Augustinian; B = Benedictine; C = Cistercian; G = Gilbertine; H = Hospitallers; P = Premonstratensian.

Parish	Order	Pre-sentations of this kind	Total pre-sentations to this parish	Reference
Great Stretton	Tupholme P	1	1	*Reg.* 25, fo. 70v
Great Stukeley	B.M. Huntingdon A	1	1	*Ibid.* fo. 355
Greetham	St Sepulchre Warwick A	1	4	*Reg.* 23, fo. 259
Hackthorn	Bullington G	1	1	*Ibid.* fo. 152
Hagworthingham	Bardney B	1	2	*Ibid.* fo. 145v
Hartford	B.M. Huntingdon A	1	1	*Ibid.* fo. 355
Ivinghoe	Ashridge Bonhommes	1	3	*Ibid.* fo. 323v
Killingholme	Newsham P	1	1	*Ibid.* fo. 15v
Kirmington	Newsham P	4	4	*Ibid.* fos. 65, 82, 85, 138
Laughton	Sempringham G	1	2	*Ibid.* fo. 144v
Legsby	Sixhills G	1	2	*Ibid.* fo. 143v
Ludgershall	St John of Jerusalem H	1	3	*Ibid.* fo. 347v
Lutton	Sempringham G	1	3	*Ibid.* fo. 108v
Messingham	Kyme A	1	3	*Ibid.* fo. 114v
Middle Rasen	Drax A	1	1	*Reg.* 25, fo. 17v
Naseby	Combe C	1	1	*Reg.* 23, fo. 170
Neots St	St Neots B	1	1	*Ibid.* fo. 381v
Northope	Newbo P	2	2	*Ibid.* fos. 156, 158
North Witham	Owston A	1	1	*Ibid.* fo. 110
Oakley	St Frideswide A	2	4	*Ibid.* fos. 316, 340v
Orby	Thornholme A	2	4	*Ibid.* fos. 56, 142
Ormesby	Ormesby G	1	1	*Ibid.* fo. 87
Over Wichendon	St Frideswide A	1	1	*Ibid.* fo. 348
Oxford St Clement	St Frideswide A	1	3	*Ibid.* fo. 279
Oxford St Mary Magdalene	Osney A	1	5	*Ibid.* fo. 305v
Scothern	Barlings P	1	4	*Ibid.* fo. 148v
Sempringham	Sempringham G	1	2	*Ibid.* fo. 138
Sibbertoft	Sulby P	1	1	*Ibid.* fo. 225
Sixhills	Sixhills G	1	2	*Ibid.* fo. 82v
South Croxton	Croxton P	1	2	*Ibid.* fo. 243
Steeple Barton	Osney A	1	1	*Ibid.* fo. 303
Stotfold	Chicksand G	1	1	*Ibid.* fo. 406v

Parish	Order	Pre-sentations of this kind	Total pre-sentations to this parish	Reference
Stow	Bourne A	1	2	*Ibid.* fo. 142
Swaton	Barlings P	1	2	*Ibid.* fo. 61v
Utterby	Ormesby G	1	2	*Ibid.* fo. 40v
Whitton	Welbeck P	3	3	*Ibid.* fos. 82, 159v; Reg. 25, fo. 19
Witham on the Hill	Bridlington A	1	2	Reg. 25, fo. 15v
Withcote	Owston A	1	2	Reg. 23, fo. 238
Worminghall	St Frideswide A	1	1	*Ibid.* fo. 315

Parishes to which religious were presented by patrons not known to be of their own house

Parish	Total pre-sentations to this parish	Presentee (with order if known)	Patron	Register
Ancaster	1	John Rydding, canon of Alvingham	Pr and C Malton	23 fo. 116
Barrowby	2	John Colby, abbot of Newburgh	Pr and C Eye	23 fo. 137
Burton Stather	3	John Penketh, canon	A and C Norton	23 fo. 126
Chacombe	3	Richard Braybrooke, canon of Owston	Pr and C Chacombe	23 fo. 178
Cotes by Stow	3	Robert Sharpe, canon	A and C Welbeck	23 fo. 149
Duston	5	Thomas Copull, prior of Caldewell	A and C St James Northampton	23 fo. 210
Kirkby Green	2	Thomas Awkeland, canon	P and C Thurgarton	23 fo. 107
Kislingbury	2	Mag. Gregory Norwich, prior of Bushmead	Lord Latimer	23 fo. 205
Langton	1	Richard Ingland, canon	Pr and C Bullington	23 fo. 104
Marton	5	Thomas Jackson, canon	Pr and C St Katherine by Lincoln	23 fo. 150v

Parish	Total number of pre-sentations to this parish	Presentee (with order if known)	Patron	Register
Milton Keynes	4	William King, canon	Abbot of St Albans	23 fo. 325 v
Owston	1	Thomas Barker, prior of Newburgh	Brian Higden	25 fo. 13 v
Saleby	1	John Smyth, canon of Sempringham	Pr and C Sixhills	23 fo. 141 v
Seaton	1	Thomas Saunders, prior of Chacombe	Thomas Emson	23 fo. 214
Shelswell	6	Stephen Verny, brother of Ashridge	Leonard Verny	23 fo. 304
Sixhill	2	Richard Whitby, canon of Sempringham	Pr and C Sixhills	23 fo. 141
Stamford St George	2	Thomas *Yeus*, abbot of Garendon	John Goldsmith	23 fo. 50
Stoke Albany	1	John Langton, abbot of St Mary Graces London	Thomas Lovell	23 fo. 169
Theddlethorpe	3	John Woodbridge, prior of Pentney	William Willoughby	23 fo. 104
Theddlethorpe	3	William Marton, abbot of Bardney	William Willoughby	25 fo. 13
Tumby	1	William Gayton, prior of Sixhills	William Littleburn	23 fo. 140
Weston	1	Richard Gresley	John Zouche	25 fo. 63 v
Withcote	2	Richard Braybrooke, canon of Owston	William Smith	23 fo. 238

NON-RESIDENTS 1514-1520/21

Abbreviations:

		Pg.	on pilgrimage
P.	Pluralist	C/RS	chaplain or in the royal
St.	studying		service
C.	canon	Dp.	parish depopulated
D.	engaged on diocesan	V.	vicarage
	administration	R.	rectory

Note: a parish will be found under the first letter of the modern place-name: e.g. Market Bosworth under M to facilitate references to L.R.S. 33. *Oxford* and *Cambridge* refer to Emden's *Biographical Registers* (see bibliography, p. 223).

	Parish	Incumbent and reason for non-residence where known	Reference
P.	Abkettleby V.	Mag. Robert Mylnys M.A.—also rector of Saxilby	*L.R.S.* 33, p. 25; Reg. 23, fo. 236
St.	Adderbury V.	Mag. Ralph Barnake —at Oxford as chancellor's commissary	*L.R.S.* 33, p. 126; Reg. 25, fo. 47; *Oxford*, I, 110
	Addington R.	Mag. William Hanwell	*L.R.S.* 33, p. 46; Reg. 23, fo. 225
P.	Addlethorpe R.	Mag. Gilbert Beken-saw—canonry at the Newarke, Leicester	*L.R.S.* 33, p. 78; Reg. 23, fo. 60
	Adstock R.	John Staple	*L.R.S.* 33, p. 47; Reg. 23, fo. 332
	Alconbury V.	Mag. Robert Tomson	*L.R.S.* 33, p. 1; Reg. 25, fo. 56; Cj. 2, fo. 77
P.	Aldbury (Herts) R.	Dom. Roger Bram-ston—another cure	*L.R.S.* 33, p. 102; Reg. 23, fo. 380v
P.	Aldenham V.	Mag. Robert Mar-shall—another benefice	*L.R.S.* 33, p. 102

	Parish	Incumbent and reason for non-residence where known	Reference
	Alkborough V.	Dom. John Belte— has not resided for 7 years	Reg. 23, fo. 160; Cj. 2, fos. 31v, 36
	Althorpe R.	Mag. Ralph Babington	*L.R.S.* 33, p. 92
	Alvescot R.	Mag. William Barowe	*L.R.S.* 33, p. 133; Reg. 25, fo. 44v; *Oxford*, 1, 233
P.	Ampthill R.	Mag. John Davidson —has not resided for 5 years; another benefice	*L.R.S.* 33, p. 107; Cj. 2, fo. 35
P.	Anderby R.	Thomas Mawdesley —cure in London	*L.R.S.* 33, p. 81; Cj. 2, fo. 35
P.	Ashby de la Zouch V.	William Skelton— another benefice	Cj. 2, fo. 77v; *Cambridge*, p. 530
C/RS	Ashwell V.	Mag. James Denton —almoner to queen of France	*L.R.S.* 33, p. 109; Reg. 25, fo. 6; *Cambridge*, p. 182
C.	Aspenden R.	John Sutton—order of St John of Jerusalem	*L.R.S.* 33, p. 110; Cj. 2, fo. 30v
	Aston Sandford R.	Dom. Christopher Tayler	*L.R.S.* 33, p. 50; Reg. 23, fo. 349
P.	Aynho R.	Richard Person— another benefice	Cj. 2, fo. 30v
C/RS	Barby R.	Mag. George Hamond—chaplain to queen of France	Cj. 2, fo. 34
	Barnoldby-le-Beck R.	Dom. William Atkynson *alias* Cooke	*L.R.S.* 33, p. 84; Reg. 23, fo. 141
P.	Barnwell R.	Mag. John William-son—another benefice	Cj. 2, fo. 34v
C/RS	Barwell R.	Dom. Thomas Angell —in royal service	*L.R.S.* 33, p. 21; Reg. 25, fo. 37; Cj. 2, fos. 25v, 31

	Parish	Incumbent and reason for non-residence where known	Reference
	Beaconsfield R.	William Delabere	*L.R.S.* 33, p. 37; Reg. 23, fo. 348
P.	Beeby R.	Laurence Potter—another cure	Cj. 2, fo. 25v
	Beelsby R.	Dom. Ralph Draper—has not taken possession since institution	*L.R.S.* 33, p. 85; Reg. 25, fo. 20v
C/RS	Begbroke R.	Richard Sutton—private chaplain; see also Odell	*L.R.S.* 33, p. 128; Cj. 2, fo. 34v
	Belton in Isle of Axholme R.	Mag. William Asheton	*L.R.S.* 33, p. 97; Reg. 25, fo. 26v
P.	Biddenham R.	Mag. Robert Halitreholme—lives at Beverley	*L.R.S.* 33, p. 105
	Bigby R.	Dom. Thomas Cooke	*L.R.S.* 33, p. 90; Reg. 23, fo. 116
P.	Bladon R.	Mag. Christopher Barnes—another living	*L.R.S.* 33, p. 130; Reg. 23, fo. 305v
P.	Blyborough R.	Richard Graunte—resides elsewhere at a chantry	*L.R.S.* 33, p. 94; Cj. 2, fo. 38
P.	Bottesford	Mag. Thomas Pert—another benefice; see Broughton, Sibstone	*L.R.S.* 33, p. 25; Reg. 23, fo. 267
P.	Bow Brickhill R.	Mag. Thomas Digent—other livings	*L.R.S.* 33, p. 51; Reg. 25, fo. 54; *Cambridge*, p. 174
St.	Bratoft R.	Mag. William Clifton—probably at Oxford	*L.R.S.* 33, p. 79; Reg. 23, fo. 132v; *Oxford*, 1, 443
	Brattleby R.	Dom. Lionel Jakson	*L.R.S.* 33, p. 100; Reg. 23, fo. 157
	Brigsley R.	Dom. John Bull	*L.R.S.* 33, p. 85; Reg. 23, fo. 146v

Parish	Incumbent and reason for non-residence where known	Reference
Brington R.	Dom. Adam Bekensaw	*L.R.S.* 33, p. 1; Reg. 23, fo. 382v
C. Brocklesby R.	Dom. Robert Esington—abbot of Newhouse	*L.R.S.* 33, p. 91
D. Broughton (Hunts)	John Galion—suffragan bishop; has another benefice	*L.R.S.* 33, p. 7; Reg. 25, fo. 58v
P. Broughton R. (Oxon)	Mag. Thomas Pert—has other benefices; see Bottesford, Sibstone	*L.R.S.* 33, p. 127; Reg. 25, fo. 46
P. Broughton R. (St Lawrence)	Dom. John Rudd—has another benefice	*L.R.S.* 33, p. 51; Cj. 2, fo. 28
D. Bucknell R.	Dom. John Galyky—probably 'Galion', suffragan bishop	*L.R.S.* 33, p. 124; Reg. 25, fo. 24
C/RS Buckworth R.	Mag. Thomas Cade—chaplain to Duke of Buckingham; see also Burford	Cj. 2, fo. 77; *L. and P.* II, pt. II, no. 3173
C/RS Burford V.	Mag. Thomas Cade—see also Buckworth	*L.R.S.* 33, p. 133; Reg. 25, fo. 44
St. Burgh on Bain V.	William Missenden—student at Cambridge	*L.R.S.* 33, p. 65; Reg. 25, fo. 44
St. Burton-by-Lincoln R.	John Sawley—at Oxford	*L.R.S.* 33, p. 99; Reg. 22, fo. 164v
P. Burwell V.	Dom. Andrew Young—other benefices	*L.R.S.* 33, p. 74; Reg. 23, fos. 78v
P. Cadeby R.	Dom. Henry Sutton—resides in benefice in Somerset	*L.R.S.* 33, p. 20; *A.A.S.R.P.* XXVIII (1905), 142
C/RS Calverton R.	Mag. Edward Cholverton—in queen's service	*L.R.S.* 33, p. 52; Cj. 2, fo. 29v
S. Careby R.	Dom. William Sharp	Cj. 2, fo. 8

	Parish	Incumbent and reason for non-residence where known	Reference
	Carlton R.	Mag. Thomas Permynter	*L.R.S.* 33, p. 195
	Castle Doning-ton V.	Henry Pemyrton	Cj. 2, fo. 86
	Catthorpe R.	Thomas Chesshyer	Cj. 2, fo. 44
D.	Chalfont St Giles R.	Mag. William Wittur —bishop's commis-sary	*L.R.S.* 33, p. 37; Reg. 25, fo. 53 v
D.	Charlbury V.	Mag. James Whit-stones—vicar general	*L.R.S.* 33, p. 135; Reg. 23, fo. 271
P.	Charlton on Otmoor R.	Mag. James Fitz-james, M.A.—benefice in London	*L.R.S.* 33, p. 124; Reg. 23, fo. 306 v
P.	Cheddington R.	Mag. James Clere-borow (Clark)—benefice in Cam-bridgeshire	*L.R.S.* 33, p. 42; Reg. 23, fo. 338 v; *Cambridge*, p. 138
P.	Chinnor R.	Mag. Robert Aisshewn M.A.—other livings	*L.R.S.* 33, p. 120
St.	Church Hand-borough R.	Mag. John Higdon—at Oxford	*L.R.S.* 33, p. 129; Reg. 25, fo. 47 v
	Clanfield V.	Dom. Miles Pryket	*L.R.S.* 33, p. 132; Reg. 23, fo. 306
	Claxby (Lincs) R.	Dom. Thomas Turpyn	*L.R.S.* 33, p. 89; Reg. 23, fo. 74
P.	Clifton R.	Mag. Ralph Cantrell B.C.L.—other benefices	*L.R.S.* 33, p. 113; Reg. 23, fo. 386; *Cambridge*, p. 121
Dp. C.	Cotes-by-Stow V.	Fr William Crosse—canon of Welbeck; no vicar for 7 years	*L.R.S.* 33, p. 96; Reg. 23, fo. 155 v; Beresford, p. 362
P.	Congerstone R.	Dom. Thomas Storar —benefice in Northampton	*L.R.S.* 33, p. 22; Reg. 23, fo. 267

	Parish	Incumbent and reason for non-residence where known	Reference
	Cornwell R.	Dom. John Beryman	*L.R.S.* 33, p. 135; Reg. 23, fo. 307v
P.	Cosgrove R.	Ralph Bedyll—resident in Gainsborough	Cj. 2, fo. 31v
P.	Courtenhall R.	William Redd—see Market Bosworth	Cj. 2, fo. 2
P.	Crick R.	Mag. David Vaughan—resident at Warwick	Cj. 2, fo. 34
	Croft V.	Mag. Richard Cartwright—resident at Mumby	*L.R.S.* 33, p. 80; Reg. 23, fo. 132v
P.	Croughton R.	Mag. Richard Skipwith—resident at Warwick	Cj. 2, fos. 26, 34
P.	Cublington R.	John Bexwick, resident at Manchester	*L.R.S.* 33, p. 44
	Cuddesdon V.	Dom. Stephen Brawderibbe	*L.R.S.* 33, p. 137; Reg. 25, fo. 44; Cj. 2, fo. 25
St.	Dean R.	Mag. Thomas Drax—probably at Oxford	*L.R.S.* 33, p. 115; *Oxford*, I, 592
Dp. St.	Denham R.	Mag. Philip Powell, B.C. & Cn.L.—probably at Oxford	*L.R.S.* 33, p. 37; Reg. 23, fo. 326; *Oxford*, II, 977; Beresford, p. 341
	Desford R.	Dom. Edmund Lacy	Cj. 2, fos. 27, 32
	Dinton V.	Mag. Edmund Horde—bishop's commissary	*L.R.S.* 33, p. 39; Reg. 25, fo. 54v
	Dodford V.	Dom. John Bowden	Reg. 23, fo. 212v; Cj. 2, fo. 31v
C/RS	Donington on Bain R.	Richard Palyn—king's service	*L.R.S.* 33, p. 66; Cj. 2, fo. 25

	Parish	Incumbent and reason for non-residence where known	Reference
	Dowsby R.	Dom. Thomas Marmyon	*L.R.S.* 33, p. 56
C.	Drayton R.	Dom. Richard Somerby, B.A.—curate not residing since canon of Wroxton	*L.R.S.* 33, p. 126; Reg. 23, fo. 289 v
	Ducklington R.	John Johnson	*L.R.S.* 33, p. 132; Reg. 23, fo. 295 v
	Dunton (Bucks) R.	Dom. Richard Alwey	*L.R.S.* 33, p. 41
	Easington R.	Mag. John Brirdenis	*L.R.S.* 33, p. 119; Reg. 25, fo. 45 v
C.	East Haddon V.	Mag. Thomas Barker —prior of Newburgh; other benefices	Cj. 2, fo. 26 v; Reg. 25, fo. 13 v
	East Keal (half of) R.	Dom. John Ruston	*L.R.S.* 33, p. 77; Reg. 25, fo. 22 v
	Eastwell R.	Dom. John Pexall	*L.R.S.* 33, p. 26; Reg. 23, fo. 268
	Edgcott R.	Dom. John Man—rector not resident on 16 May 1519, but resident by January 1519/20	*L.R.S.* 33, p. 47; Reg. 23, fo. 347 v; cf. Cj. 2, fo. 106 v
	Ellesborough R.	Nicholas Tetryll	*L.R.S.* 33, p. 40; Reg. 25, fo. 54 v
St.	Ellington R.	Mag. John Stanley—probably at Cambridge	*L.R.S.* 33, p. 1; Cj. 2, fo. 34 v; *Cambridge*, p. 550
P.	Emington R.	John Stratton—has chantry at Winchester	*L.R.S.* 33, p. 119; Cj. 2, fo. 27
	Faldingworth R.	William Wood	*L.R.S.* 33, p. 100; Reg. 23, fo. 45
	Faringdon R.	Mag. Thomas Falk	Cj. 2, fo. 26

Parish	Incumbent and reason for non-residence where known	Reference
Fawley R.	Mag. Robert Colyns —no resident rector for 30 years	*L.R.S.* 33, p. 37; Reg. 25, fo. 53 v
P. Fillingham R.	Mag. Thomas Scisson —another benefice	*L.R.S.* 33, p. 94; Reg. 25, fo. 26
Dp. P. Fleet Marston R.	Dom. Robert Hewys—resides in another benefice	*L.R.S.* 33, p. 50; Reg. 23, fo. 345; Beresford, p. 341
D. Flixborough R.	Mag. Geoffrey Hennage—possibly bishop's chaplain	*L.R.S.* 33, p. 93; Reg. 23, fo. 118 v; Reg. 25, fo. 76 v
C/RS Folkingham R.	Dom. Thomas Hall— in king's chapel	*L.R.S.* 33, p. 56
Foston R.	Henry Riding	*L.R.S.* 33, p. 15; Reg. 22, fo. 212 v
C. Fritwell V.	Dom. Robert Brice— canon of St Frideswide's	*L.R.S.* 33, p. 124; Reg. 25, fo. 48 v
Garsington R.	Mag. John More— provost of Oriel	*L.R.S.* 33, p. 137; Reg. 25, fo. 46
Gayhurst R.	Dom. John Wode	*L.R.S.* 33, p. 51; Reg. 25, fo. 53
St. Grafham R.	Mag. William Wylton, M.A.—probably at Cambridge	*L.R.S.* 33, p. 1; Reg. 23, fo. 373; *Cambridge*, p. 658
C/RS Grainsby R.	Dom. John Gascoigne —in service of Mr Tailboys	*L.R.S.* 33, p. 87
Grayingham R.	John Comys *alias* Thomson	*L.R.S.* 33, pp. 97–8; Reg. 23, fo. 157 v
P. Great Billing R.	Mag. John Egerton— lives at Lichfield	Cj. 2, fo. 34
C/RS Great Bowden (Leics.) R.	Mag. John Chambre —has never yet been there—royal physician	*L.R.S.* 33, p. 13; Reg. 23, fo. 260 v; *Oxford*, 1, 385

	Parish	Incumbent and reason for non-residence where known	Reference
P.	Great Horwood R.	Mag. Andrew Benstead—other livings	*L.R.S.* 33, p. 44; *Oxford*, 1, 169
P.	Great Linford R.	Mag. Brian Darley—other livings	*L.R.S.* 33, p. 51; Reg. 25, fo. 53v; *Cambridge*, p. 177
St.	Great Paxton V.	Thomas Erle—studying	Cj. 2, fo. 31v
	Grendon Underwood R.	Dom. Richard Hunteley	*L.R.S.* 33, p. 50; Reg. 25, fo. 51
	Hambleden R.	Mag. Lancelot Claxton	*L.R.S.* 33, p. 36
Pg.	Hamerton R.	Dom. Robert Appulby—on pilgrimage	*L.R.S.* 33, p. 2; Cj. 2, fo. 84
St.	Handborough Church R.	Mag. John Higden—at Oxford	*L.R.S.* 33, p. 129; Reg. 25, fo. 47v
	Harringworth V.	Henry Newman—at Cambridge	Cj. 2, fo. 29v
	Harston R.	Dom. Richard Brown	*L.R.S.* 33, p. 25; Reg. 25, fo. 40v
	Haversham R.	Dom. John Clement —resident in Leicester	*L.R.S.* 33, p. 51; Cj. 2, fo. 30
P.	Hawridge R.	Dom. Christopher Mitchell—has cure in London	*L.R.S.* 33, p. 44; Cj. 2, fo. 30
	Haynes V.	Dom. Thomas Burley	*L.R.S.* 33, p. 109; Reg. 25, fo. 61
P.	Heapham R.	Dom. Thomas Pain—resident in Lincoln cathedral	*L.R.S.* 33, p. 97; Reg. 25, fo. 29
P.	Heather R.	Dom. Thomas Day—in Cornwall	*L.R.S.* 33, p. 20
Pg.	Helpston R.	Henry Wylson—on pilgrimage to Rome	Reg. 23, fo. 210; Cj. 2, fo. 32
P.	Hemswell R.	Dom. Roger Adamson—rector at St Stephen's Westminster	*L.R.S.* 33, p. 94; Reg. 23, fo. 156v

	Parish	Incumbent and reason for non-residence where known	Reference
	Hertford, St Andrew R.	Dom. Thomas Bell	*L.R.S.* 33, p. 111; Reg. 23, fo. 382
P.	Hockliffe R.	Dom. Edmund Wyngate—resides at Chalgrove	*L.R.S.* 33, p. 102; Reg. 23, fo. 391
C.	Holcot R.	Mag. Robert Pocapart—order of St John of Jerusalem	Cj. 2, fo. 30v; Beresford, p. 339
P.	Horncastle V.	Mag. Richard Denham—another benefice	*L.R.S.* 33, p. 65; Reg. 25, fo. 17v; *Oxford*, I, 570
	Houghton Conquest R.	Mag. William Frankleyn	*L.R.S.* 33, p. 106
P.	Houghton on the Hill R.	Mag. Thomas Wygeston—at the Newarke, Leicester	*L.R.S.* 33, p. 12
P.	Hungerton V.	John Hammond—resides elsewhere	Cj. 2, fo. 28
	Husbands Bosworth R.	Thomas Clark	Cj. 2, fo. 64
	Ibstone R.	Ralph Meddey—old and ill	*L.R.S.* 33, p. 119
P.	Ibstock R.	Dom. William Watson—another benefice	*L.R.S.* 33, p. 21
	Iffley V.	Mag. Richard Apjohn B.Cn.L.—both rector and vicar non-resident	*L.R.S.* 33, p. 137; Cj. 2, fo. 44v; Reg. 22, fo. 219
D.	Islip R.	Mag. Peter Potkyn—special commissary—other benefices	*L.R.S.* 33, p. 122; Reg. 25, fo. 48; Cj. 2, fo. 45 ff.
	Kegworth R.	Dom. Thomas Leson	*L.R.S.* 33, p. 27
C/RS	Kelshall R.	Dom. William Atkinson—in queen's service	*L.R.S.* 33, p. 110; Reg. 23, fo. 380
	Kempston V.	Thomas Taillor	*L.R.S.* 33, p. 106

	Parish	Incumbent and reason for non-residence where known	Reference
	Keyston R.	Dom. Bromewiche—has not been there for 20 years	*L.R.S.* 33, p. 3
St.	Kidlington V.	Mag. Laurence Stubbys—president of Magdalene	*L.R.S.* 33, p. 128; Reg. 23, fo. 298
C.	Killingholme V.	Dom. Robert Esington—canon of Newhouse	*L.R.S.* 33, p. 91; Reg. 25, fo. 15 v
P.	Kingham R.	Mag. Thomas Bowden, M.A.—probably other benefices	*L.R.S.* 33, p. 134; Reg. 22, fo. 223 v; *Cambridge*, p. 82
	King's Langley V.	Hugh Newton	Cj. 2, fo. 31
P.	King's Ripton	Dom. Robert Wicheham—rector of Hemingford but does not reside there	*L.R.S.* 33, p. 6; Reg. 25, fo. 56 v
	Kirton in Holland V.	Mag. Robert Collys	*L.R.S.* 33, p. 70; Reg. 23, fo. 72 v
P.	Kislingbury R.	Mag. Robert Wambresley—vicar of Pomfrey	Cj. 2, fo. 26
Dp.	Knaptoft R.	Mag. John Nevell	*L.R.S.* 33, p. 18; Reg. 25, fo. 38; Beresford, p. 360
	Langton by Horncastle R.	Dom. William Watkynson	*L.R.S.* 33, p. 68; Reg. 23, fo. 118
	Langton Church R.	Mag. Polidore Vergil—papal collector	*L.R.S.* 33, p. 9
	Langton by Partney R.	Dom. John Bonde	*L.R.S.* 33, p. 66; Reg. 25, fo. 14 v
	Launton R.	Mag. John Hawkesford—held Marsh Gibbon	Cj. 2, fo. 5

	Parish	Incumbent and reason for non-residence where known	Reference
C.	Laughton V.	Dom. William Cuthbert—canon of Sempringham	*L.R.S.* 33, p. 98; Reg. 23, fo. 144 v
	Lea R.	Dom. Robert Dowghtfyer	*L.R.S.* 33, p. 98
P.	Leckhampstead R.	Mag. Robert Ashcombe—other livings	*L.R.S.* 33, p. 46; *Oxford*, I, 55
St.	Letchworth R.	Joseph Stepney—studying	*L.R.S.* 33, p. 113; Cj. 2, fo. 32
	Lilley R.	Mag. Hugh Ellys	*L.R.S.* 33, p. 112
	Lillingstone Lovell R.	Dom. Laurence Dobson	*L.R.S.* 33, p. 122; Reg. 23, fo. 278
P.	Little Gaddesdon R.	John Wyon—resides at Oakley (Beds)	*L.R.S.* 33, p. 101; Cj. 2, fo. 27 v
	Little Grimsby V.	Dom. John Todd	*L.R.S.* 33, p. 74; Reg. 22, fo. 141 v
	Little Kimble R.	Dom. Nicholas Thomson	*L.R.S.* 33, p. 39
	Little Munden R.	Charles Smith	*L.R.S.* 33, p. 109; Reg. 25, fo. 58
P.	Little Steeping R.	Dom. Thomas Austen—has farm of rectory at Waynfleet All Saints	*L.R.S.* 33, p. 77; Reg. 23, fo. 382 v
P.	Little Stewkeley R.	Dom. William Redd—see also Market Bosworth and Courteenhall	Cj. 2, fo. 29
St.	Loddington R.	Mag. Thomas Crokar—at New College, Oxford	Cj. 2, fo. 26 v
	Lower Gravenhurst R.	Dom. Edward Wodward	*L.R.S.* 33, p. 108; Reg. 23, fo. 403 v
	Ludborough R.	Dom. Ralph Bakar	*L.R.S.* 33, p. 73; Reg. 25, fo. 12 v
C.	Ludgershall R.	Mag. John Mableston—order of St John of Jerusalem	*L.R.S.* 33, p. 50

	Parish	Incumbent and reason for non-residence where known	Reference
	Lusby R.	Dom. John Somerby	*L.R.S.* 33, p. 76; Reg. 25, fo. 12 v
P.	Lutterworth R.	Dom. John Parsons —resides at another benefice at Rotheley	*L.R.S.* 33, p. 16; Reg. 23, fo. 253 v
	Liddington V.	Mag. Robert Purey	Cj. 2, fo. 29
	Mablethorpe St Mary R.	Dom. Robert Bulmer	*L.R.S.* 33, p. 82
St.	Manton R.	Mag. Thomas Topclyff—at Cambridge	*L.R.S.* 33, p. 93; Reg. 25, fo. 27
	Mareham-le-Fen R.	Dom. William Browne	*L.R.S.* 33, p. 65; Reg. 25, fo. 20 v
	Market Bosworth R.	William Redd—see also Courteenhall and Little Stukeley	*L.R.S.* 33, p. 10; Cj. 2, fo. 2
	Maulden R.	William Westerdale	Cj. 2, fo. 86 v
P.	Medbourne R.	Mag. Roger Pisford —at the Newarke, Leicester	*L.R.S.* 33, p. 12
St.	Meppershall R.	Mag. John Fitzherbert—at Louvain	Cj. 2, fo. 35
P.	Middle Claydon R.	William Brodehed— another benefice	*L.R.S.* 33, p. 50
	Middleton Stony R.	Dom. Richard Walton	*L.R.S.* 33, p. 125; Reg. 23, fo. 306 v
	Milton Keynes R.	Dom. William Poullam	*L.R.S.* 33, p. 52; Reg. 23, fo. 347
P.	Misterton R.	Mag. William Walker —another benefice	Cj. 2, fo. 28 v; Beresford, p. 360
St.	Mixbury R.	Mag. James Gilbert— other livings; probably at Oxford	*L.R.S.* 33, p. 123; Reg. 23, fo. 307; *Oxford*, III, 1643
C/RS	Moorby R.	Richard Ward— steward to John Husy, see also Pickworth	*L.R.S.* 33, p. 66; Cj. 2, fo. 31

Parish	Incumbent and reason for non-residence where known	Reference
C/RS Moulton V.	Mag. William Bond —possibly chaplain to Thomas Sutton	*L.R.S.* 33, p. 60; *Cambridge*, p. 72
P. Mursley R.	Dom. John Cleydon —another benefice	*L.R.S.* 33, p. 42; Cj. 2, fo. 103 v
St. Muston R.	Mag. William Clifton—at Oxford	*L.R.S.* 33, p. 25; Reg. 25, fo. 3 v; *Oxford*, I, 276
P. Narborough R.	Dr Darley—see Great Linford; other benefices	*L.R.S.* 33, p. 17
Newton Purcell R.	Dom. William Lacy *alias* Clark—cure in London	*L.R.S.* 33, p. 122; Reg. 23, fo. 307 v
Newton by Toft R.	Dom. Robert Wilkynson	*L.R.S.* 33, p. 89; Reg. 23, fo. 146
North Aston V.	Dom. Giles Toofte	*L.R.S.* 33, p. 129; Reg. 23, fo. 276
North Cotes R.	Dom. Thomas Briayn	*L.R.S.* 33, p. 87
North Crawley R.	Dom. Edward Apjohn	*L.R.S.* 33, p. 52; Reg. 23, fo. 346
Northmoor V.	Mag. John Taylor— probably at Oxford	*L.R.S.* 33, p. 133; Reg. 23, fo. 285 v; *Oxford*, III, 1851
P. North Mimms V.	Mag. Hugh Walter— another benefice	*L.R.S.* 33, p. 102; Reg. 25, fo. 57 v
P. Odell R.	Dom Richard Sutton —also rector of Begbroke	*L.R.S.* 33, p. 123; Cj. 2, fo. 34 v
P. Oddington R.	Mag. John Leicester	*L.R.S.* 33, p. 113; Reg. 25, fos. 48 v, 49
P. Offord Cluny R.	Mag. Thomas Bedyll —other benefices	*L.R.S.* 33, p. 117
P. Orton Longueville R.	Mag. Christopher Hubbert—benefice in Devon	*L.R.S.* 33, p. 3; Reg. 23, fo. 379; Cj. 2, fo. 30

	Parish	Incumbent and reason for non-residence where known	Reference
	Oxford St Giles V.	Mag. Thomas Wode	*L.R.S.* 33, p. 140; Reg. 25, fo. 47 v
P.	Oxford St Michael R.	Mag. Richard Gurle, M.A.—other benefices	*L.R.S.* 33, p. 139; Reg. 23, fo. 306 v; *Oxford*, II, 793
	Pertenhall R.	Richard Hode	*L.R.S.* 33, p. 117; Cj. 2, fo. 86 v
C/RS	Pickworth (Lincs) R.	Richard Ward—see also Moorby; steward to John Husy	*L.R.S.* 33, p. 56
	Pitchcott R.	Dom. Robert Lyne *alias* Lyons	*L.R.S.* 33, p. 49; Reg. 23, fo. 342
P.	Puttenham R.	Dom. Roger Talons—has cure at Hackney, London	*L.R.S.* 33, p. 102; Reg. 25, fo. 58 v
	Quadring V.	Mag. Robert Hansard	*L.R.S.* 33, p. 70
	Radnage R.	Dom. Thomas Jones	*L.R.S.* 33, p. 36
	Radwell R.	Dom. Walter Jeffrey	*L.R.S.* 33, p. 110; Reg. 23, fo. 355 v
St.	Rand R.	Edward Fulnetby—student at Oxford	*L.R.S.* 33, p. 65; Reg. 23, fo. 134
C.	Ravensthorpe V.	Mag. Robert Wodilove—order of St John of Jerusalem	Cj. 2, fo. 34
P.	Rearsby R.	Mag. John Barton—benefice in Lincoln Cathedral	*L.R.S.* 33, p. 33
Dp. C.	Risby V.	Robert Barthelernew (*sic*)—canon of Thornholme	*L.R.S.* 33, p. 92; Reg. 23, fo. 155; Beresford, p. 362
	Rockingham R.	William Addeson	Cj. 2, fo. 25
C/RS	Rothwell R.	Dom. Thomas Lewys—in Lord Derby's household	*L.R.S.* 33, pp. 35, 86
	Rousham R.	Dom. Humphrey Wever	*L.R.S.* 33, p. 130; Reg. 23, fo. 307

	Parish	Incumbent and reason for non-residence where known	Reference
D.	Saddington R.	Mag. John Silvester—commissary	*L.R.S.* 33, p. 12
P.	Sapcote R.	Mag. John Shorthose—another benefice	Cj. 2, fo. 24v; Reg. 25, fo. 39; *A.A.S.R.P.* xxviii, 211
	Sawtry, All Saints R.	Hugh Bulkeley—said 'dared not reside'	Cj. 2, fos. 76v, 77; Reg. 23, fo. 368
	Scothern V.	Dom. John Bell	*L.R.S.* 33, p. 99
	Scotter R.	Ralph Stevenson	*L.R.S.* 33, p. 97; Reg. 23, fo. 143v
St.	Shabbington R.	Rector John Kale—at Cambridge; vicar John Berde—private chaplain	*L.R.S.* 33, p. 49; Reg. 23, fo. 332v
	Shangton R.	William Hawkrigge	Cj. 2, fo. 30
	Sheepy R.	Dom. John Vincent	*L.R.S.* 33, pp. 20, 22; Reg. 25, fo. 40v
P.	Shelton R.	Dom. Robert Coren—resides at Billesdon, Leicester	*L.R.S.* 33, p. 116; Reg. 23, fo. 394v
P.	Sibstone R.	Mag. Thomas Port—other benefices; see Bottesford and Broughton	*L.R.S.* 33, p. 19; Reg. 23, fo. 267v; *Oxford*, iii, 1501
P.	Skegness R.	Mag. John Marshall—resident at Tattershall	*L.R.S.* 33, p. 79
	Sotby R.	Dom. Thomas Yorke	*L.R.S.* 33, p. 64; Reg. 23, fo. 130v
St.	Souldern R.	Mag. John Chilcott—student at Oxford	*L.R.S.* 33, p. 123; Reg. 25, fo. 48v
	Southoe R.	Dom. Nicholas Both	Reg. 23, fo. 376; Cj. 2, fo. 77
	South Somercotes R.	Dom. Henry Rowte	*L.R.S.* 33, p. 74; Reg. 25, fo. 22

Parish	Incumbent and reason for non-residence where known	Reference
St. South Willing-ham R.	Thomas Compton —student at Cambridge	*L.R.S.* 33, p. 65; Reg. 25, fo. 21
Spelsbury V.	Mag. Robert Charde	Cj. 2, fo. 34v; Reg. 25, fo. 46v
P. Stallingborough V.	Mag. Vincent Totofte —resides in another benefice	*L.R.S.* 33, p. 90; Reg. 23, fo. 141
Stamford St George R.	Roger Saule	Cj. 2, fo. 91
Dp. P. Stantonbury V.	Dom. William Foster —was vicar of Bradwell	*L.R.S.* 33, p. 54; Beresford, p. 342
Stanton Harcourt V.	Dom. Richard Cowland	*L.R.S.* 33, p. 129; Reg. 23, fo. 280; Cj. 2, fo. 77
P. Stathern R.	Mag. William Tailand—other livings	*L.R.S.* 33, p. 27; Reg. 23, fo. 249v; *Cambridge*, p. 578
P. Stewton R.	Dom. Richard Daddy—resides elsewhere	*L.R.S.* 33, p. 73; Reg. 23, fo. 146
C/RS Stickney R.	Christopher Cudde-worth—chaplain to John Husy	*L.R.S.* 33, p. 76; Reg. 25, fo. 29v
P. Stilton R.	Mag. John Dunham —another benefice	Cj. 2, fo. 77
Stockerston R.	Benedict Davy	*L.R.S.* 33, p. 11; Reg. 25, fo. 38
Stoney Stanton R.	Mag. Christopher Fowler	*L.R.S.* 33, p. 15
Stoke Talmage R.	Mag. Thomas Haropp M.A.— resides at Haseley	*L.R.S.* 33, p. 120; Reg. 22, fo. 227v
St. Surfleet R.	Mag. William Clyf-ton B.C. & Cn.L.— see Muston	*L.R.S.* 33, p. 59; Reg. 23, fo. 131

Parish	Incumbent and reason for non-residence where known	Reference
Sutton in Marisco R.	Dom. Elisha Symon	*L.R.S.* 33, p. 83; Reg. 23, fo. 132 v
Swallow R.	Dom. Walter Curtesse —at Grimsby *ad libitum suum*	*L.R.S.* 33, p. 84
Swaton V.	Dom. John Thomas— canon of Barlings	*L.R.S.* 33, p. 56
P. Swerford R.	Dom. Bartholomew Tatton—another benefice	*L.R.S.* 33, p. 135; Reg. 23, fo. 302
Swineshead V.	Dom. Thomas Garton	*L.R.S.* 33, p. 2; Reg. 23, fo. 136
P. Swinhope T.	Dom. Richard Tomlynson—serves cure at West Randall	*L.R.S.* 33, p. 84; Cj. 2, fos. 77 v, 84
P. Swithland R.	Dom. William Hebb —benefice in Essex	*L.R.S.* 33, p. 28; *A.A.S.R.P.* XXVIII, 24
P. Tackley R.	Mag. Thomas Hulse —other livings	*L.R.S.* 33, p. 128; Cj. 2, fo. 29; *Oxford*, II, 981
Tadmarton R.	Dom. John Belamy	*L.R.S.* 33, p. 127; Reg. 23, fo. 227 v
P. Tathwell V.	Mag. John Falowes, M.A.—rector of S. Ormesby	*L.R.S.* 33, p. 75; Reg. 23, fo. 133
C/RS Therfield R.	Mag. Henry Rawlins —chaplain to the bishop of Salisbury	*L.R.S.* 33, p. 110; Reg. 25, fo. 56 v; *Oxford*, III, 1550
Thoresway R.	Richard Dawson	*L.R.S.* 33, p. 91; Reg. 23, fo. 144 v
Thurning R.	Mag. John Kidwell	*L.R.S.* 33, p. 2; Reg. 23, fo. 382 v
C/RS Tichmarsh R.	Richard Cobb— chaplain	Cj. 2, fo. 25

	Parish	Incumbent and reason for non-residence where known	Reference
	Tilbrook R.	Mag. Robert Gurnell	*L.R.S.* 33, p. 116; Reg. 23, fo. 397
	Tingrith R.	Dom. Robert Jesse	*L.R.S.* 33, p. 108; Reg. 25, fo. 52
	Toddington (part of) R.	Dom. Thomas Browne	*L.R.S.* 33, p. 104; Reg. 23, fo. 400 v
P.	Toft by Newton R.	Mag. William Billisby—another benefice	*L.R.S.* 33, p. 88; Reg. 23, fo. 110; *Cambridge*, p. 62
	Tothill R.	Dom. Henry Colyns	*L.R.S.* 33, p. 82; Reg. 23, fo. 46
St.	Tring V.	Mag. William Haryngton—probably at Oxford	*L.R.S.* 33, p. 101; Reg. 23, fo. 363
P.	Ulceby V.	Dom. Richard Clark—another benefice	*L.R.S.* 33, p. 91; Reg. 23, fo. 110 v
P.	Waddington St Mary R.	Dom. William Tupholm—another cure	*L.R.S.* 33, p. 93; Reg. 23, fo. 7 v
	Wallington R.	Dom. Richard Lofts	*L.R.S.* 33, p. 110; Reg. 23, fo. 381
St.	Waltham R.	Mag. John Fitz-herbert—in Paris; see Meppershall and Whilton	*L.R.S.* 33, p. 85; Cj. 2, fo. 35
	Wanlip R.	John Sherman	*L.R.S.* 33, p. 29
P.	Warkton R.	Mag. William Hillyer—another benefice	Cj. 2, fo. 31
St.	Watlington V.	Mag. John Scotte—probably at Oxford	*L.R.S.* 33, p. 120; Reg. 23, fo. 288; *Oxford*, III, 1656
	Waveden R.	Dom. John Milward —serves cure at Dodford, Northants	*L.R.S.* 33, p. 52

	Parish	Incumbent and reason for non-residence where known	Reference
St.	Welwyn R.	Mag. Thomas Thomson, B.Th.—probably at Cambridge	*L.R.S.* 33, p. 111; Reg. 23, fo. 369; *Cambridge*, p. 582
	Wendlebury R.	Mag. Griffin David	*L.R.S.* 33, p. 123; Reg. 23, fo. 307
	West Keal R.	Dom. Richard Witton	*L.R.S.* 33, p. 76; Reg. 23, fo. 101v
	Westmill R.	Mag. Robert Carleston—friend of Mag. Grene, commissary	*L.R.S.* 33, p. 110; Reg. 25, fo. 57v
	Westwell R.	Dom. John Horblery	*L.R.S.* 33, p. 132; Reg. 23, fo. 195
St.	Whilton R.	Mag. John Fitzherbert—see Meppershall and Waltham	Cj. 2, fo. 34
P.	Whipsnade R.	Robert Hoon—has cure in Norwich diocese	*L.R.S.* 33, p. 103; Cj. 2, fo. 35
P.	Whitchurch V.	Antony Cassewell—cure in Abingdon	*L.R.S.* 33, p. 45
	Wigginton R.	Mag. John Mogryche, B.C.L.	*L.R.S.* 33, p. 126; Reg. 23, fo. 299
P.	Willingham-by-Stowe R.	Miles Willen—another benefice	*L.R.S.* 33, p. 99; Reg. 25, fo. 16
C/RS	Willoughby Waterless R.	Mag. Peter Bek—chaplain to Marquis of Dorset	*A.A.S.R.P.* xxviii (1905), 135; Reg. 23, fos. 257, 266
St.	Wing V.	Stephen Farant—at Oxford	*L.R.S.* 33, p. 43; Cj. 2, fos. 31v, 29; Reg. 25, fo. 30v
P.	Winterton V.	Dom. Robert Wright—farmer of rectory of Barton Stather	*L.R.S.* 33, p. 92
	Winwick R.	Dom. John Rarson	*L.R.S.* 33, p. 1; Reg. 23, fo. 371

	Parish	Incumbent and reason for non-residence where known	Reference
C/RS	Witherley R.	Dom. William Marshall—private chaplain	*A.A.S.R.P.* xxviii (1905), 141
P.	Witney R.	Mag. Richard Sydnor	*L.R.S.* 33, p. 133; Reg. 25, fo. 49; *Oxford*, iii, 1839
	Woodwalton R.	Dom. John Hiham—has benefice at Luton	*L.R.S.* 33, p. 3; Reg. 23, fo. 380
	Wootton (Beds.) V.	Hugh Reve	*L.R.S.* 33, p. 105; Reg. 23, fo. 389
D.	Wootton (Oxon.) R.	Mag. Henry Wilcocks—one time vicar general and archdeacon Leicester	*L.R.S.* 33, p. 131; Reg. 23, fo. 292
	Woughton on the Green R.	Dom. James Wylson	*L.R.S.* 33, p. 52; Reg. 23, fo. 348
	Wrangle V.	Dom. Robert Walker	*L.R.S.* 33, p. 71; Reg. 23, fo. 136v
	Wymington R.	John Stokes	Cj. 2, fo. 86v
	Yarburgh R.	Mag. Robert Wade	*L.R.S.* 33, p. 73; Reg. 23, fo. 143
	Yelford R.	Dom. William Wynter	*L.R.S.* 33, p. 132; Reg. 25, fo. 49v

BIBLIOGRAPHY

MAIN WORKS USED OR CITED

Manuscripts

Lincoln Record Office

Register 22	Register of John Russell 1480–94
Register 23 and 24	Register of Bishop Smith 1495–1514
Register 25	Register of Bishops Wolsey and Atwater 1514–20/21
Register 26	Register of Bishop Longland 1520/21–1547
Robert Toneys *Repertorium*	An early sixteenth-century collection containing valuable indices to benefices in the Bishop's collation or appropriated to monastic houses
Additional Register 7, Bishop Fuller's Transcripts	Seventeenth-century transcripts of some sixteenth-century documents, now lost in their original
P.D. 1482-	Presentation Deeds
I.B. 1501-	Institution Bonds
Resignations. Box 1 Bundle 1482–	Resignations
Convocation. Box 1	Documents connected with Convocation, mainly concerned with the election of proctors
Bishops' Rentals, 1	Accounts of late fifteenth-century or early sixteenth episcopal dues
Bishops' Accounts, Misc. 6	Accounts of fees due to the bishop 1492–
Bishops' Accounts, Misc. 7	Accounts of fees due to the bishop 1499–1500
Bishops' Accounts, Misc. 8, 9, 10, 11, 12	Accounts of episcopal manors
Bishops' Accounts, Misc. 18	Thomas Darby's Book of Costs, an account book of episcopal household expenditure, 1508–9
For. 1, 2, 3	Early sixteenth-century Formulary Books

Protocols of Appeal. Box 74. 1514	Appeals to Canterbury and Rome
Religious Houses 2, 3	Notices of projected visitations and injunctions by Bishop Smith
Religious Houses 6	Receipts and Accounts for various religious houses in the early sixteenth century
Religious Houses 7	Documents relating to appropriations of churches by religious houses
Subsid. 1, 3, 4, 5, 6, 7a	Late fifteenth-century lists of exemptions from the clerical tenth
Viv. 2, 3, 4, 5	Archidiaconal visitation returns 1489–1510
Vj. 5	Episcopal visitation returns of the archdeaconries of Lincoln and Stow and some religious houses, 1500
Vj. 6	Episcopal Visitation Returns 1507–36
Vj. 7	Episcopal Visitation Returns 1515–21
Cj. 1	Proceedings in the court of the prebendal church of St Peter and St Paul, Buckingham, 1493–1504
Cj. 2	Bishop's Court of Audience Book 1514–19/20
Cj. 3, 4	Bishop Longland's Court Book 1525–30
Penances, Box 3	Certificates of the performance of penance —notices of purgation
Visitation Monitions 1500–1739	Notices of projected visitations
Inventories, Boxes 2 and 3	Inventories 1500–
Rev/L/1, 2, 3	Lincoln archdeaconry accounts
Rev/S/1	Stow archdeaconry accounts
Monson MSS. LXXVIII	Gild Accounts of Holy Trinity Louth

Lincoln Cathedral Muniments

A. 3. 2, 3, 4	Dean and Chapter Act Books. 3 vols. 1496–1520
Bj. 3. 3	Accounts of the common fund 1500–20
Bj. 5. 16. 4	Inventory of offerings to the shrine of St Hugh
A. 4. 7. 9	Account of the clerk of the fabric

Parochial Records
Kirton Lindsey   Churchwardens' and Gild Accounts 1495–

Aylesbury Record Office
D/A/V. 1   Buckingham Archidiaconal visitation pro-
                              ceedings 1491–
D/A/We. 1   Proceedings before the bishop's commis-
                              sary 1519
D/A/C. 1   Proceedings before the bishop's commis-
                              sary 1521

Lambeth Palace
Archbishop Warham,   Material relating to the probate disputes
Register 2 vols.   1500–15
CM/VI/75; CM/XI/83,
84, 85

Bodleian Library, Oxford
MSS. Barlow, 54   Accounts for the commissary for North-
                              ampton
MSS. Browne Willis, 39   Collections for the Cathedral and Diocese
                              of Lincoln
MSS. Ashmole, 858   Grants of coats of arms
MSS. Rawlinson, A. 370   *Oculus Sacerdotis*
MSS. Bodley, 282   Sixteenth-century letters

Oxford University
Register D 1485–1505   University Register

British Museum
Lansdowne MSS. 978   Bishop Kennet's transcripts
Harleian MSS. 5398   Fifteenth-century sermons

Public Record Office
REQ 1/3; 1/4; 1/5   Court of Requests proceedings
C 85/115   Significations of Excommunication
K.B. 27/998–   Proceedings of the court of King's Bench
  K.B. 29/140–154
E. 36/55/   1522 Rutland Muster Roll

Salisbury Cathedral Muniments

Harward's Memorials   Chapter Act book
1497, Chapter Acts
Tom 14

Westminster Abbey Muniments

16038   Letter from Bishop Smith to Sir Reginald
                                             Bray

Cambridge University Library

Ely Diocesan Documents Registers of Bishops Alcock and West
G. 1. 6, 7

Eton College

E. A. 19, 20, 21, 22, 23,   Audit Rolls 1480–90
24

Vatican Archives (microfilm)

MS. Otto Lat. 2948   Accounts of the papal collector in the
                                             early sixteenth century

Early printed books

Bodleian Library

Bishop Atwater's Books

Th. Seld. U. 1. 6   *Thomas Valois et Nicholas Triveth in libros
                                             beati Augustini de Civitate Dei.* Toulouse,
                                             1488

Early Devotional Literature

S. Seld. d. 8   *Mirkus Festial.* Caxton, 1483
S. Seld. d. 5   *The Mirror of the World.* Caxton, 1480/1
S. Seld. d. 10   Lydgate, *Life of Mary.* Caxton, n.d.
Auct. QQ. sup. 1. 15   *Cordiale of the Four last things.* Caxton, 1479
S. Seld. d. 11   Clement Maidstone, *Directorium sacer-
                                             dotum.* Caxton
Douce MM. 493   Life of St Margaret. Pynson, n.d.
S. Seld. d. 11   *The arte and crafte to know well to deye.*
                                             Caxton, 1490
S. Seld. d. 82   *Quattuor Sermones.* Caxton, 1483

Lincoln Cathedral Library

C. I. I–
SS. I. I–15
SS. 2. I–
SS. 3. I–
SS. 4. I–
SS. 5. I–

The entire collection of books published before 1520 examined to see whether they were owned by priests from the diocese[1]

Brasenose College Library

Bishop Atwater's Books

U. B. S. I. 27	Jo. Duns Scotus, *Super III^or Sententiarum.* Venice, 1477
U. B. S. I. 16	Alex. de Hales, *Summa Theologiae.* 4 vols. Nuremberg, 1481–2
U. B. S. I. 35–6, 49, 52, 61	Gaietanus, *Phisicorum Metheororum, de Reactione, de Celo et Mundo,* Venice, 1498. *de Anima,* Bergamo, 1493. Jo. de Grandavo *de Substantia orbis*
U. B. S. I. 28	Jerome, *Epistolae.* Venice, 1476
U. B. S. I. 65	Albertus, *de Animalibus.* Mantua, 1479
U. B. S. I. 70–	Nich. Florentinus, *Sermo tertius de dispositionibus medicinalibus.* Pavia
U. B. S. I. 89	Petrarch, *Res memorandae*
U. B. S. I. 56	Lactantius Firmianus, *Opera.* Venice, 1497

Cambridge University Library

Pr. Bk. 1734   Vergil, *Opera.* Venice, *c.* 1486

Printed sources

Anstey, H. ed. *Epistolae Academicae.* 2 vols. Oxford Historical Society, vols. xxxv, xxxvi, 1898.

Bannister, A. T. ed. *Register of Richard Mayhew Bishop of Hereford, 1504–1516.* Canterbury and York Society, vol. 27, 1921.

—— ed. *Register of Thomas Myllyng 1474–1492.* Canterbury and York Society, vol. 26, 1920.

Bateson, M. ed. *Cambridge University Grace Book B.* Parts I and II, Cambridge Antiquarian Society, Luard Memorial Series, II, III, 1903, 1905.

[1] The books are too numerous to be listed separately.

Bliss, W. H. and Twemlow, J. A. ed. *Papal Letters 1396–1404*. Calendar of Papal Registers, vol. v, London, 1904.

Boase, T. ed. *Register of the University of Oxford 1449, 1505–1571*. Oxford Historical Society, vol. I, 1884.

Bradshaw, H. and Wordsworth, C. *Statutes of Lincoln Cathedral arranged by the late Henry Bradshaw*, edited by C. Wordsworth. 3 vols. Cambridge, 1892–7.

Brewer, J. S., Gairdner, J. and Brodie, R. H. ed. *Letters and Papers Foreign and Domestic of the reign of Henry VIII preserved in the Public Record Office, the British Museum and elsewhere.* Vol. I catalogued by J. S. Brewer, 2nd edition by R. H. Brodie, London, 1920. Vols. II–IV catalogued by J. S. Brewer, London, 1864–72.

Calendar of Patent Rolls, Henry VII. Vol. II, 1494–1509, Record Commission, 1916.

Campbell, W. E. ed. *The Dialogue of Sir Thomas More concerning Tyndale.* London, 1927.

Cattley, S. R. ed. *Acts and Monuments by John Foxe.* 8 vols. London, 1837.

Cole, R. E. G. ed. *Chapter Acts of the Cathedral Church of St Mary of Lincoln 1520–1536.* Lincoln Record Society, vol. 12, 1915.

Cowper, J. M. ed. *A Dialogue between Cardinal Pole and Thomas Lupset, Lecturer in Rhetoric at Oxford, by Thomas Starkey.* Early English Text Society, extra series, vol. XII, 1878.

Dickens, A. G. ed. *The Register or Chronicle of Butley Priory, Suffolk.* Winchester, 1951.

Dilks, T. B. ed. *Bridgwater Borough Archives*, 1200–1468, 3 vols. Somerset Record Society, vol. 48, 1933; vol. 58, 1943; vol. 60, 1945.

Dudding, R. C. ed. *The First Churchwardens' Book of Louth 1500–1524.* Oxford, 1941.

Dugdale, W. *Monasticon Anglicanum.* 6 vols. London, 1817.

Ellis, W. P. and Salter, H. E. ed. *Liber Albus Civitatis Oxoniensis.* Oxford, 1909.

Fletcher, C. R. L. ed. *The Day Book of John Dorne, Bookseller in Oxford 1520, Collectanea I.* Oxford Historical Society, vol. v, 1885.

Foster, C. W. ed. *The State of the Church in the Reigns of Elizabeth and James I as illustrated by documents relating to the Diocese of Lincoln.* Lincoln Record Society, vol. 23, 1926.

Foster, C. W. ed. *Lincoln Wills 1271–1530.* 2 vols. Lincoln Record Society, vol. 5, 1914; vol. 10, 1918.

Foster, C. W. and Thompson, A. H. ed. 'The Chantry Certificates of Lincoln and Lincolnshire, returned in 1548 under the Act of Parliament of I Edward VI'. *Associated Architectural Societies Reports and Papers*, vol. XXXVI, pt. II, and vol. XXXVIII, pts. I and II, 1921–5.

Gibbons, A. ed. *Liber Antiquus de ordinationibus vicariarum tempore Hugonis Wells, Lincolniensis episcopi 1209–35.* Lincoln, 1888.

Howden, M. P. ed. *Register of Richard Fox, Bishop of Durham 1494–1501.* Surtees Society, 1932.

Jacob, E. F. ed. *The Register of Henry Chichele, Archbishop of Canterbury 1414–1443.* 4 vols. Oxford, 1937–47.

James, M. R. ed. *Horman's Vulgaria Puerorum.* Roxburghe Club, 1926.

Journal of the House of Lords, vol. I.

Leach, A. F. ed. *Educational Charters and Documents 598–1909.* Cambridge, 1911.

Leadam, I. S. ed. *Select Cases in the Court of Requests 1497–1569.* Selden Society, vol. XII, 1898.

Leathes, S. M. *Cambridge University Grace Book A*, vol. I. Cambridge Antiquarian Society, Luard Memorial Series I, 1897.

Lyndwood, W. *Provinciale.* Oxford, 1679.

Maddison, A. R. ed. *Lincolnshire Pedigrees.* 4 vols. Harleian Society, 1902–6.

Maxwell-Lyte, H. C. ed. *Registers of Oliver King and Hadrian Castello, Bishops of Bath and Wells.* Somerset Record Society, vol. 54, 1939.

Mellows, W. T. ed. *Peterborough Local Administration. The last days of Peterborough Monastery.* Northamptonshire Record Society, 1947.

More, A. Percival. 'Proceedings of the Ecclesiastical Courts in the Archdeaconry of Leicester, 1516–1534'. *Associated Architectural Societies Reports and Papers*, vol. XXVIII, 1905–6.

Nugent, E. M. ed. *The Thought and Culture of the English Renaissance.* Cambridge, 1956.

Page-Turner, F. A. ed. 'The Bedfordshire Wills and Administrations proved at Lambeth Palace and in the Archdeaconry of Huntingdon'. *Bedfordshire Historical Record Society*, vol. 2, 1914; vol. 4, 1917.

Pantin, W. A. ed. *Canterbury College Oxford.* 3 vols. Oxford Historical Society, new series, vol. VI, 1946; vol. VII, 1946; vol. VIII, 1950.

Peacock, E. ed. *Instructions for Parish Priests by John Myrc.* Early English Text Society, vol. XXXI; Revised edition, 1902.

Phillimore, W. P. W. ed. *Rotuli Hugonis de Welles I*, Lincoln Record Society, vol. 3, 1912.

Richards, G. C. and Salter, H. E. ed. *The Dean's Register of Oriel 1446–1661*. Oxford Historical Society, vol. LXXXIV, 1926.

Rymer, T. *Foedera, conventiones, literae, et cujuscunque generis acta publica.* Tom. 1–20, 1704–35.

Salter, H. E. ed. *Cartulary of Oseney Abbey*, vol. VI. Oxford Historical Society, vol. CI, 1936.

Salter, H. E. ed. *A Subsidy Collected in the Diocese of Lincoln in 1526.* Oxford Historical Society, vol. LXIII, 1913.

Searle, W. G. ed. *Cambridge University Grace Book* vol. LV. Cambridge 1908.

Shilton, D. O. and Holworthy, R. ed. *Wells City Charters.* Somerset Record Society, vol. 46, 1932.

Statutes of the Colleges of Oxford, 1853.

Statutes of the Realm. 9 vols. 1810–28.

Tanner, J. R. *Tudor Constitutional Documents 1485–1603.* 2nd edition, Cambridge, 1930.

Thompson, A. Hamilton, ed. *Visitations in the Diocese of Lincoln 1517–1531.* 3 vols. Lincoln Record Society, vol. 33, 1940; vol. 35, 1944; vol. 37, 1947.

Valor Ecclesiasticus. 6 vols. Record Commission, 1825–34.

Weaver, F. W. ed. *Somerset Medieval Wills.* Somerset Record Society, vol. 16, 1901.

Wilkins, D. *Concilia Magnae Britanniae et Hiberniae.* 4 vols. London, 1733, 1737.

Secondary works

Absil, J. 'L'absentéisme du clergé paroissal au diocèse de Liége au XVe siècle et dans la première moitié du XVIe siècle', *Revue d'histoire Ecclésiastique*, vol. LVII. Louvain, 1962.

Anstis, J. *The Register of the Most Noble Order of the Garter.* 2 vols. London, 1724.

Baldwin, T. W. *William Shakspere's Small Latine and Lesse Greek.* Illinois, 1944.

Bell, H. E. 'The Price of Books in Medieval England'. *Transactions of the Bibliographical Society.* vol. XVII, 1936–7.

Bennett, H. S. 'Medieval Ordination Lists in the English Episcopal Registers'. *Studies presented to Sir Hilary Jenkinson*, ed. J. C. Davies, London, 1957.

—— *English Books and Readers 1475–1557.* Cambridge, 1952.

Beresford, M. *The Lost Villages of England*. London, 1954.

Blench, J. W. *Preaching in England in the Fifteenth and Sixteenth Centuries*. Oxford, 1964.

Bloxam, J. R. *Register of the Members of St Mary Magdalen College, Oxford*. 7 vols. Oxford, 1853–85.

Bond, M. F. 'Chapter Administration and Archives at Windsor'. *Journal of Ecclesiastical History*, vol. VIII, 1957.

Boulay du, F. R. H. 'Charitable Subsidies granted to the Archbishop of Canterbury 1300–1489'. *Bulletin of the Institute of Historical Research*, vol. XXIII.

Boyle, L. 'The Constitution "Cum ex eo" of Boniface VIII: Education of Parochial Clergy'. *Medieval Studies*, vol. 24, Toronto, 1962.

Bridges, J. *History and Antiquities of Northamptonshire*. 2 vols. Oxford, 1791.

Chambers, R. W. *Sir Thomas More*. London, 1935.

Churchill, I. J. *Canterbury Administration*. 2 vols. C.H.S., 1933.

Churton, R. *Lives of William Smyth, Bishop of Lincoln, and Sir Richard Sutton, Founders of Brasen Nose College*. Oxford, 1800.

Constant, G. *The Reformation in England*, trans. R. E. Scantlebury, London, 1934.

Coxe, H. O. *Catalogi Codicum Manuscriptorum Bibliothecae Bodleianae*. 4 vols., 1854.

Cutts, E. L. *The Parish Priests and their People in the Middle Ages in England*. London, 1898.

Dalton, J. N. *Manuscripts of St George's Chapel Windsor*. Windsor, 1957.

Dansey, W. *Horae decanicae rurales*. 2 vols. Rivington, 1844.

Deanesly, M. *The Lollard Bible and other medieval biblical versions*. Cambridge, 1920.

Dickens, A. G. *Lollards and Protestants in the Diocese of York 1509–1558*. Oxford, 1959.

—— *The English Reformation*. London, 1964.

Dictionary of National Biography.

Dictionnaire de Théologie Catholique.

Dietz, F. C. *English Public Finance 1485–1641*. Cass reprint, 1964.

Du Cange, *Glossarium mediae et infimae latinitatis*. Paris, 1883.

Dunham, W. H. Jnr. 'The Members of Henry VIII's whole Council 1509–1527'. *English Historical Review*, vol. 59, 1944.

Edwards, K. *The English Secular Cathedrals in the Later Middle Ages*. Manchester, 1949.

Emden, A. B. *A Biographical Register of the University of Oxford to* A.D. *1500.* 3 vols. Oxford, 1957–9.
—— *A Biographical Register of the University of Cambridge to* A.D. *1500.* Cambridge, 1963.
Etoniana.
Eubel, C. *Hierarchia Catholica Medii et recentioris Aevii.* 4 vols. 1898–1935.
Fines, J. 'Heresy Trials in the Diocese of Lichfield 1511–1512'. *Journal of Ecclesiastical History*, vol. XIX, 1963.
Foster, C. W. *Calendar of Lincoln Wills 1320–1600.* Index Library, British Record Society, vol. XXVIII, 1902.
Fotheringhay, History of. London Society of Antiquaries, 1786.
Gabel, L. C. *Benefit of Clergy in England in the Later Middle Ages.* Smith College Studies in History, vol. XIV, nos. 1–4, Northampton, Massachusetts, 1928–9.
Giuseppe, M. S. *A Guide to the Manuscripts preserved in the Public Record Office.* 2 vols. London, 1923–4.
Harrison, F. L. *Music in Medieval Britain.* London, 1958.
Hartridge, R. A. R. *A History of Vicarages in the Middle Ages.* Cambridge, 1930.
Hill, J. E. C. *Economic Problems of the Church from Archbishop Whitgift to the Long Parliament.* Oxford, 1956.
Hill, J. W. F. *Medieval Lincoln.* Cambridge, 1948.
—— *Tudor and Stuart Lincoln.* Cambridge, 1956.
Hillerbrand, H. J. *The Reformation in its own Words.* London, 1964.
Hoare, S. *History of Modern Wiltshire.* 5 vols. London, 1822–43.
Hoskins, W. G. *Essays in Leicestershire History.* Liverpool, 1950.
—— 'Harvest Fluctuations and English Economic History 1480–1619'. *The Agricultural History Review*, vol. XII, 1964.
Hughes, P. *The Reformation in England.* 3 vols. London, 1950–6.
Jacob, E. F. *Essays in the Conciliar Epoch.* Manchester, 1943.
—— 'On the Promotion of University Clerks during the Later Middle Ages'. *Journal of Ecclesiastical History*, vol. I, 1950.
—— 'University Clerks in the Later Middle Ages, the Problem of Maintenance'. *Bulletin of the John Rylands Library*, vol. XXIX, 1926.
James, M. R. *Catalogue of the Manuscripts of Lambeth Palace Library.* 2 vols. London, 1930–2.
—— *Catalogue of the Manuscripts of Corpus Christi College, Cambridge.* 2 vols. Cambridge, 1912.

James, M. R. *Catalogue of the Manuscripts of St John's College, Cambridge.* Cambridge, 1913.

—— *Catalogue of the Manuscripts of Magdalene College, Cambridge.* Cambridge, 1909.

—— *Descriptive Catalogue of the Library of Samuel Pepys.* 4 vols. London, 1923.

Janelle, P. *L'Angleterre Catholique au Veille du Schisme.* Paris, 1935.

Jones, W. H. *Fasti Ecclesiae Sarisberiensis.* Salisbury, 1879.

Jordan, W. K. *Philanthropy in England.* London, 1959.

Kennett, W. *The Case of Impropriations and of Augmentation of Vicarages.* London, 1704.

Kingsford, C. L. *Prejudice and Promise in Fifteenth Century England.* London Reprint, 1962.

Knowles, D. *Religious Orders in England.* 3 vols. Cambridge, 1955–9.

Lawson, J. *A Town Grammar School through Six Centuries.* Oxford, 1963.

Le Neve, J. *Fasti Ecclesiae Anglicanae, Lincoln Diocese I.* New edition compiled by H. P. F. King, London, 1962.

Leach, A. F. *The Schools of Medieval England.* London, 1915.

Loades, D. M. 'The Press under the Early Tudors'. *Cambridge Bibliographical Society*, vol. IV, pt. I, 1964.

Longden, H. I. *Northamptonshire and Rutland Clergy.* 16 vols. Northampton, 1938–52.

Lunt, W. F. *Financial Relations of the Papacy with England 1327–1534.* Cambridge, Massachusetts, 1962.

Macray, W. D. *Register of the Members of St Mary Magdalen College, Oxford.* 7 vols. New series, Oxford, 1894–1911.

Maddison, A. R. *A Short Account of the Vicars Choral, Poor Clerks, Organists and Choristers of Lincoln Cathedral.* London, 1878.

Major, K. *A Handlist of the Records of the Bishop of Lincoln and of the Archdeacons of Lincoln and Stow.* Oxford, 1953.

—— 'Resignation Deeds of the Diocese of Lincoln'. *Bulletin of the Institute of Historical Research*, vol. XIX, 1942–3.

—— 'The Office of Chapter Clerk in the Middle Ages'. *Medieval Studies presented to Rose Graham.* Ed. V. Ruffer and A. J. Taylor, Oxford, 1950.

Marrat, W. *History of Lincolnshire.* Boston, 1814.

Maxwell-Lyte, H. C. *History of Eton College.* London, 1911.

Maynard-Smith, H. *Pre-Reformation England.* London, 1938.

Moorman, J. R. H. *Church Life in England in the Thirteenth Century.* Cambridge, 1946.

Morris, C. 'The Commissary of the Bishop in the Diocese of Lincoln'. *Journal of Ecclesiastical History*, vol. x, 1959.

—— 'A Consistory Court in the Middle Ages'. *Journal of Ecclesiastical History*, vol. xiv, 1963.

Mullins, E. L. C. *Texts and Calendars*. London, 1958.

Mumford, A. E. *Hugh Oldham 1452?–1519*. London, 1936.

Myers, A. R. *The Household of Edward IV. The Black Book and the Ordinance of 1478*. Manchester, 1958.

Oates, J. C. T. *Cambridge University Library, Fifteenth Century Printed Books*. Cambridge, 1954.

Ogle, A. *The Tragedy of the Lollards Tower*. Oxford, 1949.

Ollard, S. L. *Fasti Wyndesorienses*. Windsor, 1950.

Owst, G. R. *The Destructorium Viciorum of Alexander Carpenter*. S.P.C.K., 1952.

Pantin, W. A. *The English Church in the Fourteenth Century*. Cambridge, 1955.

Phelps Brown, E. H. and Hopkins, S. V. 'Seven Centuries of the Prices of Consumables, compared with Builders' Wage Rates'. *Essays in Economic History*, ed. E. M. Carus-Wilson, vol. ii, London, 1929.

Pollard, A. F. *Wolsey*. London, 1929.

—— *The Reign of Henry VII from Contemporary Sources*. London, 1913.

Powicke, F. M. *A Handbook of British Chronology*. 2nd ed. London, 1961.

Proctor, R. *An Index to the Early Printed Books in the British Museum*. London, 1898.

Purvis, J. S. *Tudor Parish Documents of the Diocese of York*. Cambridge, 1948.

Rashdall, H. *The Universities of Europe in the Middle Ages*. Ed. F. M. Powicke and A. B. Emden, Oxford, 1936.

Richardson, H. G. 'Business Training in Medieval Oxford'. *American Historical Review*, vol. xlvi, 1940.

Scarisbrick, J. J. 'Clerical Taxation in England 1485–1547'. *Journal of Ecclesiastical History*, vol. xi, 1960.

—— 'The Pardon of the Clergy of Canterbury 1531'. *Cambridge Historical Journal*, vol. xii, 1956.

Shull, V. 'Clerical Drama in Lincoln Cathedral 1311–1561'. *Modern Language Association of America*, vol. lii, 1937.

Skeel, C. A. J. *The Council in the Marches of Wales*. London, 1964.

Simon, J. 'A. F. Leach on the Reformation'. *British Journal of Educational Studies*, vol. 3, 1955.

Simon, J. *Education and Society in Tudor England*. Cambridge, 1966.

Smith, J. C. C. *Prerogative Court of Canterbury Wills 1383–1558*. Index Library, British Record Society, 3 vols. vol. x, 1893; vol. xi, 1895; vol. xviii, 1897.

—— 'Calendar of Lambeth Wills'. *Genealogist*, vols. 35, 36, 37, 1918–21.

Smith, L. B. *Tudor Prelates and Politics 1506–1558*. Princeton, 1953.

Stanier, R. S. *Magdalen School*. Oxford Historical Society, new series, vol. iii, 1940.

Stone, L. 'The Education Revolution in England 1560–1640'. *Past and Present*, no. 28, 1964.

Sterry, W. *The Eton College Register 1441–1698*. Eton, 1943.

Storey, R. L. *Diocesan Administration in the Fifteenth Century*. St Antony's Press, 1959.

Strickland Gibson. *Statuta Antiqua Universitatis Oxoniensis*. Oxford, 1931.

Swan, R. *A Practical Treatise on the Jurisdiction of the Ecclesiastical Courts, relating to the Probates and Administration with an Appendix containing an account of all the Courts in the Diocese of Lincoln, the extent of their Jurisdiction and the Place where the wills are proved and deposited*. London, 1830.

Thirsk, J. *English Peasant Farming*. London, 1957.

Thompson, A. Hamilton. *The English Clergy and their Organisation in the Later Middle Ages*. Oxford, 1947.

—— *The History of the Hospital and New College of St Mary in the Newarke Leicester*. Leicester, 1937.

—— *The Manor, Castle and Church of Tattershall*. Lincoln, 1928.

—— *Song Schools in the Middle Ages*. S.P.C.K., 1942.

—— 'Diocesan Administration in the Middle Ages: Archdeacons and Rural Deans'. *Proceedings of the British Academy*, 1943.

—— 'The Manor of Noseley with some account of the free chapel of St Mary'. *Transactions of the Leicestershire Archeological Society*, vol. xii, 1921–2.

—— 'An Early History of the College of Irthlingborough'. *Associated Architectural and Archeological Societies Reports and Papers*, vol. xxxv, 1919–20.

—— 'Pluralism in the Medieval Church with notes on Pluralists in the diocese of Lincoln 1366'. *Associated Architectural and Archeological Societies Reports and Papers*, vols. xxxiii–xxxvi, 1915–21.

Venn, J. and J. A. *Alumni Cantabrigienses*. Part I. 4 vols. Cambridge, 1922–7.

Victoria County Histories.

Watson, A. G. 'A Sixteenth Century Collector; Thomas Dackomb 1496–1572'. *Transactions of the Bibliographical Society.* V, vol. XVIII, no. 3, 1963.

Weiss, R. *Humanism in England.* Oxford, 1957.

Westlake, H. P. *The Parish Gilds of Medieval England.* S.P.C.K., 1919.

Wharhirst, G. A. 'The Reformation in the Diocese of Lincoln as illustrated by the life and work of Bishop Longland'. *Lincolnshire Architectural and Archeological Societies Reports and Papers,* vol. I, pt. II, 1937.

Wise, C. *Rockingham Castle and the Watsons.* London, 1891.

Wood, A. *Athenae Oxonienses.* Ed. P. Bliss, 4 vols., Oxford, 1813–20.

Woodcock, B. L. *Medieval Ecclesiastical Courts in the Diocese of Canterbury.* Oxford, 1952.

Unpublished theses

Blatcher, M. 'The Working of the Court of King's Bench'. Ph.D. Thesis, London University, 1936.

Knecht, R. J. 'The Political and Intellectual Activities of Cardinal John Morton and his Episcopal Colleagues'. M.A. Thesis, London University, 1953.

Scarisbrick, J. J. 'The Conservative Episcopate in England 1529–1535'. Ph.D. Thesis, Cambridge University, 1956.

INDEX

Place names are indexed under the main part of the name
e.g. Market Bosworth under Bosworth

Bond, William, 81, 206
Bonde, John, 203
Boniface VIII, Pope, 42 n.
Books
  bequests of, 54
  grammar, 51
  text, 51
  vernacular, 52
  written for priests, 53
Boone, Robert, 157 n.
Booth Charles, vicar general, 13 n., 27 n., 28, 28 n., 29
  bishop of Hereford, 124
Boothby Pagnell, Lincs., 89, 187
Boston, Lincs., 35, 50, 61, 71, 72
Bosworth, Husbands, Leics., 202
Bosworth, Market, Leics., 95, 132 n., 205
Both, Nicholas, 208
Boton, William, 61
Bottesford, Leics., 92 n., 132 n., 167 n., 195
Bourchier, Humphrey, Lord Cromwell, 156
Bourne, Lincs., 73
  Augustinian abbey of, 191
Bowden, Great, Leics., 93, 200
Bowden, John, 198
Bowden, Thomas, 203
Bowman, Ralph, 11
Bracebridge, Lincs., 189
Bradbridge, Nicholas, 53, 163, 163 n., 164
Bradwell, Bucks., 102
Bramston, Roger, 193
Bransfort, John, 24
Brant Broughton, Lincs., 92 n.
Bratoft, Lincs., 87, 195
Brattleby, Lincs., 87, 195
Braunceton, Rutland, 105 n.
Brawderibbe, Stephen, 198
Bray, family of, 187
Bray, Sir Reginald, 4, 17
Braybrooke, Northants., 187
Braybrooke, Richard, Canon of Owston, 191, 192
Brayfield, Northants., 51
Brentingby, Leics., 128 n.
Briayn, Thomas, 206

Brice, Robert, 200
Brickhill, Bow, Bucks., 28 n., 195
Bridlington, Yorks., Augustinian priory of, 191
Bridport, Dorset, 137
Bright, Robert, 80
Brigsley, Lincs., 195
Brill, Bucks., 105 n.
Brington, Hunts., 79, 92 n., 97, 127 n., 187, 196
Brinknell, Thomas, Headmaster of Magdalen school, 159
Brirdenis, John, 199
Britwell Salome, Oxon., 71 n.
Brocklesby, Lincs., 189, 196
Brodshed, William, 205
Brokesby, family of, 82
Brokesby, Richard, 160 n.
Bromewiche, Mr, 203
Bromham, Beds., 134
Bromyard, Heref., 112 n.
Broughton, family of, 187
Broughton, Hunts., 79, 187
Broughton, Oxon., 196
Broughton Astley, Leics., 92 n.
Broughton St Lawrence, Bucks., 196
Brown, Richard, 201
Browne, Edward, 150
Browne, Thomas, 211
Browne, William, 205
Broxholme, Lincs., 92 n.
Brudenell, Drogo, 83
Brudenell, George, 83
Bruntingthorpe, Leics., 92 n.
Buckden, Hunts., 23 n., 40, 187
Buckingham, 48, 51, 95, 187
  archdeacon of, 36
  Duke of, 80
  prebendal court of, 33
Buckinghamshire, 48, 54, 149, 150
Buckminster, Leics., 34, 127 n., 128 n., 130 n.
Bucknell, Oxon., 128 n., 129 n.
Buckworth, Hunts., 101, 196
Bulkeley, Hugh, 208
Bull, John, 195
Bullington, Gilbertine priory of, 192
Bulmer, Robert, 205

Priests, beneficed (*cont.*)
 reform of morality of, 124–6
 responsibility for fabric, 129–36
 saying of offices, 112–15
 sociability of, 117
 stipends of, 139
 too old or infirm to perform duties,
  114
 visitation of sick, 113
 witness wills of parishioners, 113
Priests, chantry, in collegiate churches,
 164 ff., 171 ff.
Priests, collegiate, duties of, 157
Priests, unbeneficed (*see also* Curates),
 103–9
Priests, unbeneficed, stipends of, 144–5
Princes Risborough, Bucks., 128 n.
Prison, episcopal, 113, 119, 122
Probate, powers of granting, 25, 31
Provost of B.M. of Lincoln, 164
 (*see also* Roston, Richard)
Pryket, Miles, 197
Pudsey, Johanna, 34
Pulloxhill, Beds., 128 n., 135
Purley, Robert, 205
Puttenham, Herts., 207
Pynnell, William, 72 n.
Pynson, Richard, printer, 14, 52
Pyrton, Oxon., 149, 151

Quadring, Lincs., 92 n., 106, 207
Queniborough, Leics., 132, 132 n.

Radnage, Bucks., 82, 207
Ramsey, Hunts., 67, 78, 79, 146
 abbot of, 7, 129
 Benedictine abbey of, 62, 64
Rand, Lincs., 92 n., 207
Rarson, John, 212
Rasen, Middle, Lincs., 141, 190
Rasen, West, Lincs., 128 n., 188
Ratcliffe on Wreak, Leics., 132 n.
Ravendale, East, Lincs., 105 n.
Ravensthorpe, Northants., 69, 69 n., 207
Rawlins, Henry, 210
Rawlins, Richard, 155 n., 158
Raye, Johanna, 119
Rearsby, Leics., 207

Rectors, dilapidations, 133
 expenses for fabric, 134
 glebe of, 140–1
 responsibility for chancel (*see also*
  Priests, beneficed), 129–30
 stipends of, 139–41
Redbourne, Lincs., 128 n.
Redd, William, 95, 198, 204, 205
Rede, Robert, 58
Redhole, William, 100 n.
Reform of Church, attempts through
  synods, 124–6
 blocked by vested interest, 125
Reginald of Gloucester, 48 n.
Registrar, episcopal (*see also* Watson,
  Edward), 37
Religious, vows of, 19
Religious orders,
 augmentation of vicarages, 143–4
 benefices in patronage of, 67
 neglect of appropriated churches,
  129–30, 132–6
 poverty of, 135
 presentation of members to benefices,
  appendix III
 profits from appropriated churches,
  134–6
 promotion of own members to
  benefices, 76–7
 powerful opposition of, 20
 right to order election in, 25
 right to receive vows of religious in,
  25
Residence
 canonical requirements for, 85
 definition of, 87
 dispensations from, 86, 93, 96; time
  limit of, 94; cost of, 95
 episcopal activities to ensure, 89
 failure of, appendix IV
 legitimate reasons for neglecting,
  88–9
 orders for, 94–6
 proportion of rectors and vicars
  neglecting, 90
Reston, South, Lincs., 92
Retford, Thomas, 166
Reve, Hugh, 213

.

For EU product safety concerns, contact us at Calle de José Abascal, 56–1°,
28003 Madrid, Spain or eugpsr@cambridge.org.

www.ingramcontent.com/pod-product-compliance
Ingram Content Group UK Ltd.
Pitfield, Milton Keynes, MK11 3LW, UK
UKHW010342140625
459647UK00010B/776